GREEN GOLD:
THE EMPIRE OF TEA

Alan Macfarlane and Iris Macfarlane

EBURY PRESS
LONDON

First published in Great Britain in 2003

10 9 8 7 6 5 4 3 2 1

Text © Alan Macfarlane and Iris Macfarlane, 2003

Alan Macfarlane and Iris Macfarlane have asserted their right to be identified as the authors of this work under the Copyright, Designs and Patents Act 1988.

First published by
Ebury Press
Random House, 20 Vauxhall Bridge Road, London SW1V 2SA

Random House Australia (Pty) Limited
20 Alfred Street, Milsons Point, Sydney, New South Wales 2061, Australia

Random House New Zealand Limited
18 Poland Road, Glenfield, Auckland 10, New Zealand

Random House South Africa (Pty) Limited
Endulini, 5A Jubilee Road, Parktown 2193, South Africa

The Random House Group Limited Reg. No. 954009

www.randomhouse.co.uk

A CIP catalogue record for this book is available from the British Library.

Cover Design by the Senate
Text design and typesetting by Textype
Picture Credits: Chapter 1: Alan MacFarlane and Iris MacFarlane. Chapter 2, 3, 4, 13, 14: The Mary Evans Picture Library. Chapter 5, 8, 9: The Advertising Archive. Chapter 6: Photograph by E. H. Wilson, Photographic Archives of the Arnold Arboretum, copyrighted by the President and Fellows of Harvard College, Harvard University, Cambridge, Massachusetts. Chapter 7: The British Library. Chapter 10, 12: The Tea Council. Chapter 11: The Indian National Congress.

ISBN 0091883091

Papers used by Ebury Press are natural, recyclable products made from wood grown in sustainable forests.

Printed and bound in the UK by Biddles of Guildford

Contents

Part III Embodied

List of Illustrations

Iris MacFarlane and her children, Assam, 1950
A London Tavern, 1600
A traditional Japanese Tea Ceremony
Clippers owned by the East India Tea Company, circa 1860
Horniman's Tea Advertisement 1880–1899
Tibetan men carrying brick tea from China, circa 1900
Elephants clearing a plantation, Assam, 1880
Pleasure Brand Advertisement, 1888
Mazawattee tea/John Bull advertisement, 1890
A typical Chinese plantation
Henry Cotton, Chief Commissioner of Assam in 1896
Women working on plantation, circa 1990
A herbal pharmacopoeia in Tokyo
Camellia Sinensis, 19th century

To the people who will never read this book,
the tea labourers of Assam

Acknowledgements

As always, this book has been enormously enriched by the help from many friends, colleagues and others. Michelle Schaffer and H .B. F. Dixon of King's College and Derek Bendall of Trinity College, Cambridge helped to check the biochemistry. Chris Bayly, Mark Elvin, Brian Harrison and David Sneath gave advice on the history and anthropology. Lipeni, Christine and Dirang Lungalong showed us Calcutta. Mr and Mrs Singh, and Lily and Smo Das advised on Assam. Babs Johnson accompanied Iris on her trip to Assam. Brynny Lyster helped with research at the India Office Library. Hilda Martin provided her usual supportive advice (and cups of tea). Lily Blakely gave us an insight into how tea is transmitted in mother's milk. David Dugan, Ian Duncan and Carlo Massarella helped in the filming of tea ceremonies and pursuing the tea theme. Andrew Morgan and Sally Dugan read the book carefully and offered excellent advice. Elizabeth Jones, then doing a dissertation in History and Philosophy of Science at Cambridge, read the text through twice and made many helpful criticisms. A number of her suggested quotations have been incorporated, especially in chapter 5. At Ebury Press, Jake Lingwood, Claire Kingston and all who helped to produce the book. Above all, much of the work came out of the discussions and careful reading and re-reading of the book by Sarah Harrison and Gerry Martin. And, of course, there are the countless people who have sacrificed their lives to produce tea over thousands of years, to a few of whom this book is dedicated. To all of them, deepest thanks.

Introduction

This book is written by a tea planter's widow, Iris, and son, Alan. It has two views and two agendas. The questions behind my writing are described here. Those behind my mother's work are described in chapter one.

When I started to write this book I had a disparate set of puzzles and memories in my head, like disconnected pieces of a jigsaw. I was born in Shillong, Assam, in 1941, in the centre of the area where tea was first discovered. I have vague memories of my childhood on a tea plantation in Assam, the son of a tea manager. The indistinct memories of wide expanses of tea and driving between them in a Jeep. The smell of the factory, full of piles of tea and ancient churning machines. Of large, cool, bungalows surrounded by beautiful flowers and tended lawns. Of visits to mountain rivers, where I swam and fished and ate cold curries. Of trips to the club to watch polo and play tennis.

All of these memories of the first five years of my life are in fact probably mainly memories from two later trips back to Assam in my teens, after I had gone to boarding school in England. Of these, I particularly remember the shock of

Calcutta, with its luxury alongside abysmal poverty. I vowed one day to return to try to improve the lives of those in the awful slums. But of the life of the labourers and servants who hovered on the edge of my privileged childhood and provided the wealth that gave me an expensive education I remember nothing. It probably never occurred to me, young as I was, to speculate about their lives. Neither did I, at that time, wonder about how the tea industry arrived in Assam, why the British were in charge, or even why tea was grown on plantations at all. This book is partly a search for answers to these unasked questions.

In my twenties I tried to return to India to learn more, but was unable to go to Assam for political reasons. So I went to work as an anthropologist in a neighbouring country in the Himalayas, Nepal, and to investigate a similar people, the Gurungs. There I studied the lives of those who, as recruits to the famous Gurkha regiments of the British Army, had helped to guard the tea gardens and their surrounding hills.

My heart was still in Assam, but without the chance of returning there, I pursued a five-year study on the history and culture of the Naga people of the area. This only brought up further puzzles. Why had the British extended their Empire so far up into the north-east? Why had they pushed up into the Naga Hills and with what consequences? My researches circled round the edges of the tea gardens, but only added to the oddness at the heart of the phenomenon, the presence of the tea gardens themselves.

In 1990 I visited Japan, and on this and three subsequent visits I began to try to understand that ancient civilisation as part of my anthropological studies. Among the most striking memories of Japan was the central place of tea in Japanese culture. We were offered it all the time and could see its widespread effects on religion, ceramics and every part of life. Attending several tea ceremonies and visiting teahouses highlighted its extraordinary importance. Trying to understand Japan led me to read books on religion and aesthetics, which suggested that tea is far more than just another hot drink, as I had previously always regarded it. It was seen by the Japanese as a medicine with almost divine properties. There was something special about tea. If it had so much effect on Japanese civilisation, could this also be true elsewhere? Was this part of the reason for the acres of green bushes of my childhood?

All of these half-formed ideas and experiences were in the back of my mind when, in 1993, I began to explore once again the question of the genesis of the Industrial Revolution. An extraordinary, unprecedented, type of civilisation emerged in the west in the eighteenth century. Why did it first emerge in Britain? Why at that time? Why at all?

As we constructed a teahouse in our Cambridgeshire garden during the summer of 1994, and I turned over the puzzles in my mind, I began to ask myself whether the answer could not quite simply lie in the tea bushes of my childhood. Was the solution to be found in the development of tea drinking?

As soon as this occurred to me, it all seemed so obvious. Tea flooded into Britain from the 1730s and spread through much of the population. This occurred just at the point when waterborne disease faded away as a major killer. Boiling water to make the tea would kill off most of the harmful bacteria in the water. It would provide a safe drink for the populace. This might be all that needed to be said.

Yet there were further puzzles. First, all of the Chinese and Japanese authors who wrote of tea, and even the European doctors who investigated it when it first arrived in Europe, were convinced that there was something extra in tea, some beneficial substance betrayed by its bitter taste, an astringent 'medicine' which did humans good. If this were true, it would help answer other puzzles – for example, why it was that even infants who were not drinking tea, but being breast-fed, increasingly escaped infant diarrhoea. Could they be being protected by whatever it was that was in the tea and flowed through their mother's milk? An investigation showed that this was indeed possible, and that the 'tannin' of tea is not actually tannin, but a substance called 'phenolics' that has powerful antiseptic and antibacterial effects.

This was just one of the jumble of questions in my mind when my mother and I sat down to write this book. How, I also wondered, had tea been discovered? Why should it contain such special properties, in particular caffeine, phenolics and flavonoids? How and why had it spread across the world? How had it become so central to British life? What effects had its production had on those who worked in tea and on their neighbours? What other effects had it had on the civilisations that had adopted it? Were there wider links between the spread of tea and the simultaneous rise of several great civilisations, for instance in China, Japan and Britain? And how far are its supposed health effects likely to be true?

My part of the book is an attempt to fit all these pieces together in a personal exploration of my own past and that of my family, which has for many generations been involved both in tea and in the area around Assam. Also, it is a theoretical exploration of what may turn out to be an important contributor to bringing about the world in which we all live. What started as a tiny set of puzzles and a scarcely-to-be-noticed leaf has ended up in this story as one of the great addictions of history.

Alan Macfarlane

Chapter One

Memoirs of a Memsahib

I was brought up with all the colonial claptrap of my kind: that 'Out There in India' there were dark people irremediably inferior, who were lucky to be ruled by Us. At the boarding schools to which I was sent I looked with pride at the large part of the world coloured pink. I breathed in from birth the assumption that Orientals were subject races, by definition. There was something called the Indian Mind which was changeless, shared by the entire sub-continent.

Parents, grandparents, uncles and brothers had been Out There and in photos they stood in sepia rows, leaning on rifles or polo sticks or dead tigers, squinting haughtily into the sun. The women lounged in deckchairs on the ship or sat sidesaddle on shiny horses, floppy hats replaced by solar topees. Under the dappled canopy of tropical trees they were serene, since turbaned men held the reins.

Other men hovered around little boys in miniature jodhpurs on the backs of donkeys – there were more servants than relatives in these photographs, standing submissively waiting for orders. Out There, India, was where the men in the family went to join the army; usually becoming officers in the Gurkha regiments whose men were believed to be attached to their white officers to the point of worship. The girls went out to have a good time and then marry. In fact, India was the bin into which was tipped the less than brilliant, the plump, the pimply and the plainly unmarriageable.

Of course we didn't see it like that – we were brought up to believe that Indians were lucky to have us, that they didn't know what was good for them until we imposed our intellectual authority over them in the shape of scholars, missionaries, businessmen, soldiers and teachers. Our menfolk were educated at the United Services College, Westward Ho, or a similar public school, drilled to be 'good with natives'. Between 1815 and1914, 85 per cent of the world's surface was colonised, so there were plenty of natives around, and there were politicians like Balfour booming 'that they have under us a better government than in the whole history of the world'. Stereotypes abounded and were continually reinforced. Europeans were 'selfless administrators' who were 'natural logicians' with 'ingrained intelligence'; white, male, wealthy. Indians were one and all 'slipshod' and, except for maharajahs, poor.

With my head stuffed with such nonsense I Went Out in 1938, as to a finishing school, to have my rough edges smoothed and my spare pounds shed, sixteen years old and ready for the long party my mother described Indian life to be. My hope and belief was that after a couple of years I would return to Britain to go to university, slim and self-possessed. My mother, on the other hand, was planning my trousseau from the moment we stepped onto the *Strathnaver*. India was well supplied with middle-aged men needing wives, not fussy about 'looks', maybe even appreciative of my good brain, a terrible handicap in the Jamesean world of matchmaking matriarchs to which she belonged.

The Cantonment in which we lived (my father had seconded from the regular army into the Cantonments Department) was an oasis of tidiness and order in the sprawling muddle around; Indians always lived untidily, it was part of being 'slipshod'. We were surrounded by white fences, trees were painted white too, and gates and doors – everything was painted and repainted white, perhaps symbolic of the superiority of our colour. We lived in white bungalows around which grew marigolds, petunias and scarlet salvias (I have disliked these ever since) and in the centre of the complex was the Club with tennis courts and a golf course. There was a church and a hospital but no shops; the cook went to the bazaar every morning and my mother wrote down his purchases in her Memsahib's Account Book. Everything was very cheap but the cook's figures were daily questioned; Indians were 'chilarky', a word that covered lying, cheating and a general (innate of course) inability to resist being saucily devious.

The Cantonment housed a regiment or two, members of the Civil Service, the Police, the Forestry Department, a couple of doctors, the Royal Army Service Corps, which arranged supplies, and, tucked out of sight, some Railway People who were always Coloured and shared an inferior club with Other Ranks. In the hot weather the whole contraption moved up into the hills, except for junior staff and the Railway Riffraff.

In the hills there was a lake, and the Boat Club became the centre of social life, a strict hierarchy being maintained. At the summit, in a house of palatial grandeur, surrounded by hundreds of acres of parkland, was the Governor. In a slightly smaller mansion the General in Charge of Eastern Command sat being rude to anyone who couldn't respond to his boorish gibes. He employed his son as his ADC and his daughter as his housekeeper. We had to accept invitations from both these grandees; it cemented status, as did the seating arrangements. The Raj was scrupulously snobbish. Doctors from the Indian Medical Association were more respectable than those of the Royal Indian Army Medical Corps and got to sit closer to the Governor or his Lady. I was put down at the bottom of the table next to the ADC who was always a dashing cavalry officer tricked out in gold braid, shiny boots and spurs. The life of tennis parties, golf matches and evening dances was little affected by the outbreak of war that first September soon after my seventeenth birthday, but it put paid to my own hopes of soon returning home. Nobody, however, thought it would last long. We heard on the wireless about Dunkirk and the Battle of Britain and rolled bandages for some possible unspecified local needs. A whole brigade arrived to train, headily filling the Cantonment with young men in uniform. When I was eighteen one of them led me to the altar, to the enormous relief of my mother.

In peacetime he was a tea planter, which was something of a pity since 'box wallahs' (businessmen) were almost *hoi polloi* in my family's vocabulary, but planters were known to be rich and to live in a remote and peaceful backwater. My mother sent me off happily with a trunkful of toast racks, entrée dishes and Chinese soup bowls to the eastern outpost, where a new regiment was being raised under planter officers to train the hill people of Assam. The Assam Regiment, along with my husband, went in various directions, I went in others, and it was five years and three children later that we started our married life together on a tea garden. I had visualised tea flowering as in an orchard, swathes of sweet-smelling landscape surrounding us and our first settled home. I had absolutely no idea of the process that turned this perfumed profusion into a drink from a pot. I arrived in July 1946 with all my misconceptions in place. I had spent most of the war with my parents, who still wouldn't – couldn't – believe in Indian independence. In their circle, Gandhi and Nehru were best behind prison bars. The talk at the Boat Club was of the amusing little processions bearing 'Quit India' placards; just children paid a few annas to shout and wave flags. My parents retired with their illusions still about them. I arrived in Assam cocooned like its silkworms in those same illusions.

At twenty-nine, with two years' planting experience, Mac, my husband took over the management of a large estate so that the couple who had been there through the war could take leave. The Manager's bungalow was almost as big as the ship, *Strathnaver*, on which I had sailed to India, and similarly constructed in wood with an upper and lower deck. We lived upstairs; the children rode tricycles round the pillars of the ground floor. In its centre was a locked storeroom. We found the key and discovered it to be packed to the ceiling with food, fridges, sewing machines, spare parts left by the departing Yanks. We filched a couple of tins of ice cream powder but had to wait for the returning Manager to buy off him a fridge and some fans.

Tea turned out to be grown on bushes some distance from the bungalow, and I saw nothing of its plucking or manufacturing. With no car and three children under five I spent my days wiping the sweat from my eyes as I kept them amused and safe. Huge black hornets nested in the ceiling, lizards the size of crocodiles wandered the verandas flicking their tongues; one day I looked down from the top veranda to see a humped bull with spreading horns leaning over the baby's pram. As gentle as all Brahman bulls he recognised a small creature and went his way. There were probable snakes and possible tigers, but the most deadly creature was the mosquito. I carried a flit gun everywhere.

As prolific as the wild life of brilliant birds, butterflies and animals, was the riot of purple, scarlet, gold, apricot and pearly-white plants. They cascaded and fountained and clambered everywhere, needing little attention from the gardeners (*malis*) who mowed the acres of grass and then sat in the shade and drank tea out of watering cans. They and the other servants were from the labour lines (living quarters), Mac told me, but to me they were just brown figures who appeared from nowhere and melted back into the same nothingness. They were not as smart as my mother's servants, who wore starched white coats with coloured cummerbunds held together with shiny brass clasps. They had lived in shacks at the bottom of the garden, called Servants' Quarters. Having accepted the myth of the Cheating Native, I counted the cigarettes in the silver box on the coffee table and measured the whisky in the decanter. A scruffy lot I thought these garden servants, and wondered if white starched coats would improve them.

I looked forward to getting a car, and after a couple of months this turned up in the shape of an old Hillman Minx from some other ex-Yank scrap heap. It would get us to the club though, and I was excited. The company of toddlers and a largely absent husband was to be enlivened by meeting other planters and their wives. I dressed us all in crisp cottons and we launched ourselves into a steamy afternoon, our first outing for eight weeks. The children sucked their thumbs and dozed grumpily, Mac cursed the wandering cows and potholes. I saw tea for the first time and women bending above it with baskets on their backs. They looked cool and pretty under the shade trees. What a pleasant life, I thought, days drifting like swans on the green sea of tea.

We reached a river and climbed into an open boat, a flimsy affair, but the children woke up to enjoy the slushy bumpy crossing. As my crispness collapsed into damp, bedraggled disarray, I cheered myself with the thought of the club. I pictured polished floors, flower arrangements, chintzy sofas, tea trays and iced drinks carried by servants in white coats and cummerbunds. I thought of a library, a card room, a children's playroom. I thought in fact of the clubs I had known on the other side of India, where magistrates, forestry officers, policemen had mixed with doctors and colonels to talk of their jobs and hobbies. Their wives sketched a bit, sailed skilfully, were keen gardeners and bridge players. The club for all its petty cliques and established racism was quite a civilised place. There was friendship and laughter and relaxation there.

When we had disembarked and climbed a muddy bank a company car drove us past some bungalows and deposited us beside one slightly bigger, flanked with tennis courts. Inside was a large room, its only furniture a circle of wicker chairs. Opening from it was a bar, and we walked past this out onto the tennis courts. We were to watch tennis, seated on a row of hard chairs, and then the men would retire to play billiards and their own bar. There was nothing for the children to do, no swings or sandpits; in fairness there were no other children. There were no interesting Empire Builders either, nothing but planters, all of a red-faced, thick-legged, sweaty Scottish variety it seemed, a stereotype that remains with me still.

After tennis a dozen women sat in a circle on the wicker

chairs; and sat and sat. The children dozed on my lap, the fan ground and squeaked, and the conversation was about servants. There were particular horror stories about the paniwallah, the man who washed up and who never learned and heavens hadn't one been telling him for years, to take the pot to the kettle. The woman on my right, who said what she didn't know about running a bungalow in Assam would go on sixpence, kindly shared her deep knowledge about *jharans*, or dusters. I must give these out every morning and get them back each evening. I must see that each servant got the *jharan* his status justified – the best to the bearers, any old rags to the sweepers. I must of course lock up food stores in the go-down, a large stone larder that came with most bungalows, and hand out flour and sugar in spoonfuls. The fridge must be locked – watering the milk was a well-known dodge. Did I sew? No? Well in that case I needn't bother to keep my cotton reels under lock and key, but the silver had to be given lynx-like attention. If any of the pieces started to move round the room be sure that they would gently disappear out of the door one dark night. The amusing thing was to pretend you hadn't noticed and then pounce at the last moment. Remember that the servants were a pretty primitive race here, not long down from the trees. Like children really, always trying on their tricks, but you had to show them you were master.

After a couple of hours with the children clammily asleep, I said I was going to get my husband. The whole circle froze. It was unheard of for a woman to enter the precincts behind the swing doors where the men had their own bar and from which they would emerge when they were ready. This they did after what seemed like a hundred years, staggering a bit but ready to drive off to their gardens. When we had crossed the river, collected the car and carried the comatose children up the stairs to bed, I leant over the veranda rail and stared down into the compound.

The old man who guarded us, the *chowkidar*, was wandering up and down with a stick, dressed in a tattered shirt, barefoot. What sort of *jharan* should I give him? What was he guarding us from anyway? Tigers? Bandits? I knew that as soon as we were asleep he would lay himself down, his head on his turban, and dream the night away. Above his sleeping head the hornets dozed in their hive, snakes lay curled in dry corners, a myriad moths opened and closed their silver wings. The warm night was a humming symphony of sound, the buzzing of insects broken by the *clack-clack* of frogs, the distant howl of jackals, the beat of drums. It was full of light from fireflies and a canopy of stars, and perfumed with moonflowers and lilies.

I breathed in the sweetness and thought this is the last hot weather I'll spend in Assam. When we went home on leave next year Mac would get another job and that would be the end of India. There would be no separations from the children, no terrible club circles waiting for the men to come and collect us, their shirts stuck to their pink stomachs, their fly buttons undone. I went to bed happily unaware that I would actually spend twenty years in tea; it would be 1966 before I was carried out on a stretcher from this beautiful, vibrant, exhausting, magical country.

It was ten years before I really started to look around the country. I taught my daughters until the elder was ten, and it was 1955 before I was alone with Assam. I had another ten years before we retired, and I sat on my veranda telling my Journal what I intended to do with my time. Mac was now Manager of a very beautiful tea garden on the edge of the Naga Hills. In the bad old days (of which I knew nothing) the Nagas had raided it, but now they only came down to a market where we bought beads and took photographs. On our fishing trips up a nearby river we watched them laying their bamboo fishtraps, and afterwards they joined us round our campfire, wet and naked. Mac had got particularly fond of them in the army, and in spite of language problems we laughed a lot as we shared our tea and sausages.

Language, my lack of it, was my concern. The labour force spoke so many dialects I was baffled at the thought of choosing one, but I would learn Assamese and go out into the villages to discover the country I had lived in so long and ignorantly. I would also see if I could help in the hospital and school. I knew nothing of the Plantation Act of 1952 with directions about housing, health and education. Mac had shown me the crèche he had built, a cement square in which no mother would leave her child so it doubled as a cattle pound.

Somewhere low down on my list was a visit to the lines. I passed these on walks with the dogs – rows of thatched hovels sharing a communal tap. No wonder the servants suffered from boils and colds, I thought, my clouded mind only mildly concerned. As I called the dogs off chasing ducks it was occupied with how to decorate my new air-conditioned room. Occasionally I considered how strange the servants must find it, leaving my taps and lamps and fans and returning to their one-roomed quarters without light or water. But that was the East for you.

The only books I could find to teach me Assamese were printed by the Catholic Church with half the pages upside-down, but Mac produced a local teacher, a schoolmaster who came up twice a week and sat on the veranda with his knees knocking together in terror. I told him very simple stories like *Cinderella* and he was too polite and frightened to correct me, so we made little progress. He wouldn't let me pay him, instead arriving at the bungalow with fifteen-pound fish as if I was doing him a favour. Mac thought he probably had his sights set on a job on the staff.

Was it a bribe that he invited me to his house for a meal? I hoped not. It was the first time I had visited a village; we drove past them quite fast in a cloud of dust, but this one was a palm-shaded clearing, my schoolmaster's house climbed over by pumpkins and morning glory. The whole village was spotless, a shadowy haven of rustling leaves, a pond at its centre on which floated waterlilies and ducks. Children played, watched over by women with bare gold arms curved round water pots. Beyond the coconut palms and banana trees, tender green tassels of rice were reflected in flooded fields. Cocks crowed, there was singing and the thump of an axe on wood.

As befitted my status I ate alone, waited on by the schoolmaster's wife with her sari drawn across her face. An old lady with a plate came to the door and was given a handful of rice. This was the custom, my schoolmaster told me, the village communally cared for the old and sick. He had three boys and was paying off interest on a debt incurred by his grandfather, but his wife had silver bracelets and earrings and he had a share in a rice field and a pair of bullocks. If he could become an Assistant Headmaster he would be satisfied.

Clutching a bag of guavas I drove home elated. The first scale had fallen from my eyes. Assamese were not the 'spineless sods' planters had led me to believe; compared to the labour force in

the lines they lived sumptuously. I could visualise retiring to a
village shaded by palms, with pumpkins, bananas, coconuts and
guavas dropping at my door. Mac, who had pitied me a dreary
afternoon of very sweet tea and stilted talk, was surprised at my
glowing demeanour.

I glowed because I had the key to escape from the club circles,
the coffee mornings, the weekend Polo Sprees when the
conversation still circled round the paniwallah. In all my years in
Assam I never met another women who wanted to escape. I was
considered eccentric and Mac was pitied. Most of the time I
didn't care, sometimes self-pity seeped from my pores as sour as
sweat.

From the village I moved on to contacting a middle-class Indian
family called Bharali. I had written to a scholar whose books I
could now read and asked if he knew of a family I could visit,
perhaps even stay with. The eldest daughter, Anima, was working
for a doctorate, a gentle bespectacled girl for whom there were no
marriage plans, it seemed. Her pretty younger sister had married,
but lost track of her husband when he went to London on a course
and never returned. She hoped I would find him for her, which I
did on our next leave, but I failed to persuade him to go back to
her.

The Bharalis' house was square and solid and we sat on the
veranda drinking lemon sherbet and talking about the things we
would do together. They had an outing lined up; at the end of the
rains when the river had subsided, we would visit a holy island in
the Brahmaputra, where a yearly drama was enacted to celebrate
the life of Lord Krishna. The island was entirely inhabited by
monks, and there was one special one Anima's mother wanted to

be blessed by. Anima herself, a graduate and from a younger generation, smiled at such old-fashioned nonsense, but thought the experience would interest me.

Mac thought the whole thing would be a 'bloody shambles', but produced a car and driver to take us to the river. We picked up Anima, her mother and an aunt who wanted to come along; and a trunk and several large bundles and a couple of chickens in a basket. Anima's mother carried a tin of cooking fat, which she intended to smear on the sacred feet of her guru, and which was already beginning to melt and smell quite pungent.

We were to spend the night in a hostel on the riverbank; our room had four beds whose sheets looked grey and crumpled and well slept in, but Anima and I sat down on a couple of them while the two old ladies went off to kill the chickens and prepare a curry. She told me the story of Lord Krishna. I knew nothing of Hinduism, vaguely connecting it with a lot of gods and some messy rituals of squirting red liquid about. Anima believed in a purified and monotheistic form of it, with Krishna as a Christ-like incarnation. The monks on the island held this view, the man her mother was wanting to see had the reputation of being impeccably holy.

After a night hemmed in by the snoring old ladies, I woke excited. In my mind the holy island would be a collection of sacred groves drifted through by gold-clad, chanting figures. An air of solemn mystery would surround us as we made our way towards a specially venerable Mahatma on a hilltop. My Christian belief was almost exhausted and I was prepared to be blessed by other gods, at least for the space of a day.

We drove to the riverbank to board the steamer; us and half the population of Assam and their livestock and their bicycles. As we scrambled aboard and fought our way to the railings I pushed to the back of my mind stories that regularly appeared in the press of boatloads of drowning passengers on just such crossings. Almost as soon as we were under way Anima's aunt said she was going to vomit, and promptly did so all over my shoes. I couldn't move to clean them, being pinned in by a bicycle and the backside of a goat. How Mac would laugh and say 'I told you so', when I described the scene to him.

A nephew was to meet us at the island; he owned a taxi, one of the few non-holy members of the community. Anima's mother had told me that he was very black and therefore difficult to fix up with a wife. Less of a problem was that he was an alcoholic, which didn't fit in very well with being a taxi driver, but there was little traffic on the island. When the crowd had dispersed he appeared, only a little tipsy, and we climbed aboard his taxi along with the luggage and the tin of Cocogem cooking fat.

As we made our rather zigzag way along the rough island roads the nephew spent a lot of time turning round to tell me that he was a poet, and a great admirer of Wordsworth. Did I not think the little houses we passed were reminiscent of the bard's lowly cot? All they lacked was daffodils, no? One day, with my help, he hoped to visit the great man's dwelling and see the daffodils.

Meanwhile, we were making little headway in finding the right dwelling of the right monk. The Cocogem was dripping down the tin as we lurched along rutted tracks and landed up in front of the wrong monastery. The island was just like any other part of Assam, with banana trees and wandering cows and clusters of houses where cocks crowed and women winnowed grain. It didn't feel holy, it felt irritating; hot, dusty, untidy. Why hadn't someone brought a map, for heaven's sake? I closed my eyes, the word 'slipshod' hovering behind my lids.

I opened them when Anima exclaimed, 'Now we are here.' Here was a small hillock with steps leading through a park where two or three scabby deer and a moulting peacock lay under the trees. We climbed up to a tin-roofed house, where a couple of disciples took our shoes and asked us to sit in an ante-room to wait for an audience. His holiness could only see a couple of people at a time. They brought us glasses of cloudy water to drink, which I sipped with closed lips, suspicious that the sacred feet might have been washed in it. The backs of my knees stuck to the wooden seat of my chair and my stomach rumbled.

Anima and her aunt were called first, and then her mother and I were led into a room where a large man wrapped in a white shawl sat on a platform. Candles and flowers were strewn around; as I touched my head to the floor in front of him I thought I should have brought a bouquet, it was only polite, an omission I hoped he wouldn't mind. I kept my eyes down as the melted fat from Mrs Bharali's tin was emptied over the holy feet. A murmuring, a stretching-out of a hand to her head, and she rose and left the room backwards.

What happened next I have remembered for the rest of my life. A hand rested on my bent head, and through it, onto my clammy forehead, into my dusty scalp, right inside my head and then flowing down my body, sweetness and strength filled me. It was like sunshine pouring into a dark room, like rain falling on dry earth. It was as if the windows of my mind had opened and all the beauty of the world blown in. It was the secret of happiness plainly revealed.

When he took his hand away the joy remained. He spoke a few halting words; his lack of English was like a rock, he said, but round it and over it would flow wisdom. Distance didn't matter, no matter the miles between us, he would always be there, his hands ready to bless. Did he know – I think he did – how often in moments of despair I would cross that great river, climb that dusty path, and lay my aching head down at his sacred feet?

When I got home next day I told Mac about the boat and the nephew and the drama that went on all night. I didn't tell him, or anyone, about the brown hand of a stranger that had blessed me forever. Looking back I wonder why I never returned to that island in person, though often in my thoughts. Perhaps I was afraid the miracle would fail next time.

Anima gave me history books to read and I learnt about the Ahom kings whose tombs were on our tea garden. They had been buried in large mounds with gold and ivory, which had been looted, but there was a temple on one of the mounds, now lost in the jungle. I would clear it and dig up the remains of the temple. I set off every morning with a picnic and spade and scraped away at the pink tiles. When I lay on my back and rested a couple of vultures would drift above me, hoping I was dead. I rubbed my hands raw and progress was slow, but I was very happy and thought that soon some government-sponsored society would move in.

Did I ask anyone's permission to begin the work? I don't think I did. Did I consider that I might be ruffling superstitious sensibilities? No, I never gave it a thought. So I was grieved when every weekend the work I had done was destroyed, my walls knocked down. Students, Mac said, undisciplined hooligans who needed their backsides skelped. He was angry over my disappointment, and sorry to see the colour fade from my cheeks, a rosy glow from being out in the fresh air all day. I wrote a huffy letter to the papers and gave up. I missed the vultures covering me with their inquisitive shadows.

The hospital was my next target. Tea estates were very proud of their hospitals, so I was surprised when I entered this one to find only two rooms, for men and women, filled with iron beds very close together. Another room behind was reserved for special cases, and there was a small dispensary. Women sat on the beds holding babies. There were no tables or chairs, relations bringing their food (not supplied by the hospital) put it on the floor. A cloud of flies hovered and crawled, the mothers waved thin arms above the babies' heads.

The Doctor Babu, who was trained in Bengal and didn't speak any of the patients' languages, told me that anaemia was a big problem. Too many children, that was the mistake. He showed me some slides of blood samples, very pale, one almost yellow. He gave injections while they were in hospital but when they returned to their houses and their work their conditions deteriorated. Nowadays with DDT they didn't get malaria, at least. In the single room a small girl lay in the bed, the only piece of furniture. TB, said the Doctor Babu, advanced, too much advanced for treatment. Her family were many and there was little room for her at home, it was better for her to be here though there was little to be done for her. She needed fresh milk but this was hard to obtain. Her name was Neelima, he told me, but when I spoke it she went on looking at the blank wall.

Mac was willing to put in fly-proof doors, but as for the rest – family planning work, some furniture, cheerful paint, a few toys for child patients – I would have to ask Dr P. He was the European in charge of all the Company hospitals, who visited once a fortnight, a nice man, a friend, who didn't even have a word of Urdu, which was not considered unusual. His job was to see that the necessary medicines were stocked and records kept.

The Company weren't keen on family planning, he said, the more the merrier – it was a mechanism for keeping wages down. With trade unions now compulsory by law there were a lot of clever dicks around advising the labour of their rights, the best thing was to have a great many people desperately looking for work. However, I would be allowed, within reason, to give family planning advice as long as I didn't expect the Company to pay for the rubber doo-dahs.

The rest of my plans – to make the hospital a bright, cheerful place with pictures and curtains – sorry, no can do. No could even understand the need of it, frankly. If Mac wanted to use a few pots of paint fair enough, but let's face it, would these people even notice? Look at where they came from. It was too soon for me to suggest that if where they came from was supplied with running water and sanitation it would save on expensive drugs. I homed in on family planning and wrote off to Delhi on the subject.

While waiting for a reply I visited the hospital every day. A simple-minded girl had given birth and had no milk for the baby. She was given a bottle, but hardly knew which end to put in the child's mouth. I sat and helped her, knowing that as soon as she got home the baby would die, what with her incompetence and no milk. I thought of the little gibbons I had reared on milk from our cows, and vowed to go down and help her keep her baby alive. Mac said, darling forget it, you can't go to the lines five times a day, it's survival of the fittest here. I knew he was right, but in a small, desperate gesture of despair saw to it that most of the milk from our cows went to the hospital.

I spent time every morning with the little TB patient. I took down paper and chalks and books and beads to thread. A friend gave me a beautiful wooden doll complete with clothes, and Neelima's face lit up with a smile at last. She held the doll in her arms all day, and it seemed that she looked less pinched and feverish. Then a couple of weeks later her bed was empty. Dead? No, her family had removed her, along with the books and the doll. The Doctor Babu could not prevent them. A couple of weeks later he was sorry to announce that she had died. I wept and he said, 'Madam, do not concern yourself; her case was hopeless.' But I had a feeling her family had taken her home because of the doll and the crayons. Perhaps I hadn't killed her, perhaps I had hastened her death.

I was cheered by the arrival of a letter from Delhi saying that a Miss Das was visiting Assam in a couple of weeks and would be happy to give a lecture to the labour force on the subject of birth control. She would come provided with all necessary materials, which she would be happy to distribute gratis. Would I put her up for the night?

Mac foresaw trouble when Father James, the Catholic priest from the Silesian mission, asked to stay the same night. Neither of us anticipated Miss Das's extraordinary enthusiasm, her laying out on the tea table within ten minutes of her arrival an array of long and round rubber objects for our inspection. Father James, a man of charm and humour, winked at me as Miss Das questioned us about the sexual habits of the labour force. Mac pointed out that they belonged to different castes and probably had different habits. Father James suggested that as we were all ignorant, God should be left in charge at which Miss Das threw up her bangled arms and quoted figures to show how much India's population had exploded, even at this minute half a million babies were being conceived.

'I think the women will be too busy preparing the evening meal at this minute,' Father James said, consulting his watch, at which Miss Das hooted with laughter. He and she, a spinster and a celibate, were rather in the dark about these things, she admitted. For that reason, she had brought with her questionnaires which Mac and his staff would please complete by midday tomorrow, when she was leaving. Looking at these later, Mac doubted if everyone really understood the word intercourse, even though it was used on every line of the questionnaires. I thought Miss Das wonderful, and very brave; a single Hindu woman travelling round with condoms was an inspiration. Well, don't let it inspire you, Mac said; I'll get the sack if my wife is known to be a commercial traveller in Dutch caps.

In spite of his reluctance to take her seriously, Mac arranged with the staff for an open-air meeting the following morning, complete with marigolds and microphones. Only women would attend, and Miss Das and I would both give speeches. A large display table was placed in front of the microphones, laid out with her wares. I spoke first, telling them that because I only had three children, I lived in a big house and ran a car. This connection was nonsense that none of us believed. My English was translated into, I suspected, something quite different and more logical. Miss Das described the use of her rubber goods, and held up a large poster of a penis and testicles to show the kind of operation men could have. The whole thing was watched in solemn silence and afterwards the women shuffled past to receive their packages. Mac said that next day the air was filled with little rubber airships whizzing about.

I was optimistic for a bit, but in the end only a handful of women were sterilised and only my cook had a vasectomy, to please me. I put the poor response down to ignorance; how could illiterate people who never read a paper, never had a wireless set, know the first thing about their bodies' rhythms; how could they understand the intricacies of organising the size of a family? Education was the priority. When we came back from leave education would be my own.

My programme was interrupted in 1962 by the Chinese invading army pouring down into Assam, and we women being flown down to Calcutta for a few weeks. Did we think we would be turned into concubines with our feet squeezed into tiny shoes? Or was it that the Chinese, being yellow, would be like the dreaded Japs, who only twenty years earlier had been presented to us as monsters of cruelty and vice. I was frightened at the time, but look back on our 'escape' with shame. We were unconcerned about what happened to the labour force or the Assamese, who didn't have Hercules aircraft provided for their exit. Quite a few Managers handed over the keys of their safes to the Head Mohurer and departed too. The gardens ran smoothly without them, the safes remained unlooted.

By then I had started on my educational mission. The garden supplied by law a primary school, after that it was the state's business to educate children up to Class Ten, when they could matriculate and go on to college. For the thousand-odd children on the garden there was a primary school the size of my sitting room. The children sat on the floor with slates and chanted. There were not a lot of them. Although it was illegal to employ a child under twelve, birth certificates were never asked for and there was plenty for them to do, looking after younger siblings, cutting fodder, fetching water. Educated or not, their parents saw no future for them in the world outside the tea garden. I could order plasticine and reading books, but they would still stay away.

The secondary school was more hopeful; it had several classrooms and a new extension for Arts and Crafts. The headmaster admitted this had never been used; its presence upped the school's status and entitled its staff to higher salaries, but still left funds short to supply an Art teacher or materials. Ah. My opening. I would be Unpaid Art Instructor, and English teacher on the side. How kind, said the headmaster, and welcomed me on my arrival with a speech and some marigolds. These stuck to my neck; under a tin roof the classrooms were suffocatingly hot.

The Art room had a large central table on which I deposited a large lump of clay and some powder paint. In no time I had half a dozen bananas to pass round. I handed out some clay to each of the children of Class Four, aged about twelve, and asked them to make something from it. One and all they produced a banana. Next day dozens more bananas piled up on the table. The headmaster, surveying the heap of phallic symbols, said how useful were extracurricular activities. He asked the children what they would like to make next and almost with one voice they said bows and arrows. This would involve bringing in quantities of bamboo and providing sharp knives, not practical we thought, and I sent for raffia and more paints. Meanwhile we made woollen balls and numbers dropped.

English was more successful; I taught Class Five grammar and Class Ten *Macbeth* and Essays. The children were from the villages and the staff, none from the lines. The girls were pretty with pink ribbons in their oiled plaits. Some of the boys looked about thirty, with bushy moustaches. They were all bright and enthusiastic and enjoyed the games I introduced into grammar lessons. *Macbeth* was a problem – how to explain a blasted heath or any of the great speeches? I broke them of the habit of copying the essay of the cleverest boy, and handing in a dozen identical pieces. I asked them to write about 'How I spend Sunday' or 'My grandfather', opening doors into their lives. I was happier than I had ever been in Assam.

Because of my interest, I was invited to speech days and prizegivings. These were something of an ordeal, sitting in a stifling tent listening to speeches given by very old, toothless men into microphones that seldom worked. The children got tattered little books as prizes and a lot of resolutions were passed and tea was handed round and aniseed chewed and it all went on for hours and hours.

Sometimes important guests turned up; one of these was the Minister of Education, a charming man who told me he was very keen to start Scouts and Guides, and disappointed at my reluctance to organise these, baffled when I told him I had hated being a Girl Guide and never learnt to light a fire with one match. After the meeting his transport failed to turn up, and we sat by the side of the road on upright chairs waiting for my car. 'In a nut I am stranded,' said the Minister cheerfully, and told me of a thesis he was writing to obtain a doctorate, and his hopes of going to England for research. The sun set, the parrots flew in their squawking rainbow back into the hills, and I had the kind of talk no planter ever provided.

One day Mac brought in a letter, which we laughed a lot about. It was a love missive stylishly written and adorned with blue tear drops down the sides. I could read it; an expression of undying devotion, harmlessly unsuggestive. But Mac said it had caused outrage among the staff, being addressed to the Head Mohurer's daughter by a classmate who could never in a million years aspire to her hand, a poor village boy from a family everyone knew to be worthless.

Moreover the boy had arranged an assignation with the girl, and had taken to it three umbrellas. Why, nobody knew, but guesses were darkly suspicious. The mystery was solved a few days later when, after cross-examination by the entire staff, he had owned up. He had taken them, he said, because it was Damn Wet. I exploded with laughter when Mac told me this, but the Head Mohurer was not amused, it seemed. He demanded that the boy be expelled before he defiled any more daughters.

When I found that the boy was from Class Ten, the clever student whose essays everyone copied, about to take his final exams and matriculate, I implored forgiveness. His life would be ruined, the punishment was far in excess of the crime; indeed what crime was there? I thought as Manager's wife my wishes would be more important than the Head Mohurer's, but I was wrong. With a mixture of frustration and genuine pain I gave up going to the school. Fortunately we went on leave soon after, which gave me time to simmer down.

We returned to our last tour before retirement, and to me it was now a different country, now that the scales one by one had fallen from my eyes. I saw the labour living in dirty shacks, the women anaemic, the children uneducated. I saw the hospital as a lot of beds, no nurses, no sustaining diet, a fortnightly visit from a doctor who couldn't even ask the patients how they were feeling. The only school was just four walls and a roof, featureless and unequipped. I started to snap at Mac: wasn't the Company making huge profits, why was nothing ploughed back, nothing, I wailed, not even a football field, not even a bus to take people to the nearest town for a change of scene? He agreed with me in everything I said, but it was the System. He took his orders from the Company, they from the ITA. At this very moment directives to build new Line houses were being argued over and would probably be evaded.

I still felt that education was the key; illiteracy left people helpless, futureless. I dreamed of a Model School staffed by VSO teachers, open to everyone irrespective of class or background. I would approach the Chairman when he came out on his winter visit. Mac produced a voice of weary disdain to imitate the Chairman's. 'This isn't a charitable concern, dear lady,' and 'Wait till the ball's in your court, my dear,' and 'With all the damn taxes we pay it's a question of tightening belts not lashing out on expensive buildings.'

Which was exactly what happened: alas, said the Chairman, Times being what they were, philanthropy was simply not on the cards. Simply there was no spondulux (cash), dear lady. I had to refrain from asking where the spondulux came for him and his Lady Wife to float out first-class every winter, drifting on to Hong Kong or Penang as the mood took them. I pointed out that the tea

industry had been in Assam for a hundred-odd years and left no
monument to their stay. A beautiful school would fill this gap. He
leaned forward and patted me on the knee and suggested that I
fill my pretty head with the things other wives were occupied
with. His wife contributed flower arrangement and tapestry. Mac
winked at me as he poured them both another gin.

I turned to Anima, and we arranged a meeting in her garden to
which were invited all the richest men we could think of – Marwaris
mostly, known to have huge sums stashed in banks all over the
world. There were speeches, all in favour of such a commendable
project; a lot of resolutions were passed, sites for the school settled,
its name (that of the richest Marwari) decided on. But somehow
nothing further happened. I spat at Mac when he said it was
Typical. Our marriage was suffering from all my failed schemes.

Anima and I went on visiting villages, to collect folklore for a
book I was beginning to write. In between, I watched polo and
had friends to dinner, a double life, which in the end was too
much for me. I was sitting on my veranda one day when panic
overcame me. The plants that twined around me were dangerous,
poisonous. There was poison everywhere, I washed my hands
incessantly to keep it at bay. As well as fear there was pain, and I
was given pills and sent to hospital for treatment. In between the
pain and panic I looked out at the beautiful garden; at jays lying
like blue fans on the lawn, their wings spread to the sun; at egrets
arriving for a tea-time ballet every afternoon; at golden orioles
drinking from the bird bath, and humming birds beating their
wings in front of orchids. I wept bitterly at the farewell meetings
laid on by the staff when they heard I was to be sent home ahead
of Mac. It was an ignominious end to life in Assam.

Four years later the Assam Company wound up most of its property, selling its gardens to Marwaris, and all the European Managers left. For most of them it had been a good life, and for their wives too, comfortably ignorant and complacently unconcerned about schools, hospitals, the lines; sensibly so it now seems to me. They didn't become ill with frustration, they enjoyed the warmth and the servants and the tennis and their sumptuous bungalows and their husbands were pleased at their pleasure.

The Indian Managers who took over continued 'to flaunt a colonial lifestyle' as a contemporary author has put it. They were without exception the product of public schools, such as the Doon School, where their heads were filled with the same nonsense mine had been. They had looked at those old maps and absorbed the history of empire as written by retired colonial officers. On the whole, they were better educated than most European planters, but just as blinkered.

However, in November 2002 I visited some Tata tea estates in southern India (Kerala) and found the conditions much better than portrayed above.

Part I
Bewitched

Chapter Two

The Story of an Addiction

'As a rule they [the English] will refuse even to sample a foreign dish, they regard such things as garlic and olive oil with disgust, life is unlivable to them unless they have tea and puddings.'

George Orwell, The Lion and the Unicorn: 'The English People', *Collected Essays*

'It was part of Kipling's "Natural Theology" that to lack tea for a week knocked the bottom out of the Universe . . .'

Daily Telegraph, 1938

Tea is an addiction, but an addiction different from all others. It is milder, a habit relatively easily broken. It is more universal. Most unusually, it is good for the addict. And it is largely unnoticed both to those addicted and others. Indeed, the conquest of the world by tea has been so successful that we have forgotten that it has happened at all. Tea has become like water or air, something that many of us take for granted.

No one on earth drank tea a few thousand years ago. A few small tribal groups in the jungles of south-east Asia chewed the leaves of the plant, but that was the nearest anyone came to tea drinking. Two thousand years ago it was drunk in a handful of religious communities. By a thousand years ago it was drunk by millions of Chinese. Five hundred years ago over half of the world's population was drinking tea as their main alternative to water.

During the next five hundred years tea drinking spread to cover the world. By the 1930s there was enough tea for 200 cups of tea a year for every person in the world. Tea is now more ubiquitous than any type of food or any drink apart from water. Thousands of millions of cups of tea are drunk every day. In Britain, for example, 165 million cups of tea a day are drunk, an average of over three per person. This means that about forty per cent of the total liquid intake of the British population is in the form of tea. Its world consumption easily equals all the other manufactured drinks in the world put together – that is, coffee, chocolate, cocoa, sweet fizzy artificial drinks and all alcoholic drinks.

So how and why did this happen? And, given the rapid and worldwide spread of this drink, what have been the consequences of this success? Tea became the first truly global product with worldwide repercussions.

In many ways, water dominates the world. Human beings consist mainly of water. They need between two and four pints of liquid per person per day, depending on the climate, work and body weight, in order to survive. About half of the daily requirement comes through the food we eat, the rest through drink. This means that more than anything else on earth, apart from air, water is essential for human survival.

For long periods of history and in many places, people drank and still drink plain water. For tens of thousands of years, hunter-gatherers had no protection against waterborne diseases, but the dangers were not so great, as the population was thinly spread and mobile. People moved on, abandoning their faeces and other potentially harmful waste; water supplies remained largely unpolluted. The rapid evolution of harmful bacteria was inhibited and mainly took place in other mammals.

When settled city civilisations emerged about ten thousand years ago a number of density-dependent diseases emerged. Many of our 'modern' diseases such as malaria, influenza, tuberculosis began to be serious hazards. Water supplies became contaminated, particularly in the cities and crowded countryside, and waterborne disease spread. As huge civilisations such as China began to emerge, the dangers from disease escalated, and by two thousand years ago the problem was widespread.

As an ideal drink, water, although it scores low in terms of taste, scores very highly in terms of cost and fluid replacement. In many parts of the world, however, it became increasingly dangerous. So what alternatives to water were available to carry humans through the last two thousand years, from a population of less than quarter of a billion to something over twenty-five times that number today?

Many of us, if asked what the simplest societies drank, might think of pastoral tribes milking their cows and sheep. Certainly milk drinking has featured as important in certain societies. Yet there were several problems with milk as a major alternative to water. One was its availability and cost. Only populations with considerable areas of free land for grazing livestock could obtain substantial amounts of milk. This basically restricted large-scale dairy farming to north-western Europe, central Asia and certain pastoral areas in the Himalayas, India and East Africa.

Furthermore, until recently, particularly in urban and crowded civilisations, milk was often a very hazardous substance, full of bacteria, some of them harmful. The rich fatty fluids are ideal for the proliferation of many kinds of micro-organism not found in water. There are even lethal kinds of organism that are specially adapted to milk, for example bovine tuberculosis. People who tried to drink unheated milk that had been stored for a few hours outside the animal would soon discover how lethal it was. And so milk-drinking only became widespread in settled civilisations about a century and a half ago, after Pasteur discovered a method of killing the germs in milk. We have forgotten the dangers that lurk in milk, or the strangeness of squirting juice from an animal into our mouths.

One more factor that rules out milk as a universal alternative to water is that not everyone likes it or can drink it. A curious feature of milk is that the enzyme necessary to digest it is not naturally present in the body after weaning – the body has to be programmed to accept and digest milk. If children are not given substantial quantities of animal milk after they are weaned they develop lactose intolerance. Hence, drinking milk or eating milk products such as cheese or butter makes many people literally sick, a condition that is extremely common in all those parts of the world where there is no dairy farming.

Imagine sitting down to design a world-conquering drink to satisfy human beings. What would one need? Cost and ease of access are the most important single factors. It must be cheap enough to become the drink of millions of relatively poor people. Whatever it is made from should grow easily and quickly over a wide ecological zone. The more of it that can be used and the more often it can be harvested the better. It must be easy to transport and store.

People should *want* to consume the product. Perhaps it should be sweet – a major appeal to human taste. Yet not all drinks are sweet, appealing rather to the pleasant sensation caused to the drinker. The drink must refresh, exhilarate, energise and relax the body and mind. It must be safe, too – many dangerous micro-organisms can be absorbed through drink. Any alternative to clean water must be relatively germ-free if it is to attract many millions of consumers.

Finally, if our miracle drink is going to become the staple liquid intake, it has to be genuinely thirst-quenching, and it must be possible to drink one or two pints of it a day without it interfering with work and concentration.

One group of drinks, invented as city civilisations emerged, showed some promise as a thirst quencher. These are the drinks where a grain or plant juice is left to ferment, often with a yeast or other substance to speed up the process – that is the beers and wines.

Yet the various 'beers' that have played such a large part in world history could not replace water. One problem was that the warm broth of mashed grains and the ensuing liquid – an ideal environment for bacteria to thrive, although this was not understood at the time – quickly went stale. In trying to find ways to combat this, people discovered, through accident and experiment, that if certain plants were added during the process they stopped the brew going bad. They often seemed to improve the taste as well, lending a tang and aroma to the beer.

The ancient Egyptians found this out, perhaps adapting

techniques first used in bread-making. Particularly effective was a climbing plant found in northern Europe some thousands of years ago – hops. The ancient Germans brewed hop-made beer. We now know that its astringent, bitter taste is an indication that it contains some kind of preserving substance. The intriguing puzzle of what this substance was and what it was destroying lay behind the decision of Louis Pasteur to do his doctoral thesis on hops and beer, a riddle which if solved could also make a substantial fortune for the scientist.

The great advantage of beer, especially when made in its mild form as in English 'small beer', was that it could be drunk right through the day without leading to excessive drunkenness. With a low alcohol content (about two or three per cent), it was safe not only for grown men, but could be drunk by women and children. Since it was also thought by many to be 'tasty', although not sweet, and left a pleasant feeling, it appeared to fit most of the criterion for a successful super-drink, especially as it was also relatively safe in that it did not seem to carry disease.

The great disadvantage of beer as a universal thirst-quencher was that huge quantities of malt, hops and above all grain were used in the process – half of the total grain harvest in seventeenth-century England was used for beer brewing. Although it is an efficient way of providing vitamins, carbohydrates and proteins, it is indeed a fortunate country that can use half of its grain harvest for drink – and still have enough grain for bread. Some tribes may have produced calabashes of beer on a wide scale, but no large peasant civilisation has ever been able to replace water with beer over a long period. So, it is really cost that, in the wider sense, is the major obstacle.

Wines offered an alternative, unfermented fruit juices originally being impractical. In European grape-based wine, the inner part of the fruit, the soft flesh, produces the liquid while the skins contain an antiseptic, antibacterial substance. While the wine is maturing this helps to prevent harmful bacteria from proliferating and the wine from going stale.

There are, however, two disadvantages with wine as a total thirst-quenching solution. Normally, wine is about two to three times as alcoholic as beer – about 10–15 per cent proof. Even seasoned drinkers who drank nothing else would become drunk after some two to four pints of wine a day and their mouths would become extremely dry. Of course, it can be mixed with water, and the protective antiseptic element in it may provide some cleansing, but the balance has to be right. Too much water and it loses much of its attractiveness.

The second problem is the production cost in terms of land and labour. To provide the whole population of a large nation with enough wine for all its drinking needs would require huge vineyards, and this would threaten arable and pastoral farming. It would also require a vast labour input, particularly at the picking and pressing stage, for it is extremely labour-intensive – large parts of the population would be tied up in wine production, and would have to be fed. Unlike that of beer, wine production is very difficult to mechanise. The grains that go into beer and bread are processed with the same types of machinery – animals, wind and water mills, and advanced reaping tools – which makes large-scale production with relatively light labour input so much easier.

For this, and perhaps other reasons, no nation, not even France or Italy, has ever had wine as its main drink for the whole population. Even the upper classes could not drink it exclusively. Until the nineteenth century, the ordinary population drank water, a little wine, and, in northern France and Germany, some pear- and apple-based drinks.

Then, there are the distilled drinks. Grain is fermented then boiled in water and liquid is condensed from its vapours. This would be sterile. The micro-organisms would be killed by the boiling and not transmitted in the vapour. All distilled drinks, such as the rice spirit of Japan, the millet spirit of Nepal and Tibet or the grain spirit of Scotland and Ireland, are generally safe from bacterial and other infections. Unfortunately, it will make you very drunk if you absorb the several pints a day needed to keep a human being alive. Furthermore, the distilled and fortified spirits consume a considerable amount of energy in their production, while the amount of liquid produced is relatively small. Though very popular for recreational or religious purposes, as a candidate for the perfect world drink to fulfil human needs for liquid, spirits are a non-starter.

Finally, there are drinks produced by infusing parts of a plant in water. This usually involves soaking the relevant parts in boiling or very hot water, which releases the active agent in the plant. Three major infusion drinks have spread widely. In two of them, chocolate and coffee, the berry or nut of a plant is ground up and water added. Both are very bitter without sugar. These drinks are extremely popular nowadays in affluent societies, but because of the costs of producing chocolate on a large scale, and the very high caffeine levels in traditional coffee, neither of them became drinks that could replace water.

The other type of infusion drinks are those which use a leaf, flower or fruit; these, termed 'teas', comprise true tea and numerous other varieties, including herbal teas. True tea, made from the *Camellia sinensis* plant, scores highly on all the criteria set out above. It can be produced cheaply. The plant which yields it is very productive, giving new leaf every six weeks or so. It grows over quite a range of climatic zones, from central China to East Africa. Just a few leaves are needed to make a good pot of tea and they can be re-used. Dry tea is very light and stores well. It is easily prepared for drinking, but its preparation is sufficiently elaborate to encourage the human love of play and ceremony. It is extremely safe to drink and indeed many believe it has special health benefits. It is attractive because it makes the drinker feel stimulated and relaxed, optimistic and focused. It is mild enough to be drunk throughout the day without any harmful side effects.

So tea was always a potential world conqueror. Over the last two thousand years its empire has spread and it has become the greatest addiction in history. As the mythical or possibly legendary Chinese Emperor Shen Nung is said to have put it: 'Tea is better than wine for it leadeth not to intoxication, neither does it cause a man to say foolish things and repent thereof in his sober moments. It is better than water for it does not carry disease; neither does it act like poison as water does when it contains foul and rotten matter.' [1]

Chapter Three

Froth of the Liquid Jade

'The progress of this famous plant has been something like the progress of truth; suspected at first, though very palatable to those who had the courage to taste it; resisted as it encroached; abused as its popularity spread; and establishing its triumph at last, in cheering the whole land from the palace to the cottage, only by slow and resistless efforts of time and its own virtues.'

Isaac D'Israeli (1766–1848)

No one knows for certain exactly where or when the tea plant, *Camellia sinensis*, originated, or even when or by whom it was first domesticated. What is known is that the tree evolved somewhere in the jungles of the eastern Himalayas, where in an amazingly rapid evolutionary development, the great varieties in temperature and micro-climate caused by the mountains rising from tropical lowlands, combined with the heaviest rainfall in the world as the monsoon clouds hit the outlying Himalayas, made it the most varied and rich region for plants in the world.

It seems likely that parts of the tea tree were first chewed by monkeys and other mammals indigenous to this region. *Homo sapiens* spread into the area between sixty and a hundred thousand years ago, and, perhaps taking their cue from the monkeys, early tribesmen began chewing tea and found it to be stimulating and relaxing to mind and body. It helped when carrying out arduous tasks, such as tramping through jungles and up mountainsides; indeed, people still chew tea leaves for this purpose: in Turkistan, for example, as Serena Hardy writes in *The Tea Book*, they chew used tea leaves, which 'helps to allay fatigue on a journey when food is scarce'.[2] The early forest dwellers may also have found that rubbing tea on to wounds, or binding up a wound with some ground-up tea inside it, helped healing, and we know from recent accounts that tribesmen in the Naga, Shan, Kachin and neighbouring hills use tea as a medicine in this way. Such vitalising and medicinal properties would have given tea-chewing humans, and tea-chewing monkeys, a competitive advantage. For thousands of years there existed a symbiosis between tea and mammals as the latter, through their consumption and handling of the plants, unconsciously encouraged widespread growth of the tea tree.

It is often assumed that tea has always been taken as an infusion of leaves in hot water. The idea of adding a leaf to boiling water, however, is not a very obvious one, and certainly not an option open to the monkeys and other mammals that first consumed tea and possibly demonstrated its attractiveness to humans. It is therefore not surprising that some of the earliest accounts we have of tea consumption among forest dwellers in the regions of northern Thailand, Burma, Assam and south-west China describe how they eat rather than drink tea. In Burma, northern Thailand and Yunan, the tribal peoples still use wild tea tree leaves to make 'small bundles of steamed and fermented tea for chewing'[3]. Early explorers who described the customs of the people living in the area give hints of the diverse ways in which the forest peoples may have consumed tea. 'The Shans of Northern Siam [Thailand] steamed or boiled the leaves of the *miang*, or wild tea tree, and molded them into balls to be eaten with salt, oil, garlic, pig fat, and dried fish – a custom still followed by their descendants.' In 1835 a writer described how the Singphos and Kamttees of the Burma border 'drank an infusion of wild tea leaves, "prepared by cutting [the leaves] into small pieces, taking out the stalks and fibres, boiling, and squeezing them into a ball, which they dry in the sun and retain for use".' These customs continue today in the Burmese *letpet*, or tea salad. 'This is a pickled tea which Pelungs long have had a custom of preparing by boiling and kneading jungle tea leaves, and then wrapping them in papers or stuffing them into internodes of bamboo, which they bury in underground silos for several months to ferment. Eventually the product is dug up and eaten as a great luxury at marriage feasts and similar festive occasions.'[4]

However it was discovered that tea could be consumed as an infusion of leaves in hot water – legends suggest that it was first discovered when a camellia leaf dropped accidentally into hot water – tea was increasingly made into a drink, and it was as such that it flowed up through China and hence into Tibet and Mongolia, and elsewhere in central Asia. When it reached those high altitudes, however, it reverted to at least a semi-food form – a mushy tea soup made with yak butter and sugar, or balls of tea leaves with other foodstuffs, comparable to the way tea was probably used by the early tribes of the eastern Himalayas.

In due course, thousands of years ago, the tribal peoples in the eastern Himalayas, including south-western China, started trading this attractive leaf to others living on the edge of their forested mountains. Among these were the settled peoples of the great civilisation of China.

There are legends of tea in Chinese sources going back to the fourth century BC and earlier. Chinese traders who brought back some of these leaves along with numerous other forest products found a particularly ready market in the temples and monasteries. Nearly all religious specialists appreciate 'medicines' or 'herbs' that will increase their success, quickly adopting plants that might shorten the climb to the spiritual world and safeguard their worldly position.

The practitioners of the forms of religion that spread in China – Taoism and, especially, Buddhism – were particularly attracted by a plant that could help meditation by increasing mental concentration and staving off sleep. So much did Buddhists come to appreciate this new elixir that, in certain sects, tea-drinking was to be elevated to one of the four ways of concentrating the mind, alongside walking, feeding fish and sitting quietly in thought.

The problem was that the leaves grew on a big tree far away in the forest. The solution was to move the tea plant, changing its shape and size from a large forest tree into a small, easily harvested, bush. This was not easy, but the wealth and organisation of the Chinese monasteries achieved it.

The obscure and little documented early period of tea is well summarised by the late nineteenth-century Japanese writer, Kakuzo Okakura.

The tea-plant, a native of southern China, was known from very early times to Chinese botany and medicine. It is alluded to in the classics under the various names of Tou, Tseh, Chung, Kha, and Ming, and was highly prized for possessing the virtues of relieving fatigue, delighting the soul, strengthening the will, and repairing the eye-sight. It was not only administered as an internal dose, but also often applied externally, in form of paste, to alleviate rheumatic pains. The Taoists claimed it as an important ingredient of the elixir of immortality. The Buddhists used it extensively to prevent drowsiness during their long hours of meditation.[5]

Between its first domestication in south-west China and about the fifth century AD, tea spread mainly through the monastic gardens. It was seen mainly as an herbal medicine and grown alongside a wide range of Chinese medicinal plants that were part of a sophisticated pharmacopoeia. All sorts of variants of tea were developed to deal with different complaints of the head, heart, liver and stomach.

But this plant was special. Unlike almost all other medical herbs it not only cured, but also made a tasty and invigorating drink that helped mental and physical work. This use could well be applied outside the monastic calling, and by the fourth and fifth centuries AD tea had become a favourite beverage among the inhabitants of the Yangtze valley. As the popularity of this wonder drink grew, it began to be produced for the largest domestic market in the world. During the Tang period (620–907), tea spread through most of the Chinese provinces, its popularity heightened by the publication in the eighth century of the first treatise on tea, Lu Yu's *The Classic of Tea*. This brilliant short

book became a bible for tea producers and consumers for a
thousand years, describing the essence of each stage of the
production and consumption of tea. The book starts by
explaining that 'Tea is from a grand tree in the south', describing
how it grows best in certain conditions and only certain leaves
should be picked.

> Tea is of a cold nature and may be used in case of blockage or
> stoppage of the bowels. When its flavor is at its coldest nature,
> it is most suitable as a drink. If one is generally moderate but
> feeling hot or warm, given to melancholia, suffering from
> aching of the brain, smarting of the eyes, troubled in the four
> limbs or afflicted in the hundred joints, he may take tea four or
> five times. Its liquor is like the sweetest dew of Heaven.[6]

When the Chinese could not obtain the camellia leaf, they made
infusions from alternative sources.

> In the mountainous parts of central and Western China many
> substitutes are employed by the peasants, who seldom taste
> the real articles. In western Hupeh the leaves of several kinds
> of Wild Pear and Apple, grouped under the colloquial name of
> 'T'-ang-li-tzu', are used as a source of tea and exported to
> Shasi for the same purpose. The infusion prepared from these
> leaves is of a rich brown colour, very palatable and thirst
> quenching. It is called Hung-ch'a (red tea), and is in general
> use among the poorer classes in the west.[7]

If there was nothing at all, people in China drank hot water as a
poor imitation of the real thing, dreaming that they were drinking

'virtual' tea, or what was called 'white tea' (*baicha*).

Many varieties of tea were grown, and it was traded over long distances. Certain varieties, particularly those with a bitter taste, were prized as medicines.

> In all the larger medicine shops in Szechuan and, incidentally, elsewhere in the Empire, a product known as 'P'uerh tea' is on sale . . . This tea is grown in the Shan states . . . has a bitter flavour, and is famous as a medicine all over China, being esteemed as a digestive and nervous stimulant. It also finds its way into the wealthy lamaseries of Thibet, where its medicinal properties are highly appreciated.[8]

The need for a safe and pleasant alternative to water was especially desirable just at the time that the Tang writers were exhorting their fellows to drink tea. Around the eighth century China's population epicentre was moving south. People were settling and multiplying in the rich lands of the central Yangtze basin, where they grew the newly improved miracle plant, wet rice. Previously, in the north, barley and millet had been grown and could supply grains for drink, at least of an alcoholic kind, and the population was quite light. But now the population expanded fast and the cities grew large. Space was scarce and all the available land was needed for rice.

Tea provided a stimulus to the production of Chinese porcelain, and the changing styles of tea production and drinking are reflected in the great eras of Chinese ceramics. Okakura discusses the relative merits of different porcelains used for teacups.

The Celestial porcelain, as is well known, had its origin in an attempt to reproduce the exquisite shade of jade, resulting, in the Tang dynasty, in the blue glaze of the south, and the white glaze of the north. Luwuh [Lu Yu] considered the blue as the ideal colour for the teacup, as it lent additional greenness to the beverage, whereas the white made it look pinkish and distasteful. It was because he used Cake-tea. Later on, when the teamasters of Sung took to the Powdered-tea, they preferred heavy bowls of blue-black and dark brown. The Mings, with their steeped tea, rejoiced in light ware of white porcelain.[9]

More broadly, Okakura suggested that the ages of tea were linked to the changing phases of Chinese civilisation.

Even as the difference in favourite vintage marks the separate idiosyncrasies of different periods and nationalities of Europe, so the Tea ideals characterise the various moods of Oriental culture. The Cake-tea which was boiled, the Powdered-tea which was whipped, the Leaf-tea which was steeped, mark the distinct emotional impulses of the Tang, the Sung, and the Ming dynasties of China. If we were inclined to borrow the much-abused terminology of art classification, we might designate them respectively, the Classic, the Romantic, and the Naturalistic schools of Tea.[10]

Tea was also increasingly viewed as a powerful medicine. For example, in a herbal by Li Shih-chen, published in 1578 but thought to contain material from a much earlier period, Li stated that tea would 'promote digestion, dissolve fats, neutralise poisons in the digestive system, cure dysentery, fight lung disease, lower fevers, and treat epilepsy. Tea was also thought to be an effective astringent for cleaning sores and recommended for washing the eyes and mouth.'[11]

As more and more tea was produced for the huge Chinese market it moved outwards. Most significantly for the Chinese, it came to the attention of its pastoral neighbours in the great uplands of central Asia, from Tibet to Siberia.

These peoples lived in an area where the bitter winds and cold winters put a great strain on the human body. They had for centuries drunk water and milk. Now they discovered this strange leaf that the Chinese were willing to sell to them in exchange for pastoral products. When mixed with their milk and butter it gave them added vigour and protection against the harsh climate of their upland ranges.

A huge trade in bricks of tea grew along the Silk Road and through many other routes, criss-crossing from south-west China to Siberia, and from China as far as the Islamic civilisations of the Middle East. Much of this merchandise was carried up to the high regions on the human back, so rough was the terrain. By about the twelfth century, the tea bricks were so ubiquitous that they became the preferred currency in many parts of central Asia. The tea coinage was perfectly suited to perform the central functions of money as a measure of value, medium of exchange and store of wealth. It was light, it could be made into uniform bricks, it was valuable. It had one great advantage over a silver coin or paper money – if one were desperate, one could eat or drink it. Alongside silk, tea became one of the few articles of value that the armed horsemen of the steppes wanted from China.

To all these advantages of tea over other currency, William H. Ukers adds one more.

Tea-money in China is almost as old as tea itself. The Chinese had bank-notes long before Western culture came into existence, but in commercial transactions with far-inland tribes, who were mostly nomadic pastoralists, paper money was of little use; the various coins, of mystic value, were equally useless. But tea – compressed tea-money – could be used as an article of consumption or for further bartering. Unlike real money which often lessens in value the farther it circulates from its point of issue, tea-money enhanced in value the farther it was carried from the tea gardens of China. The first tea-money consisted of crude cakes made in ox-presses. These have been superseded by machine-made, hard-as-granite tea blocks.[12]

Even to this day, brick tea is used as currency in some of the remoter areas of Central Asia.

There are a number of descriptions of how the tea was prepared in these upland areas, including Tibet, which indicate both its importance and the way in which it was combined with other foodstuffs. In the 1930s, Ukers wrote, the 'Mongols and the other Tartar tribes make a kind of soup from powdered brick tea, which they boil with alkaline steppe water, salt, and fat. Then they strain it and mix it with milk, butter, and roasted meal.' It was sometimes mixed with rice and ginger. The author comments that 'boiled and churned butter-tea continues the great stand-by of the Tibetans. No Tibetan drinks less than fifteen or twenty cups a day, and some even seventy or eighty.'[13]

The following description by an early nineteenth-century traveller in Tibet, William Moorcroft, gives a more detailed account. 'At breakfast each person drinks about five to ten cups, each containing about one-third of a pint; and when the last is half finished, he mixes with the remainder enough barley meal to bring it to the consistency of paste . . . At the midday meal, those who can afford it take tea again, with wheaten cakes, accompanied by a paste of wheat, flour, butter, and sugar, served hot.'[14]

The importance of the drink was noted by Colonel Laurence Waddell in his *Lhasa and its Mysteries* (1905). Describing the Tibetans, he wrote that 'As a beverage he drinks, all day long, cupfuls of hot buttered tea, which is really a soup or broth . . . no doubt it is wholesome; for it is not merely a stimulating hot drink in the cold, but overcomes the danger of drinking unboiled water in a country where the water supply is dangerously polluted.' [15]

Tea was also important in terms of nutrition; particularly in the way it was prepared and consumed in this area. Tea contains vitamins, magnesium, potassium and other nutrients in the leaf that are lost or diminish greatly when the substance is drunk in strained form. Furthermore, the leaf when mixed with curdled milk and vegetables radically improved the nutritional value of the vegetables, helping the absorption of vitamin C. Indeed it may have formed an important supplement for green vegetables in arid zones.

The American historian, S. Wells Williams, remarks on one more constituent.

A remaining ingredient worthy of notice in tea, in common with other food-plants, is gluten. This forms one-fourth of the

weight of the leaves, but in order to derive the greatest good
from it which proper methods of cooking might bring out, we
must contrive a mode of eating the leaves. The nutritious
property of the gluten accounts for the general use of brick tea
throughout the Asiatic plateau. Huc [the great traveller
through China] says he drank the dish in default of something
better, for he was unaccustomed to it, but his cameleers would
often take twenty to forty cups a day.[16]

Finally, it is known that tea has an especial benefit as a
protection against extremes of climate, in particular the cold. The
Eskimos became avid tea drinkers when it was introduced and
the nomadic herdsmen, however thick their fleeces, would have
benefited from the mixture of tea and butter.

By the fifteenth century, tea drinking had deeply influenced a
great part of the world's population. In a large area – from
northern Burma in the south to Siberia in the north, from the
coast of China in the east to eastern Russia in the west – people
were drinking tea. It was in Japan, however, that tea had its
profoundest effect on culture and economy.

Tea was probably introduced into Japan in about 593 AD. The
importation of the leaves and plant grew during the eighth and
ninth centuries, which had seen one of the strongest waves of
Chinese influence on Japan. As in China, the plant was
cultivated in monastery gardens as a medicinal herb, to heal
sickness and to help keep the monks alert during meditation. Yet
at this time its use and influence was restricted to courtly and
monastic circles. It does not seem to have followed the Chinese
route of becoming a national drink.

A number of reformed sects of Buddhism grew in the late twelfth century. Zen and other variants of reformed Buddhism flourished and the monks practised extremely demanding forms of withdrawal and meditation. In 1191 the monk Eisai returned to Japan from China, bringing with him Rinzai Zen Buddhism and green powdered tea. Eisai gave detailed advice on how tea should be grown, picked, prepared and drunk so that its virtues would be maximised. 'Eisai also taught the Japanese the Chinese way of preparing the leaves: gather them early in the morning before dew-fall, then roast them on a sheet of paper over a very gentle heat so that they do not burn, and keep them in a pot with a stopper made from bamboo leaves.' Tea was soon incorporated into an elaborate tea ceremony and it came to affect much of Japanese cultural life.[17]

Eisai wrote a two-volume work called *Kissa-yojo-ki*, or *Notes on the curative effects of tea*, in which he argued forcefully for its curative effect in many types of illness. 'Tea is the most wonderful medicine for preserving health; it is the secret of long life. It shoots forth its leaves on the hillside like the spirit of the earth. Now, as in the past, it possesses these same extraordinary qualities, and we should make much greater use of it.' He argued that 'the health of the five human organs is strengthened through the plentiful intake of the five flavours they each respectively enjoy . . . But, whilst people absorb the four flavours of sharp, sour, sweet and salty, the bitter flavour necessary for the heart is unpleasant and cannot be taken in. This is the reason,' Eisai writes, 'why Japanese hearts are afflicted and Japanese lives short. We are fortunately able to learn from the people of the continent and we must make our hearts healthy absorbing the bitter flavour of tea.'[18]

Eisai interprets 'tea drinking as a secret technique for the prolongation of life'. It gave health to many other parts of the body as well as the heart; 'it was believed to banish sleep and to be effective against liver and skin complaints, rheumatism and beri-beri.' He strongly recommended it 'as a cure for five types of disease: loss of appetite, drinking water disease, paralysis, boils and beri-beri'. Tea, he added, is a 'remedy for all disorders . . .' Eisai's ideas were given a large boost when he sent some tea and a copy of his book to the great military ruler or Shogun of Japan, Sanetomo (1203–19), thereby curing the Shogun of a serious stomach ailment caused by bad food. When Sanetomo recovered he became a tea devotee and helped to spread the custom of tea drinking through Japan.

The Japanese cult of tea began. Tea became like the hallucinogenic drugs that have helped shamans in many other parts of the world to enter or communicate with the spirit world. It constituted the mystical centre of the rites of withdrawal, self-abnegation and the attainment of nothingness in the new sects. To have its full effect, to release the maximum amount of caffeine and other relaxants and stimulants, tea had to be prepared in its purest and most powerful form. So it was ground into powder and used as fresh as possible. It was also prepared and served in an almost sacred manner, emphasising and encouraging the belief in its mystical power. So the whole elaborate tea ceremony developed. As an old Buddhist saying put it, 'The taste of *ch'an* [Zen] and the taste of *ch'a* [tea] are the same.'[19]

By the Muromachi period (1336 onward), all classes in Japan drank tea.[20] The teahouse or tea stall appeared along the streets and roads of Japan. Tea was easily grown, for the bush could be trimmed to keep it small, very productive (for all the surface of the bush could produce leaves), and it grew well over most of Japan except the far north. In many ways Japan resembles quite closely the warm, wet, mountainous country where tea first evolved and the plant took quickly to its new quasi-Himalayan home. So, through the thirteenth to sixteenth centuries, the tea bush colonised a new Empire.

Every household that had a few feet of spare land could have a bush or two and supply its own needs, and the bush made an attractive, consumable, hedge. Since only a leaf or two were needed for this stimulating and healthful infusion, and the leaves could be re-used, it soon became an economical and enjoyable part of Japanese life.

One of the greatest puzzles is why tea has spread so quickly and has conquered such different cultures. An important part of the explanation of this success lies in the way in which it is served. Most drinks are prepared in one place and then stored and served at a later date – in other words poured out of a jug, bottle or barrel at the time and place of drinking. The action is simple and takes only a second or two. This gives little chance for social interaction around the procedure of preparing the drink and serving it to the guests. There can be little embellishment or social ritual. The human desire to create ceremonial can be seen in attempts to drag out the process through such customs as 'passing the port', the rituals of de-corking, and so on. The preparation of tea, on the other hand, allows for a spot of elaboration.

The famous tea ceremony of Japan shows the most extreme form of the ritualisation of the consumption of any food or drink in historian. Here is a summary of only small parts of what happens at a traditional Japanese tea ceremony as witnessed by an American scholar, Edward Morse, visiting Japan in the 1870s: 'In brief, the party comes about by the host inviting a company of four to attend the tea-ceremony, and in their presence making the tea in a bowl after certain prescribed forms, and offering it to the guests.' Morse then describes the ceremonial objects which are such an important part of the event.

The tea is first prepared by grinding it to a fine, almost impalpable, powder . . . This material, always freshly ground for each party, is usually kept in a little earthen jar, having an ivory cover, – the well-known *cha-ire* of the collector. Lacquer-boxes may also be used for this purpose. The principal utensils used in the ceremony consist of a *furo*, or fire-pot, made of pottery (or use may be made of a depression in the floor partially filled with ashes, in which the charcoal may be placed); an iron kettle to boil the water in; a bamboo dipper of the most delicate construction, to dip out the water; a wide-mouthed jar, from which to replenish the water in the kettle; a bowl, in which the tea is made; a bamboo spoon, to dip out the powdered tea; a bamboo stirrer, not unlike certain forms of egg-beaters, by which the tea is briskly stirred after the hot water has been added; a square silk cloth, with which to wipe the jar and spoon properly; a little rest for the tea-kettle cover, made of pottery or bronze or section of bamboo; a shallow vessel, in which the rinsings of the tea-bowl are poured after washing; a brush, consisting of three feathers of the eagle or some other large bird, to dust the edge of the fire-vessel; and finally a shallow basket, in which is not only charcoal to replenish the fire, but a pair of metal rods or *hibashi* to handle the coal, two interrupted metal rings by which the kettle is lifted off the fire, a circular mat upon which the kettle is placed, and a small box containing incense, or bits of wood that give out a peculiar fragrance when burned.

Around these objects and the serving and receiving of the tea is an elaborate set of ceremonial movements which can take several hours to perform. Just the preparation of the tea can take an hour or more. 'With the exception of the fire-vessel and an iron kettle, all these utensils have to be brought in by the host with great formality and in a certain sequence, and placed with great precision upon the mats after the prescribed rules of certain schools. In the making of the tea, the utensils are used in a most exact and formal manner.'

It all seems rather convoluted and formal, an extraordinary display of behaviour when we remember that a host is merely giving his or her guest a cup of tea. 'To watch the making of the tea, knowing nothing about the ceremony, seems as grotesque a performance as one can well imagine. Many of the forms connected with it seem uselessly absurd . . .' Yet if one learns more about it, the whole complicated ceremony begins to be comprehensible and deeply meaningful. Edward Morse goes on to write that:

Having taken many lessons in the art of tea-making, I found that with few exceptions it was natural and easy; and the guests assembled on such an occasion, though at first sight appearing stiff, are always perfectly at their ease. The proper placing of the utensils, and the sequence in handling them and making the tea are all natural and easy movements, as I have said. The light wiping of the tea-jar, and the washing of the bowl and its wiping with so many peripheral jerks, the dropping of the stirrer against the side of the bowl with a click in rinsing, and a few of the other usual movements are certainly grotesquely formal enough; but I question whether the etiquette of a ceremonious dinner-party at home, with the decorum observed in the proper use of each utensil, does not strike a Japanese as equally odd and incomprehensible when experienced by him for the first time.[21]

What seems to be special about tea is the simplicity of its preparation and the spirit in which it is served, beautifully summarised by the greatest Japanese tea master, Rikyu, in the early seventeenth century. The whole art of tea consisted of gathering firewood, boiling water, pouring it on the tea and serving the guests. Very simple equipment is combined with very simple action, but there is also care, attention and skill. This gives scope for creativity and allows one human to impress others. The procedure is also drawn out while the tea water boils, and then when it acts on the tea. This turns the making of tea into something that can be elaborated and embellished.

A glimpse of its inner meaning emerges from the seven tea rules which Sen Rikyu inscribed on the wall of the cell in the temple at Sakai.

When the guests have arrived at the waiting-lodge and all the like-minded participants are assembled there, the host announces himself by sounding a wooden gong.

As far as washing the hands is concerned, what really matters on this Way is the purification of the heart.

The host must approach the guests with every respect and conduct them to the tea-room. If the host is a person without composure and imagination, if the tea and eating utensils are of bad taste, and if the natural layout and planning of the trees and rocks in the tea-garden are unpleasing, then it is as well to go straight back home.

As soon as the boiling water sounds like the wind in the pine trees and the sound of a gong rings out, the guests enter the tea-room for the second time. It is unforgivable to let slip the right moment as regards water and fire.

Neither inside nor outside the tea-room let the conversation turn to worldly things: this is a commandment of old.

At a true gathering neither guest nor host has recourse to fine words or smooth airs.

A gathering may not exceed two double hours in length. If, however, this time is exceeded in the course of discussion of the Buddha's teachings and aesthetic matters, that is not objectionable.[22]

The best single description of the philosophical progress and effects of tea is in Kakuzo Okakura's, *The Book of Tea* (1906).

Tea began as a medicine and grew into a beverage. In China, in the eighth century, it entered the realm of poetry as one of the polite amusements. The fifteenth century saw Japan ennoble it into a religion of aestheticism – Teaism. Teaism is a cult founded on the adoration of the beautiful among the sordid facts of everyday existence. It inculcates purity and harmony, the mystery of mutual charity, the romanticism of the social order. It is essentially a worship of the Imperfect, as it is a tender attempt to accomplish something possible in this impossible thing we know as life.

He explains how tea, religion and culture became intertwined.

The Philosophy of Tea is not mere aestheticism in the ordinary acceptance of the term, for it expresses conjointly with ethics and religion our whole point of view about man and nature. It is hygiene, for it enforces cleanliness; it is economics, for it shows comfort in simplicity rather than in the complex and costly; it is moral geometry, inasmuch as it defines our sense of proportion to the universe. It represents the true spirit of eastern democracy by making all its votaries aristocrats in taste.

Okakura suggests that the Japanese continued the tradition of early Chinese civilisation, which had been cut off in China itself by the Mongol invasions.

Tea with us became more than an idealisation of the form of drinking; it is a religion of the art of life. The beverage grew to be an excuse for the worship of purity and refinement, a sacred function at which the host and guest joined to produce for that occasion the utmost beatitude of the mundane. The tea-room was an oasis in the dreary waste of existence where we travellers could meet to drink from the common spring of art appreciation. The ceremony was an improvised drama whose plot was woven about the tea, the flowers, and the paintings. Not a colour to disturb the tone of the room, not a sound to mar the rhythm of things, not a gesture to obtrude on the harmony, not a word to break the unity of the surroundings, all movements to be performed simply and naturally – such were the aims of the tea-ceremony. And strangely enough it was often successful.

Its appeal lay very considerably in the fact that it was based on religious sentiments, but in a way that fitted with the form of Buddhist religion. This was a religion that emphasised the illusion behind all things, including the Buddha, so that the religious element subsequently seemed to disappear, leaving just the ceremony.

All our great tea-masters were students of Zen and attempted to introduce the spirit of Zenism into the actualities of life. Thus the room, like the other equipments of the tea ceremony, reflects many of the doctrines. The size of the orthodox tea-room, which is four mats and a half, or ten feet square, is determined by a passage in the Sutra of Vikramadytia. In that interesting work, Vikramadytia welcomes the Saint Manjushiri and eighty-four thousand disciples of Buddha in a room of this size – an allegory based on the theory of the non-existence of space to the truly enlightened. Again the roji, the garden path which leads from the machiai to the tea-room, signified the first stage of meditation – the passage into self-illumination.

The roji was intended to break connection with the outside world, and to produce a fresh sensation conducive to the full enjoyment of aestheticism in the tea-room itself . . . One may be in the midst of a city, and yet feel as if he were in the forest far from the dust and din of civilisation.

Yet the influence of tea was not merely on religion and high culture, on painting, ceramics and literature. It spread throughout all of Japanese culture, as Okakura explains:

> Great as has been the influence of the tea-masters in the world of art, it is as nothing compared to that which they have exerted on the conduct of life. Not only in the usages of polite society, but also in the arrangement of all our domestic details, do we feel the presence of the tea-masters. Many of our delicate dishes, as well as our way of serving food, are their inventions. They have taught us to dress only in garments of sober colours. They have instructed us in the proper spirit in which to approach flowers. They have given emphasis to our natural love of simplicity, and shown us the beauty of humility. In fact, through their teachings tea has entered the life of the people.[23]

Edward Morse, who made similar claims, drew on an analogy with his own puritan New England background, he concluded that 'Indeed, it has had an effect on the Japanese almost equal to that of Calvinistic doctrines on the early Puritans. The one suppressed the exuberance of an art-loving people, and brought many of their decorative impulses down to a restful purity and simplicity; but in the case of the Puritans . . . their sombre dogmas crushed the little love for art that might have dawned . . .'[24]

The teahouse is a place where class and caste barriers are temporarily suspended. It is a neutral, empty space, an arena where you communicate in the language of movement and gesture. It is both private space, very intimate, yet public space, where non-family members and even strangers can be safely absorbed. The teahouse is the outside world (as opposed to the inside, domestic, sphere), but it is nevertheless safe and neutral and allows the kind of deep intimacy of communication that normally could only occur in the home.

It is said that 'there is no religion in Japan'. There is no established formal religion; no holy book, no proper priesthood, no extensive dogma, little interest in the after-life. Japan is a society where aesthetics and etiquette seem largely to have taken the place of religion. The 'tea ceremony' is a purely secular occasion, without God or a priest, yet with a quasi-sacred atmosphere because of the heavy formality of the proceedings, the smoking incense, the offering of an apparent sacrifice (the tea), the presence of a kind of altar (the *tokonoma*), which contains a 'religious' writing.

Thus the Zen ascetic spirit spread out throughout all of Japanese society and culture by way of tea. What adds to the interest of the story is that many of the same effects were to be found on another island – Britain. Tea became much more than a drink with pleasant bodily and mental effects. As in Japan, it became a 'way', almost a 'way of life'. Although not a religion, it certainly became a passion, a curious blend of a game, a creed and an entertainment.

Chapter Four

Tea Comes to the West

'[Mrs Jesse] poured tea. The oil-lamps cast a warm light on the teatray. The teapot was china, with little roses painted all over it ... There were sugared biscuits ... Sophy Sheeky watched the stream of topaz-coloured liquid fall from the spout, steaming and aromatic. This too was a miracle, that gold-skinned persons in China and bronze-skinned persons in India should gather leaves which should come across the seas safely in white-winged ships, encased in lead, encased in wood, surviving storms and whirlwinds, sailing on under hot sun and cold moon, and come here, and be poured from bone china, made from fine clay, moulded by clever fingers, in the Pottery Towns, baked in kilns ... '

A. S. Byatt, 'The Conjugal Angel', *Angels and Insects*

Tea was first mentioned in European sources in 1559.[25] In 1678 a Dutchman, William Ten Rhijne, described and imported the first specimens of the tea plant to come to the West. Just a few months after his arrival at Nagasaki he sent an essay on the tea plant, a branch of a camphor tree, and a batch of twigs, leaves, and flowers back to a friend.[26] Engelbert Kaempfer, a German doctor, botanist and polymath, who was employed by the Dutch East India Company and lived in Japan in the late seventeenth century, was one of those who were most effective in spreading an understanding of tea to the West. In his great history of Japanese civilisation he described the history, politics, crafts, government and economy with enormous care. At the end of the volumes he included detailed appendices on several important subjects, including tea. Likewise, missionaries, diplomats and others who visited and wrote about China described the wonderful Chinese plant that seemed to cure so many different diseases.

The records of the use of tea suggest that it first arrived at Amsterdam in 1610, in France in the 1630s and in England in 1657. It was 'brewed, kept in a cask, then drawn and warmed up for customers as they asked for it'. Milk was probably not added at this stage. As with many new technologies, in fact, it was at first assimilated into techniques already in use, being treated as a kind of warmed-up beer, still served from a barrel.

In the 1660s it was advertised as 'That excellent and by all Physicians approved, China drink, called by the Chineans, Tcha, by other Nations Tay or Tee', and was sold at the Sultans Head near the Royal Exchange.[27] The first overview of its medical effects and virtues was given in the tea broadsheet by Thomas Garway, published in 1657 to advertise the first public sale of tea in Garway's coffee house. A list of the medical benefits of tea, similar to those given by Garway, was transcribed from a Chinese source in 1686 by T. Povey, a Member of Parliament.[28]

1 It purifyes the Bloud of that which is grosse and Heavy.
2 It Vanquisheth heavy Dreames.
3 It Easeth the brain of heavy Damps.

4 Easeth and cureth giddinesse and Paines in the Heade.
5 Prevents the Dropsie.
6 Drieth Moist humours in the Head.
7 Consumes Rawnesse.
8 Opens Obstructions.
9 Cleares the Sight.
10 Clenseth and Purifieth adults humours and a hot Liver.
11 Purifieth defects of the Bladder and Kiddneys.
12 Vanquisheth Superfluous Sleep.
13 Drives away dissines, makes one Nimble and Valient.
14 Encourageth the heart and Drives away feare.
15 Drives away all Paines of the Collick which proceed from Wind.
16 Strengthens the Inward parts and Prevents Consumptions.
17 Strengthens the Memory.
18 Sharpens the Will and Quickens the Understanding.
19 Purgeth Safely the Gaul.
20 Strengthens the use of due benevolence.

As tea began to be introduced into Europe the argument about its virtues and possible dangers increased. In Holland it was recommended by physicians like Johannes van Helmont as a restorative against loss of body fluids. Dr Nikolas Dirx (1593–1674) wrote a widely read eulogy on tea in his *Observationes Medicae* under the name 'Nikolas Tulp'.

Nothing is comparable to this plant. Those who use it are for that reason, alone, exempt from all maladies and reach an extreme old age. Not only does it procure great vigour for their bodies, but also it preserves them from gravel and gallstones, headaches, colds, ophthalmia, catarrh, asthma, sluggishness of the stomach and intestinal troubles. It has the additional merit of preventing sleep and facilitating vigils, which makes it a great help to persons desiring to spend their nights writing or meditating.[29]

One of the most extended treatments was by the Dutch physician Cornelis Bontekoe (alias Cornelis Dekker) who published a *Tractaat* on the excellence of tea, coffee and chocolate in 1679. Bontekoe held green tea of Bohea in such high esteem that in one of his works he seriously recommended the sick to take 50, 60, up to 100 cups without stopping, a feat he had accomplished himself in one morning. He had suffered cruelly from stones, and believed that he had been cured by the copious use he made of the Chinese drink. He defended it strongly against those who said it caused convulsions and epilepsy; on the contrary, he attributed to it all sorts of therapeutic virtues. Bontekoe also recommended drinking two glasses of strong tea before an attack of malaria and a number of glasses afterwards.[30]

A number of British doctors also investigated its properties. Thomas Trotter in his *View of the Nervous Temperament* (1807) argued that tea, as well as other commodities, like coffee and tobacco, 'had once been used as medicines, but had been reduced to necessities'.[31] Thomas Short in his *Dissertation upon Tea* of 1730 reported various experiments that showed that when tea was added to blood, it separated the 'blood serum'. It furthermore helped to preserve meat from becoming rotten. He listed the diseases for which it was a remedy, including 'diseases of the head', 'thickness of the blood', diseases of the eye, ulcers, gout, the stone, obstructions of the bowels and many others.[32] In

1772 Dr Lettsom wrote a *Natural History of the Tea-Tree, with Observations on the Medical Qualities of Tea* along the same lines. He similarly undertook experiments to show that beef immersed in green tea water took 72 hours to become putrid, while beef immersed in ordinary water was rotten in 48 hours. From this and other experiments he concluded that 'It is evident from these experiments, that both green and bohea Tea possess an antiseptic (Experiment 1) and astringent (Experiment 2), applied to the dead animal fibre.' His third experiment, injecting tea and ordinary water from the first experiment into the abdomen of a dead frog, showed that while tea had no effect, the ordinary water led to rigidity and loss of motion in the frog's legs.[33]

Tea spread fairly slowly at first in Britain, largely because of the cost. It was a luxury item. Famously Mrs Pepys drank it, as Pepys recorded in his *Diary* on 25 September 1660; she took it partly for medicinal reasons as it was thought that it would be good for her cough. When it first reached the London market 'it was sold for the remarkable price of £3 10s a pound'. Then 'the price dropped to about £2 in nine or ten years', when it became available in every coffee house. Yet it remained a luxury drink throughout the seventeenth century and into the early eighteenth.

The great surge in tea importation and the drop in its cost occurred from the 1730s onwards, soon after the direct clipper trade to China was opened. By the end of the eighteenth century, the Secretary on Lord Macartney's Mission to China, Sir George Staunton, estimated that 'more than a pound weight each, in the course of a year, for the individuals of all ranks, ages and sexes' was consumed in England.[34] Other estimates are higher than this.

Some suggest that the average consumption was over two pounds per person per annum. 'By the end of the century the amount imported was over twenty million pound, that is, about 2 lb per head of the population.' But this was only the official figure. 'It was estimated that in 1766 as much reached England illegally as came through the proper channels.'[35] A pound of tea can make between 200 and 300 cups of tea. This would imply that an adult, on average, was drinking at least two cups of tea a day. The chronology indicates an amazingly rapid growth from the 1730s onwards, with tea spreading through the whole population.

Contemporary comments suggest the rapid spread of tea drinking throughout all parts of Britain. In a model diet of a typical middle-class family of 1734, a contemporary allocated some 5.25 pence per head per week for bread and 7 pence per week for tea and sugar.[36] A similar model budget for a tradesman's family in 1749 allocated three shillings per week for the family to buy bread, and four shillings a week to buy tea and sugar.[37] Very early on, in the middle class at least, tea and sugar were the staff of life.

In the middle of the eighteenth century the Scottish philosopher Lord Kames observed how even the poorest recipients of charity would drink tea twice a day.[38] The comments of those opposed to tea suggest how widely tea drinking had spread. In 1744 the judge and writer Duncan Forbes wrote that the 'the opening a Trade with the *East-Indies* . . . brought the Price of Tea . . . so low, that the *meanest* labouring Man could compass the Purchase of it . . .'[39]

In 1751 Charles Deering, author of a book about Nottinghamshire, wrote:

The People here are not without their Tea, Coffee and
Chocolate, especially the first, the Use of which is spread to
that Degree, that not only the Gentry and Wealthy Traders
drink it constantly, but almost every Seamer, Sizer and
Winder, will have her Tea and will enjoy herself over it in a
Morning . . . and even a Common Washerwoman thinks she
had not had a proper Breakfast without Tea and hot buttered
white Bread . . .[40]

The agricultural writer Arthur Young was disturbed by the
growing custom 'of men making tea an article of their food,
almost as much as women, labourers losing their time to come
and go to the tea-table, farmers' servants even demanding tea for
their breakfast!'[41]

In 1784 Rochefoucauld wrote: 'Throughout the whole of
England the drinking of tea is general. You have it twice a day
and, though the expense is considerable, the humblest peasant
has his tea twice a day just like the rich man; the total
consumption is immense.' Even more specifically he later
observed 'that it is reckoned that in the course of the year every
single person, man or women, on the average consumes four
pounds of tea. That is truly enormous.'[42]

By the end of the eighteenth century, the writer on the poor, Sir
Frederick Eden, wrote, 'Any person who will give himself the
trouble of stepping into the cottages of Middlesex and Surrey at
meal-times, will find, that, in poor families, tea is not only the
usual beverage in the morning and evening, but is generally
drunk in large quantities at dinner.'[43] In 1809 a Swedish visitor,
Erik Gustav Geijer, described how 'Next to water tea is the
Englishman's proper element. All classes consume it, and if one

is out on the London streets early in the morning, one may see in many places small tables set up under the open sky, round which coal-carters and workmen empty their cups of delicious beverage.'[44]

Both the demand and the supply of tea rose rapidly from the later seventeenth century. In terms of demand, particularly in Holland and England, the disposable income of all classes had been rising for some centuries so they could afford the small luxuries of life – good meat, good bread, beer and ale, coal or peat in the fire, good warm clothing, leather shoes and well-made houses. This process continued so that by the later seventeenth century in much of north-western Europe the effective demand for the new products of colonial expansion was considerable. Tobacco, coffee, chocolate, silks, spices were all in great demand and so, increasingly, was tea.

The demand was, however, curiously lop-sided within Europe. Only in the Netherlands[45] and Britain did tea drinking become widespread, while neither France, Germany, Spain nor Italy really took to the drink at all seriously. This is one of the most curious and unexplained parts of the story. Why was tea largely restricted to the British at first? It is true that the Dutch drank tea, particularly the women, but the men preferred beer and went on drinking it, while exporting the tea to England. Why did tea not take off in France or Germany? One might surmise that the peculiar set of conditions that encouraged it in England – the abhorrence of drinking water, the rising price of beer because of the malt taxes, the trade system based on the sea – led to a different outcome. If we add to this the relative affluence of the British middling sorts, who could afford to experiment with the new drink, the fact that the British were already used to hot drinks such as heated ale, possets, toddies and punches, and the enormous push given to tea by the East India Company, who had a monopoly of the import, we can see some of the reasons for its success.[46] As is often the case in history, starting from almost imperceptible differences, the gap grew greater. So the French drank coffee as their luxury, as did the Germans. The fact that the Dutch and the British had interests in the Far East, where tea grew, while the French, Germans, Italians and Portuguese, in so far as they had trade connections, mainly focused on Africa, parts of India and South America, is clearly very important.

It is equally puzzling if we put the question the other way round. Coffee took off faster than tea in the half-century after 1660, with coffee houses proliferating. Then it faded away and tea came to dominate in Britain. Why was this? There are a number of possible reasons. Tea is easier to prepare at the point of consumption; there is no roasting and grinding required. Tea comes by sea, and this ensured a more dependable route (for the British at least), than across land from the Middle East (whence coffee came to central and southern Europe). Tea stretches further; it can be diluted and used again and it is relatively cheap to produce, partly because the tea tree is so prolific. The production of tea became associated with the Eastern trade, and hence was promoted, as we have noted, by the powerful East India Company. Politics and capital were on its side and the price fell and the government supported it as an important source of tax revenue. Advertising and marketing pushed this commodity more than coffee, though cocoa was equally widely advertised in the nineteenth century.

Politics was also important. A great deal of the early tea

imports were re-exported to America and it looked as if the Americans, like the British, would become a great tea-drinking people. In many ways they did become so. In the nineteenth century, with a relatively much smaller population, very considerable amounts of tea continued to be imported into America. Yet after the tossing of the chests of tea into the harbour at Boston – the famous Boston Tea Party – tea became a symbol of British arrogance and taxation without representation. So the Americans, despite their widespread private use of tea, have represented themselves publicly as coffee drinkers, in opposition to the British tea drinkers.

Another factor that altered the equation was the supply of tea. During the later seventeenth and early eighteenth centuries, there was a breakthrough in the safety of sea travel and hence the profits to be made from long-distance navigation. A combination of improved maps, ship construction, cannon for defence against pirates, sextants to determine latitude and later the chronometer to determine longitude, opened up a direct sea route round the Cape of Good Hope. Alongside this, new forms of commercial organisation, the joint stock company, the increasingly efficient facilities for borrowing through such institutions as the Bank of England or the large Dutch banks, all made it easier to organise and finance long-distance trading ventures. The great trading companies of the Dutch and British were looking for profitable activities and were in a position to invest in them.

This meant that the first direct cargoes of tea from China began to arrive in Europe in the 1720s. Tea leaves were light to carry, easy to store and to keep over long distances, and sold well. Tea became increasingly valuable, this new precious commodity, flooding into Europe, alongside chinaware and silks. For a while there was sufficient silver – the only commodity China desired from the west – from South American and central European mines, to pay for the tea.

We can see the effects in terms of prices and volumes. Although the British government tried to make a profit through excise duties, it was far more difficult to do in the case of tea than it had been with the malt that was necessary for beer. Tea is very easy to smuggle, being light and concentrated. Smuggling put a check on taxes. As today with cigarettes or wine, if the government raises the taxes too high it actually reduces its income, since the profits from smuggling increase, the volume of smuggled goods swells, and in consequence the taxed legal trade declines.

So tea complemented beer as the British national drink. There is not much evidence that it was specifically drunk on a large scale for its perceived medicinal value, despite the exhortations on the subject. It seems to have been its stimulating and pleasant effects and relative cheapness that made it attractive. This attraction was increased by the fact that, unlike in China and Japan, tea was soon drunk with milk and sugar. In a pastoral nation, which was rapidly developing the colonial trade in sugar, this increased the energy and protein value of the tea.

Part II

Enslaved

Chapter Five

Enchantment

'A bus took him to the West End, where, among the crazy coloured fountains of illumination, shattering the blue dusk with green and crimson fire, he found the café of his choice, a teashop that had gone mad and turned Babylonian, a white palace with ten thousand lights. It towered above the older buildings like a citadel, which indeed it was, the outpost of a new age, perhaps a new civilisation, perhaps a new barbarism . . . Such was the gigantic teashop into which Turgis marched, in search not of mere refreshment but of all the enchantment of unfamiliar luxury.'

J. B. Priestley, *Angel Pavement*

Like the Chinese and Japanese, the British became enchanted with tea soon after it arrived in their country. Two main locations for the celebration of tea drinking developed in Britain. One was the public arena – the teashop or garden. Tea was originally served alongside coffee and other drinks in the coffee shop, particularly in the period when such shops flourished between about 1660 and 1720. These coffee and teahouses had an important role in the growing prosperity of Britain, as they were the place where many great international institutions were born, including Lloyd's insurance and the Bank of England. They were also the nucleus of many political clubs and hence contributed to the rise of parliamentary democracy. They were the seeds from which grew missionary movements – indeed, a special teapot was given as a founding gift to the Eclectic Society early in the eighteenth century. The first meetings of the Society, at the Castle and Falcon Tavern, took place over cups of tea, and out of its discussions there emerged the Church Missionary Society. Furthermore, such coffee- and teashops developed into meeting places for writers and scientists and as a result became centres for the circulation of ideas.

The coffee houses started to decline in importance after the first two decades of the eighteenth century. Tea, on the other hand, did not decline, but moved out to new venues, from the coffee shops and taverns where it had first been welcomed into pleasure gardens at Vauxhall, Ranelagh, Marylebone, Cuper's, White Conduit House, Bermondsey Spa. In these gardens, Londoners were able to promenade, look at interesting objects such as the latest stationary steam engine or piece of sculpture, and drink tea. Tea was a central focus. With their groves, walks, arbours, surprises and tea areas these gardens often covered several acres – bringing the elegant aristocratic parks of the countryside into the town. There the gentry and middle classes congregated, to 'take tea', to gossip and exchange information, and to listen to music. In particular, these gardens were places where wives and children as well as men were welcome.

The coffee houses were adult male meeting places, as coffee shops still are in many Islamic and Catholic countries. Perhaps because of its cost and rapidly stimulating action, coffee was always equated with men and, in England, was seen as a luxury drink of the rich. Tea, on the other hand, was soon perceived to be a 'gentler' drink, milder in its effect, as well as cheaper, and hence quite suitable for women and children. It may have been known that men in the Arab lands where it was first cultivated drank coffee, but that tea was the universal drink of all ages and both genders in China and Japan. So the English could enjoy a day out in the tea gardens with the family, flaunting and comparing their domestic happiness, and go to parties in tearooms to see and be seen.

The pleasure gardens also became the magnet for many of the greatest literary, musical and artistic figures of the early eighteenth century – Pope and Handel, for instance – who would meet there and exchange ideas. They became garden universities of a sort. The pleasure came not just from the tea, but from the architecture and landscape, so that the tea gardens strongly influenced the dramatic developments in British gardening, which culminated in the eighteenth century with 'Capability' Brown and his 'natural' style of landscape gardening. It was appropriate also that an exotic Chinese drink, tea, should be the catalyst for places which helped to channel the growing obsession with 'things Oriental' that spread through Britain and other parts of the West at this time. Drinking a Chinese beverage in Chinese ceramics was naturally linked to admiring Chinese things, new designs, lacquer, silks and Chinese gardens.

An early example, which shows the way in which the adherence of women made a large difference, occurred in 1717 when Thomas Twining converted Tom's Coffee House into The Golden Lyon, the first teashop in London, from where tea had begun to be sold in 1706. This shop still sells tea in the Strand in London.[47] Unlike the coffee house, it was frequented by both sexes: 'Great Ladies flocked to Twining's house. . .' The rapid growth of the elegant, middle-class teashop, occurred in the later nineteenth century, famously associated with Lyons Corner Houses.[48] Again these teashops provided a place where whole families could entertain themselves and meet friends. If a respectable middle-class family went on a trip to London, or travelled by the new railways or visited the seaside, they could not drop into the local pub, where alcohol was served, or go into the bar of the inn. Nor could they enter the all-male London clubs of the various professions. But they could go to a teashop.

The teashop and pleasure garden were well-suited to the British system of domestic-centred companionate marriage in the middle classes. It allowed the family of parents and children to rest and enjoy themselves together. In many civilisations, including much of Catholic Europe, the women stay at home and the men go off to the public sphere of the coffee shop or bar. In Britain, tea drinking helped to establish an arena where men and women, adults and children could be together in public.

Tea drinking also spread at the semi-private level. Before the arrival of tea, if a middle-class family, and particularly its women, wanted to entertain other families or individual friends in the private space of their own home, all that could be offered were alcoholic drinks. Now, at last, there was a calming infusion drink, which could be served with a degree of elaborate ceremonial. The serving provided an opportunity to display all the accoutrements of good breeding, manners and etiquette. The custom had been originated and patronised by royalty, for

Princess Catherine of Braganza, wife of Charles II, had originally propagated tea as a useful temperate drink at court in the later seventeenth century. Tea was early on associated with the aristocracy and gentry. An important innovator in tea etiquette, for example, was Anna, wife of the seventh Duke of Bedford (1788–1861), who encouraged the serving of tea and cakes in the middle of the afternoon because she had a 'sinking feeling'. From its high-class roots it spread down to humble households. Indeed the over-enthusiasm of the poor for a middle-class drink and its associated rituals was resented and criticised as the poor imitating their betters in a pretentious way.

In a class-conscious yet mobile society where tiny signs in language, gesture and objects were constantly being interpreted to place people socially, tea became an important mechanism for inclusion and exclusion. The exact shape and style of the tea service and furniture, the flavour of the tea (the lighter and more bitter the higher the class – like sherry), everything down to the way in which the fingers were used to pick up the teacup would indicate which social stratum a person came from.

Later, in the World Wars of the twentieth century, the officers drank tea out of china cups, while the ordinary troops were served very strong, sugary tea out of large metal mugs from a bucket.[49] Yet very often the differences were much more subtle; the art of impressing and indicating that one was of the right background had to be learnt very explicitly, rather like playing a musical instrument, flower arranging, the art of polite conversation and other appropriate female accomplishments. It was not as intense a course as that for the Japanese tea ceremony, which can take years, but it was an art that had rules and needed practice.

The 'afternoon tea party' developed many small ceremonial forms similar to those in Japan. There was the special tea equipment: the cups, plates, tea caddy and teapot, the table and chairs all set out in a special room. The social importance of the way in which people took tea led to a mass of writing devoted to explaining the art of tea preparation and serving. Authors explained how a person was to be invited, what utensils should be laid out, how a person should be asked if they would like tea or more tea. Particularly important was how to deal with different ranks of guest, how to address titled folk, bishops, judges, and the order of precedence in serving the guests. Instruction was also needed on how to serve the accompanying food and what foods they should be, how to thank one's hostess and how to depart.

Lady Troubridge in her two-volume *Book of Etiquette* (1926) devotes a chapter to teas and other afternoon parties. 'The guests may gather round the table, or the hostess may place a little table or stool by the chairs for the reception of teacup and a tiny tea-plate . . . Little tea-napkins are sometimes used, but, as a rule, they are considered unnecessary. If jam is served, tea-knives (very small knives with plated or silver blades) are provided.'[50]

A more recent *Complete Guide to Etiquette* (1966) by Betty Messenger, outlines various aspects of the occasion, including what to say when the important part of serving the guests occurred. 'The correct thing to say when you are asking anyone if they want more is: "Lady Bland, will you have another cup of tea?" When you hand sandwiches, do say what is in them. Lady Bland, who may be allergic to crab paste, does not want to have to ask what is in them when her hostess offers a plateful of sandwiches.'[51] All of this may seem to be trifling. But a whole social system depended on such small signs, as Sarah Maclean explains in *Etiquette and Good Manners*: 'Tea parties today are informal affairs. But there are three small points of etiquette. It is "not done" to crook your little finger as you drink your tea – a ridiculous affectation which is fairly considered "genteel". The more "upper class" the home, the more likely is the milk to go in last. "Just as it comes" is another class pointer. What you are supposed to do when your hostess asks you how you like it is to tell her exactly – "weak", "strong" or "very little milk, please".'[52]

The aim was to produce a certain atmosphere. 'There ought to be an air of refinement in the room in which it is partaken, the guests should be neat and well chosen, and the tea itself the finest and best procurable for love or money. No need to say what the hostess should be; she will be natural, that is enough.'[53]

Much of this formal behaviour performed a similar social function to the tea ceremony in Japan. That is to say, with a reserved and status-conscious people, much could be said through things, through small politenesses and marks of esteem and favour, which could not be expressed in words. The tea party conveyed an atmosphere of amity, even cordiality, but this was often combined with preservation of boundaries through gossip and criticism, as numerous scenes in the novels of Jane Austen, Trollope and Dickens show.

The gossip would vary according to the nature of the tea itself. Thomas De Witt Talmage (1879) wrote:

the style of the conversation depends very much on the kind of tea that the housewife pours for the guests. If it be genuine Young Hyson . . . the talk will be fresh and spirited and sun-shiny. If it be . . . Gunpowder, the conversation will be explosive and somebody's reputation will be killed before you get through. If it be green tea . . . you may expect there will be a poisonous effect in the conversation and the moral health damaged.[54]

So the whole business of taking tea became a national obsession in the eighteenth century, filling the long, enforced leisure hours of millions of women. Taking tea together became, as in Japan, the occasion for signifying friendship, hospitality, a communion of closeness through things and actions, communicating through consumption. It was, in particular, the way in which middle-class women could escape the loneliness of their homes by inviting in other women or going out to tea.

These sociable meetings were often just occasions for display, gossip and friendship. They could provide for women a counter to the men's congregating round drink. In William Congreve's play *The Double Dealer* (1694), someone asks where the women are, to be told that 'they are at the end of the gallery, retired to their tea and scandal, according to their ancient custom'. These get-togethers could also give women an area of control. In *Lady Audley's Secret* (1862), Mary Elizabeth Braddon wrote: 'Surely a pretty woman never looks prettier than when making tea. [This is] . . . the most feminine and domestic of all occupations . . . To do away with the tea-table is to rob woman of her legitimate empire.' [55]

They could also give women the arena within which to develop co-ordinated action. It does not seem far-fetched to suggest that many of the notable achievements of the great women of nineteenth-century England, many of them – like the writer and social commentator Harriet Martineau – known to be avid tea drinkers, owed a fair bit to communal tea drinking. The successful actions of women in widening democracy, in setting up social and charitable concerns, in organising mission work and literary endeavours, the Women's Institute, the Girl Guides and many other notable institutions, was partly made possible by meeting over tea.

The rise of women in the private world was also linked to tea. The tea party was the one occasion where they were mistress. She who wields the teapot has a powerful weapon in her hand, and even the most bullying of men will defer to her during that limited period. Furthermore, it altered the relations of the age groups. The nursery tea was the time when parents, especially mothers, and children who were looked after by servants could meet. Similarly, the generations and the genders were brought together on festive occasions such as birthday tea parties or Christmas tea with Christmas cake.

It was not just the upper and middle classes whose daily lives were shaped by tea, for tea drinking spread right through the population and is important in another institution, which also played a notable part in the growth of modern British economy and society – the worker's tea break. The development of the 'tea break' made life more bearable, gave workers something to look forward to and became the central social ceremony during the long hours of drudgery in factory, small workshop, office or mine. Fortified by the caffeine and the sugar, relaxed and re-invigorated by the drink and the exchange of banter and information within the small group, the workers could return to the relentless task and do things that would have been beyond endurance without the tea break. At the end of a long day, grimy and exhausted, a 'nice cup of tea' with the meal would refresh tired limbs and avoid the expense and health dangers of alcohol.

It is no wonder that tea was later to become one of the central symbols and weapons of the large temperance movement of the nineteenth century that fought against the abuse of alcohol. One of the safest drinks that could be recommended as stimulating, cheap but cheering, was tea. Temperance campaigners held tea parties, both to raise money and to recruit members. The gin craze of the mid-eighteenth century had been overcome largely through the rise in the price of gin and the consequent substitution of tea as the drink of the poor. A similar process occurred, but on a larger scale in a far bigger population, in the nineteenth century. There was a complex link between tea, morality and temperance.[56]

It is intriguing to speculate on the effect this might have had on the national character. From aggressive, belligerent, red-meat-and-beer sort of people, did the British become gentler, less volatile? The impact of changing a national drink is suggested in accounts of the great tea-drinking civilisations of Japan and China.

The American historian of China, S. Wells Williams, argued that the influence of tea 'among occidentals cannot be overlooked'.

The domestic, quiet life and habits of the Chinese owe much of their strength to the constant use of this beverage, for the weak infusion which they sip allows them to spend all the time they choose at the tea-table. If they were in the habit of sipping even their weak whiskey in the same way, misery, poverty, quarrels, and sickness would take the place of thrift, quiet, and industry. The general temperance seen among them is owing to the tea much more than any other cause . . . If one passing through the streets of Peking, Canton, or Ohosaka [Osaka], and seeing the good-natured hilarity of the groups of laborers and loiterers around the *cha-kwan* and the *cha-ya* of those cities, doubts the value of tea as a harmonizer and satisfier of human wants and passions, it must be taken as a proof of his own unsatisfied cravings.[57]

It was a point which had been made at the end of the seventeenth century by Sir John Ovington in his book on tea: 'For where can a Stranger that was always bred among a People the most polite of any in the World, expect a kind Reception with more Assurance than from a Person whose Conversation is adorn'd with all that Civility that even China it self can boast of?'[58] Likewise, John Sumner in 1863 had enquired, 'Is it going too far to inquire whether Tea may not have borne an important part in the formation of the gentleness and tractability of character, which keeps the Chinese calm and orderly, even in the midst of political revolutions?'[59]

Later, Dr G. G. Sigmond discussing temperance societies in *Tea: Its Effects, Medicinal and Moral* (1839), was full of praise for tea.

Tea has in most instances been substituted for fermented or spirituous liquors, and the consequence has been a general improvement in the health and in the morals of a vast number of persons. The tone, the strength, and the vigour of the human body are increased by it; there is a greater capability of enduring fatigue; the mind is rendered more susceptible of the innocent pleasures of life, and of acquiring information.

Whole classes of the community have been rendered sober, careful and provident . . . Men have become healthier, happier, and better for the exchange they have made. They have given up a debasing habit for an innocent one. Individuals who were outcast, miserable, abandoned have become independent and a blessing to society.[60]

Another writer on tea, W. Gordon Stables, in 1883 quotes the author Douglas William Jerrold: 'Of the social influence of tea, in truth, upon the masses of the people in this country, it is not very easy to say too much. It has civilised brutish and turbulent homes, saved the drunkard from his doom, and to many a mother, who would else indeed have been most wretched and most forlorn, it has given cheerful, peaceful thoughts that have sustained her.' [61]

So the drinking of tea altered work patterns, the status of women, the nature of art and aesthetics, and possibly even national temperament. Much of life was altered, as it had been in Japan and China, by the rise of tea, even if in each case the effects were substantially different because of the cultural history of each civilisation. 'Tea is the beverage of ceremonious peoples, and like the dense monsoon rains, it is both calming and stimulating, encouraging conversation and relaxation . . .' wrote Pascal Bruckner. 'Ideas and traditions steep slowly in its steamy transparence.'[62] It altered the tone of a society, as the French commentator Guillaume Raynal suggested in 1715, for though there might be inconveniences in the new craze for tea, he pointed out that 'it cannot be denied that it has contributed more to the sobriety of the nation than the severest laws, the most eloquent harangues of Christian orators, or the best treatises of morality.'[63]

While the way one drank tea was a way of marking the differences between the social classes, through minor signs and symbols, it also played a part in covering over some of the 'hidden injuries of class'. Like discussions about the weather, which unite all of the British across their various divides, so tea, it can be argued, became a point of unity. As the author, J. M. Scott wrote in *The Tea Story*, 'Essentially, classlessly, it belongs to every home. It is the form of hospitality that can be offered by the rich to the poor or the poor to the rich, equally and without embarrassment on either side.' [64]

The profound influence of tea on Chinese and Japanese ceramics is widely acknowledged, the requirements for drinking it having a very strong influence on the quality and quantity of pottery in those civilisations. The effect of tea drinking on European ceramics was almost as dramatic.

If we concentrate on Britain and leave aside the discovery of the porcelain-making process in Germany in the middle of the eighteenth century, we still find a great influence exerted by tea. Part of this was in fact through the ceramics that accompanied the tea on the ships coming back from China. These ships needed ballast alongside the very light tea chests. So they were packed with Chinese pottery and porcelain, which was heavy and additionally had some re-sale value in Europe. The quantity of these ceramics was staggering. In his book *Seeds of Change*, the author Henry Hobhouse estimates that probably over five million pieces of Chinese porcelain were imported a year, on average, from China to Europe during the first half of the eighteenth century. In the whole period 1684 to 1791, he reckons that about 215 million pieces of Chinese porcelain were imported into

Europe.[65] As a result the British never drank from such fine chinaware before or after the eighteenth century.

The second effect was directly on the production of ceramics within Britain. A very considerable new consumer demand was created. Tea is best drunk from china and pottery. Glass is used in Turkey and tin mugs can be used, but on the whole brass, pewter, enamel, glass and vessels made of other materials are not really suitable for this hot drink. As the passion for tea grew in a new setting, the tea-serving equipment became more complex and many features were added to the simple, elegant, cups of China and Japan. The Chinese and Japanese drank from tea bowls without handles. The British were already used to glasses and other vessels with handles and preferred to adapt these to deal with a very hot drink. The Chinese had traditionally brewed their tea in a large bowl on which they had placed a separate cover, like a saucer but on the top. The tea was then poured from this into smaller bowls for drinking. The Chinese style of teapot was modified so that tea could be poured through a spout. Because the British decided to add sugar and milk, spoons were necessary for all the guests, saucers were added to the cups to hold the spoons. Sugar bowls and milk jugs accompanied the teapot. Here was a whole new world for silversmiths and potters to exploit. It was also a way in which conspicuous display of wealth and taste could establish status through the ceremony of tea.

In addition, the containers holding the tea, the tea caddies, had to be made, and the tables for serving the tea from, and the biscuits and cakes to accompany the drinking on appropriate side-plates, and the chairs and screens and fireplaces which would provide the elegant or cosy setting. So a consumer boom was launched in the first third of the eighteenth century, serviced by craftsmen and the expanding profession of general grocers, tea tasters and auctioneers.

Tea became the backbone of one of the most important industrialised production developments of eighteenth-century England: pottery and porcelain manufacture. Josiah Wedgwood was but the most notable example. At the heart of his business was the tea ware that his firm manufactured with fine classical designs and colours, made relatively cheaply for the middle classes. There had been a notable development of tea ceramics, including experimentation with form, materials and patterns, from 1672 onwards. Poole, Worcester, Spode, Chelsea and numerous other firms showed how making tea ware and making money could go together. Many technical improvements were made and the mass production of what had hitherto been a craft item expanded. England had a new industry. Eventually this would make the importation of chinaware unnecessary and certainly drove down its price to a pitiful level.

As the drinking of tea became a central social event, it altered the rhythm of the British day and the nature of meals. In the upper and middle classes, breakfast had previously been a heavy meal with meat and ale; it was transformed into a lighter meal with bread, cakes, preserves and a hot drink, particularly tea.[66] Previously, the long gap between lunch and bed was filled by a rather early supper. Now it was possible to put the evening meal or 'dinner' back to seven or eight in the evening, for tea at about four or five in the afternoon meant that there was a bridging refreshment available; often bread, cakes, biscuits accompanied the tea, which turned it into a small meal.

All this was appropriate for the higher ranks in society, but a rather different pattern developed in the working class. Here an exhausted manual worker, who returned from the mine or factory after a shift ending at say five or six in the evening, would want to eat and relax straight away. Accordingly there developed, particularly in the factory and mining areas of northern England and southern Scotland, a meal named after its central ingredient, the 'tea' or 'high tea' as it was often called. The mug of tea, bread, a small amount of vegetable, cheese and occasionally meat – this was what brought the exhausted workers back from the edge of collapse and made it possible to recover and face another day. So while tea became a social necessity for the middle classes, it literally became a lifesaver for many working-class families throughout the later eighteenth and the nineteenth century, who spent up to half their food-and-drink budget on this one substance, cheap though it was. This was not because they were improvident or stupid as many of their critics alleged, but because they knew from bitter experience that only tea made life bearable.

This deep bond between tea and the working class may also be one of the factors that lie behind the affection for tea seen in certain parts of the British Empire. For many years the most avid tea-drinking nation outside Asia was not England, but Australia. Largely populated by working-class British emigrants, they took their dependence on tea with them.

There has been much interest recently in a phenomenon which occurred roughly in the hundred years after 1650 and which helped to prepare the way for, and increase the efficiency of, the industrial revolution, namely the consumer revolution. It would be fairly useless to devise methods to mass-produce cheap consumer goods, particularly clothes and ceramics, if there was no market for them. Goods needed to be sold, and for this one had to develop taste and discrimination, and above all desire, in people – the consumers. So alongside the increase in industrial production, there was a great surge in consumption practices.

This required a number of organisational and communication changes. Building on hundreds of years of quite sophisticated market retailing and skills, a set of devices was further refined or invented. These included advertising, storage, packaging and distribution. One of tea's many roles was to be a major vehicle for the experiments to establish a new consumer world. That tea should be the focus of the consumer revolution is not altogether surprising. People in seventeenth-century England did not need a new and improved method in order to help them to know about and discriminates between, or even to know how to buy and consume, beer, bread or woollen clothing. All these practices and substances were well known. On the other hand, to convert a population to an exotic, hitherto unknown leaf – a strange bit of black stuff looking like dirt, which was dropped into hot water – or to other new substances such as coffee or tobacco, required a special effort.

First one had to advertise, to explain what the product was and why sensible people should desire and buy it. Reputedly the 'first advertisement for any commodity in a London newspaper' (the *Mercurius Politicus* of 1658) was for tea.[67] From then on there was a non-stop advertising campaign, still alive on television and the World Wide Web today, to explain, coax and exhort people to buy tea. The wealth and power of the East India Company and a number of large firms gave it particular force.

Then there was the retailing. In the early eighteenth century tea became something which grocers, of whom there was now a new brand called 'tea grocers' to distinguish themselves from general grocers, sold in new ways. They began to develop specialist shops which pre-packaged the tea in attractive boxes and bags rather than scooping the substance out and weighing it. Tea became the foundation for many of the great retailing firms, such as Lipton's in the early eighteenth century. A century and a half later, another retailing giant, Tesco, also emerged out of the selling of tea.

Tea had to make new channels for itself alongside long-established commodities – in the country where and at the time when the greatest transformation in human history since farming was occurring. Just as, for the first time on this planet, humans were moving from agriculture to industry and from a country-based to city-based civilisation, tea emerged as the world's favourite drink. Thus tea was able to set the patterns and trends that many other commodities would follow. The conversion of a nation within a couple of generations to a new basic drink, little known in 1650, yet widespread a hundred years later, was one of the most dramatic consumer revolutions in British history.

Tea transformed Britain as it had done China and Japan. 'In no instance has a greater revolution taken place in the habits of a people than that which tea has effected within the last hundred years among the English,' wrote John Davis, the historian of China, in the middle of the nineteenth century.[68] Alongside that transformation there emerged the most powerful capitalist and imperial nation in world history. The anthropologist Sidney Mintz described how the 'first sweetened cup of hot tea to be drunk by an English worker was a significant historical event, because it prefigured the transformation of an entire society, a total remaking of its economic and social basis.'[69] Tea changed everything.

Chapter Six

Replacing China

Britain needed more tea. The British population was growing rapidly and the number of emigrants to the British colonies and dominions grew from small numbers to a huge potential market in the Americas and Asia. The amount of tea drunk per person also increased very fast.

Tea from China kept the West, and particularly Britain, satisfied until the late eighteenth century. The East India Company was not enthusiastic about investigating alternative sources for this commodity. It had the monopoly of the China trade and not surprisingly did not want this threatened. Between 1711 and 1810, £77,000,000 in taxes had been collected from the tea trade, which indicates its value. Yet against this reluctance there was a growing conviction among traders and entrepreneurs that China should not be allowed to reap all the benefits from one of the most profitable, and yearly more profitable, commodities in the world.

Europeans could not see why eastern countries should make fortunes out of their own products, and it became their aim to seek out and control the production of sugar, opium, rubber, coffee, cocoa and other necessary plant products. In Britain, Kew Gardens was established, and lesser offshoots elsewhere, where 'collectors' could send specimens to which the British could lay claim as soon as they were in possession of the place where they grew. The naturalist Sir Joseph Banks, president of the Royal Society from 1778, had plant hunters scouring the world for such specimens; many 'explorers' were on the same mission.

As early as 1778 the East India Company asked Banks's advice on tea. He told them it grew best between 26 and 30 degrees of latitude, and advised that it might grow in Bihar, Rungpor and Coochbihar in India. Green tea (which was then thought to be a different species) would thrive in the mountains; 'proper inducements' would ensure that the people of Bhutan would grow it. He pointed out that Chinamen often came as sailors. 'We may therefore safely conclude that their neighbours at Honan may be induced by the offer of liberal terms to follow their example' and bring tea shrubs, and tools to the Botanic Gardens in Calcutta, where they would teach the natives how to process them. Tea, he insisted, 'was of the greatest national importance' to Britain.

China was more difficult to deal with than other eastern countries. It was a powerful, self-confident nation that could not be overrun by small armies. It was also 'vain' and presumed to think it could manage its own affairs. Pulling down 'the haughty pride of the Chinese' was necessary but difficult. The only way tea could be grown elsewhere was by taking plants and putting them in similar situations in the European colonies, or in climates that suited them further afield, like Rio de Janeiro or St Helena.

The Dutch were the first to carry Chinese tea bushes to other parts of the world. As early as 1728 they were taking them to the

Cape of Good Hope and Ceylon. Yet it was not until 1828 that they established tea estates seriously, and these were much closer to China, in Java. It was a hazardous process, carrying off plants and seeds from Canton; the Chinese government put a price on the head of any merchant thought to be trying this botanical sabotage and tried to capture their ships. However, the Javanese plantations thrived since there was cheap labour available, but, ironically, tea growing only really took off in Java when tea plants from India were introduced in 1878.

So when two British embassies went to China they were each encouraged to investigate the possibility of bringing out tea. Banks accompanied Lord Macartney on the first embassy in 1792 and brought back tea seeds and plants for the botanical gardens in Calcutta. The plants sent from Lord Amherst's embassy of 1816 were lost in transit through the difficulties of the voyage.

The major pressure to bypass Chinese tea production was economic, in many ways similar to the desire to manufacture cotton in Britain rather than depend on Indian weavers. The growing dissatisfaction with Chinese production can only be understood if we realise the dramatic changes that were going on at precisely this period in Britain, with the first industrial revolution occurring roughly between 1750 and 1850. Its essence was the replacement of human labour, which was expensive, slow and often untrustworthy, by machines, which were driven by non-human power, and hence cheaper, faster and more dependable.

The industrial method not only led to a revolution in the production of factory goods, at the start mainly cotton items. The parallel agricultural revolution started as a method that was centred on improved rotation and use of crops and artificial fertilisers. Farms became outdoor factories for the production of plants. Everything was designed to maximise efficiency, jobs were carefully divided into their constituent parts, the application of the maximum amount of machinery and non-human energy was worked out to reduce costs.

So the British had seen in their own country how their agriculture had been made vastly more productive, both in terms of crops per acre and crops produced per person, by using machines and intensive methods. They had become the most powerful nation on earth by tapping large coal reserves to supplement animal, wind- and waterpower. As their consumption of tea increased, so a number of entrepreneurs began to turn to the question of how the extraordinary new power released by mechanisation, new sources of energy and a new organisation of labour could be used in the production of tea itself.

What was increasingly obvious was that this maximisation of efficiency and profit could never happen if tea was grown and processed within the traditional and apparently unchanging framework of Chinese civilisation.

The haphazard way in which the tea bushes were planted in China is shown in an early photograph. The implements used in the various stages of the process were of the very simplest kind, and scarcely changed over the thousand years from the ninth to nineteenth century. Family groups would often go out to do the picking together. [70]

One description of the scene and the immense labour involved is provided by the British lady traveller, Constance Gordon Cumming, in the 1870s.

I am greatly struck by the number of girls whom we meet working as tea-coolies, and by the enormous burdens which they carry slung from a bamboo which rests on their shoulder. Each girl carries two bags thus slung, the weight of a bag being half a *picul*, which is upwards of 60 lb. Thus heavily burdened, a party of these bright, pleasant-looking young women march a dozen miles or more, chatting and singing as they go . . . The tea-plantations are scattered over the hills, forming little dotted patches of regularly planted bushes. Here the girls and women are busy selecting the young green leaves, which they pick and collect in large basket-work trays of split bamboo.[71]

The early twentieth-century naturalist, Ernest Henry Wilson, writing of higher-altitude tea growing, describes how 'The culture extends up to 4000 feet altitude, the bushes being planted round the sides of the terraced fields on the mountain-sides. Very little attention is given them and they are usually allowed to grow smothered in coarse weeds to a height of from 3 to 6 feet.'[72]

The actual method of processing the tea once it was picked was enormously laborious. An 'early' manuscript gives the following instructions for commercial tea manufacture.

Spread the leaves about five or six inches thick on bamboo trays, in a proper place for the air to blow on them. Hire a workman, or *ching fu*, to watch them. Thus, the leaves continue from noon until six o'clock, when they begin to give out a fragrant smell. They are then poured into large bamboo trays, in which they are tossed with the hands about three or four hundred times: this is called *to ching*. It is this operation which gives the red edges and spots to the leaves. They are now carried to the *kuo* and roasted; and afterwards poured on flat trays to be rolled. The rolling is performed with both hands in a circular direction about three or four hundred times, when the leaves are again carried to the *kuo* and thus roasted and rolled three times. If the rolling be performed by a good workman, the leaves will be close and well twisted; if by an inferior one, loose, open, straight, and ill-looking. They are then conveyed to the *poey long*, the fire fierce, and the leaves turned without intermission until they are nearly eight-tenths dried. They are afterward spread on flat trays to dry until five o'clock, when the old yellow leaves and the stalks are picked out. At eight o'clock they are '*poeyed*' again over a slow fire. At noon they are turned once, and then left in this state to dry until three o'clock, when they are packed in chests.[73]

These methods had probably been in use for a thousand years. Towards the end of the nineteenth century, as the following description by Constance Gordon Cumming shows, they had changed little.

The leaves are then spread on mats, and are left in the sun till they are partially dried. After this, they are placed in very large flat circular trays, and barefooted coolies proceed to use their feet as rollers, and twirl the leaves round and round, till each has acquired an individual curl . . . Then the whole process is repeated a second time. The leaves have another turn in the sun, another foot-curling, and a more elaborate hand-rubbing. Then once more they are exposed to the sun, till they are so dried that no trace of green remains. They are then packed in bags, and are sent off to the tea merchants to be fired under their own supervision in the great tea *hongs*, where the hitherto unadulterated leaf receives that coating of indigo and gypsum . . . Some of the tea farmers have charcoal stoves in their own houses, where firing is done on a small scale – but this is exceptional.[74]

Despite the immense amount of human labour required in the process, there was no move towards any labour-saving machinery over the hundreds of years during which tea was produced in this way. Under pressure from the mechanisation of these stages in the Assamese industry in the later nineteenth century, attempts were made in some parts of China to substitute machines for humans; but they all failed for various reasons.[75]

From the British point of view, all this was very inefficient. Their own agricultural revolution had been brought about by the application of capitalist methods and the consolidation of small farms into larger ones. The domestic or peasant way favoured by the Chinese was deemed grossly unproductive. What was needed were large estates, or plantations, where economies of scale and real 'scientific' production could take place. The British could never achieve this in China. The tea must obviously be moved to a new site where it could be grown properly and efficiently. It should be treated as if it was wheat or maize growing on an East Anglian farm in Britain, where a few labourers with efficient machines and mills produced a huge amount per head and hence kept production costs down and quality up.

In Britain, the use of water and of wheeled carts on reasonable roads kept the transport costs to a minimum. But in China, the cost of tea was raised by the difficulty of getting the tea from the growing areas to the coast. It is worth quoting Samuel Ball's fairly detailed description written in the late 1840s since it quickly dispels any lingering nostalgia we might have for the supposed pleasures of tea production in its homeland.

> The usual route by which the black teas are sent to Canton, is through the province of Kiang-sy. They are first transported down the river Min in Fokien to the small town of Tsong-gan-hien, whence they are carried, by porters, an eight days' journey, over mountain passes to Ho-keu, and the rivers of Kiang-sy, which conduct to Nan-chang-foo and Kan-chew-foo; and then, suffering many transhipments on their way, to the pass of Ta-moey-ling, in that part of the same chain of mountains which divides Kiang-sy from Quon-tong. At this pass the teas are again carried by porters – the journey occupies one day – when they are re-shipped in large vessels which convey them to Canton. The time occupied in the entire transport from the Bohea [tea] country to Canton is about six weeks or two months.[76]

Thus tea passed through this immensely difficult terrain using largely sweated, semi-bonded, human labour. At times it was poled down a river, but even here immense labour was needed, for the boats might go down relatively easily – but they had to be taken up again. Isabella Bird's extraordinary account of the labour involved in the later nineteenth century takes some three pages to describe the agonies of the work.

On a tiny amount of food and wages, 'these men do the hardest and riskiest work I have seen done in any country . . . week after week, from early dawn to sunset.'

Away they go, climbing over the huge angular boulders of the riverbanks, sliding on their backs down spurs of smooth rock, climbing cliff walls on each other's shoulders, or holding on with fingers and toes, sometimes on hands and knees, sometimes on shelving precipices where only their grass sandals save them from slipping into the foaming race below . . . these poor fellows who drag our commerce up the Yangtze amidst all these difficulties and perils, and many more, are attached to a heavy junk by a long and heavy rope, and are dragging her up against the force of a tremendous current, raging in billows, eddies, and whirlpools; that they are subject to frequent severe jerks; that occasionally their burden comes to a dead stop and hangs in the torrent for several minutes; that the tow-rope often snaps, throwing them on their faces and bare bodies on jagged and rough rocks; that they are continually in and out of the water; that they are running many chances daily of having their lives violently ended; and that they are doing all this mainly on rice![77]

The terrain was far too difficult here and elsewhere for animals. Over many of the other parts of the routes, the porters carried huge loads on their backs. Ernest Henry Wilson described how they were carrying an average load of over 150 kg (twice their own body weight). On one part of the route, of less than 140 miles, it took the laden porters some twenty days. 'With their huge loads they are forced to rest every hundred yards or so, and as it would be impossible for the carrier to raise his burden if it were once deposited on the ground he carries a short crutch, with which he supports it when resting, without releasing himself from the slings.' A porter received about one English shilling for this gruelling twenty days of carrying, and 'out of this he has to keep himself and pay for his lodgings'.[78] Photographs of the carriers show the huge burdens and emaciated bodies, both on their voyages to and from the trade ports and on their equally arduous journeys up into Tibet. The numerous middlemen who organised the porters and allowed the tea through their areas, exacting tolls and taxes and protection money, added to the cost.

The advantage of this system was that all the tiny trickles of tea produced by millions of households in the end produced a vast river of tea flowing to the ports. It was relatively cheap to produce, in terms of both labour and land. It was also very important as a supplementary source of income for peasant households and all the middlemen on the route. The disadvantage from the British point of view was that there was no central control over production, no way in which quality could be systematically improved or monitored and no way to apply systematic knowledge and scientific management to the growing and protection of tea against the various pests which attacked it.

Finally, the British were outraged that the Chinese merchants at the ports should make a further, substantial, profit. 'Thus one considerable item which entered into the cost of tea to the foreigner, was the Hong merchant's profit,' remarked Samuel Ball, writing in the mid-nineteenth century.[79]

He gave the average costs of each stage of this process in Chinese currency as follows.

Cost of growth and manipulation	12	0	0	0
Cost of chests, canisters, and packing	1	3	1	6
Expense of transport to Canton	3	9	2	0
Charges at Canton on account of govt. Duties, Hong merchants' expenses, and Boat hire to the ships. . .	3	0	0	0
Total	20	2	3	6

It was these costs which the British hoped to undercut. This was a task made increasingly more necessary as economic and political difficulties of other kinds began to build up.

While tea was yearly becoming more of a necessity for the British, they were dependent for its supply on the one country in the world which they found too powerful, at first, to control. But the situation was changing rapidly, and the growth of industrial and military power in the period between the time of Macartney's mission to China in 1792 and the 1830s is well shown by one famous episode.[80]

When small quantities of tea were being imported into Europe, it could be paid for by trading several commodities. In the second half of the eighteenth and the start of the nineteenth century, Britain could use its increasing hold over India to pay for tea with cotton exported from Bengal to China. But this trade dwindled as the Chinese improved their own cotton manufacturing and undercut the cheap Indian goods, just as the British themselves were starting to do.

The major commodity, which had always been the mainstay of Western trade with China, was silver. This worked for a while — basically for the first fifty years of the direct clipper trade between China and Britain, from about 1720 to 1770. Then various things happened which meant that it was no longer practicable to use silver directly. Then the American Revolution in 1776 cut off the supply of silver from Mexico, one of the major sources. The cost of silver also rose through inflation. Furthermore, the amounts of tea now being demanded in Britain rose enormously each year. There was not enough silver to pay for it and there was a crisis. Tea was desperately needed, but there was nothing to buy it with. The solution that emerged was to exchange tea for another far more addictive drug.

In 1758 Parliament gave the East India Company the monopoly of the production of opium in India. Although the importation of opium was banned in China, the Portuguese were engaged in the illegal trade of this substance to China. In 1773 the British wrested it from them, and by 1776 the British were already exporting some sixty tons, and double that amount by 1790. Producing opium became an immense industry, employing nearly a million people in Bengal where it was mainly grown. By 1830 the British exported nearly 1500 tons of opium to China – worth several billion dollars in present money. As the nineteenth-century historian, John Davis, wrote, 'The pernicious drug, sold to the Chinese, has exceeded in market-value the wholesome leaf that has been purchased from them; and the balance of the trade has been paid to us in silver.' In 1833, just before the Opium Wars, the imports of opium into China were worth eleven and a half million dollars in currency of that time, the exports of tea just over nine million dollars.[81]

On the face of it, there was no direct connection between the East India Company's monopoly in opium production and its monopoly in tea trading. The Company merely sold the opium to

British merchants in India. These merchants then took it to China where corrupt officials handled it. So the Company was not officially involved – but of course it knew what was going on. The merchants received silver coin that was then sold back to the East India Company. The silver went back to London where it was given to those who went to China to buy tea on behalf of the Company. Plausible denial was always possible. Protests from the Chinese were ignored, or they were told that it was nothing to do with the British Government or the Company. American merchants practised an almost exactly similar system, but used less-pure opium from the Ottoman Empire.

The British increased the export of opium by a thousand times in the fifty years up to the 1830s. All efforts by the Chinese authorities to curb this devastating plague failed. In the end they took drastic measures, burning a year's supply of opium in a vast bonfire and arresting the British and Chinese involved. War was declared. In the Opium War of 1839–42 British warships pulverised the Chinese fortifications and forced the Chinese government into humiliating concessions, including the paying of huge reparations and the ceding of Hong Kong. Finally, Amoy, Fuchow, Ningpo and Shanghai were made 'open ports', a further indemnity was paid and the Chinese customs were forced to accept British supervision.

It is impossible to estimate the cumulative effect of the mass addiction of the population to opium and the political instability caused by the apparently mighty and invincible Chinese empire being defeated in war by a tiny far-off island. The terrible devastations and turmoil of Chinese history from the middle of the century, with the massive mortality of the Taiping rebellion and later the Boxer uprising, in which many millions died, cannot be unconnected to these events. Hobhouse suggests that 'China, a repository of arts and artefacts, of craftsmanship, design, ingenuity, and philosophy, was raped for a few years' increase in the national income of the white man. For a pot of tea, one could say, Chinese culture was nearly destroyed.'[82]

Other historians would add qualifications. They point out that at all times more opium was produced internally than externally. The import was only made possible because of the demand in China and the collusion of Chinese merchants. The British did not force opium on China, though they fed the desire. By the end of the nineteenth century, the Chinese production had more or less replaced foreign imports. Yet even if we accept these revisions, it does not alter the fact that the link between tea and opium was very close and that it was the British desire for tea that lay along the causal chain that led to the Opium War and all the subsequent effects on China.

Ironically, the Opium War only helped to underline the fragile nature of the tea trade and the dependence on Chinese producers. 'In 1822, the Royal Society of Arts offered fifty guineas to whoever could grow and prepare the greatest quantity of China tea in the British West Indies, Cape of Good Hope, New South Wales or the East Indies. The prize remained unclaimed,' the author Edward Bramah tells us.[83] Competition added to the urgency. The Dutch were setting up a successful alternative in Java. Furthermore, in 1833 the East India Company's monopoly in China was ended by Parliament. The field was open and huge profits might be made. But was it possible that the Chinese could be undercut? Would tea grow successfully in India? Could the incredibly cheap Chinese labour costs be undercut? Two detailed reports on the possibilities give a flavour of the arguments that were used in support of the new venture.

In 1828 Lord Bentinck, Governor-General of India, set up a Committee to look into the matter. He chose businessmen and botanists – the most prominent of these being Nathaniel Wallich, who was in charge of the Botanic Gardens in Calcutta – and showed them a report sent to him by a Mr Walker. This began with a diatribe against China: 'the jealous policy of the Chinese Government in her intercourse with all nations; the apprehensions which she had always entertained of our formidable Empire in the East Indies; the ignorance, pride and prejudice of the Government; . . . the rapacity and corruption of her officers; and occasionally the misconduct of our own people' had hampered efforts to date. But he produced all sorts of convincing arguments to counter these handicaps.

Tea plants could be transplanted easily, unlike other things they had tried, such as mangosteens. The problem lay in the resistance of the Chinese. Outsiders were not allowed into the country but confined to Canton 'where they see as much of China as a Chinese would of England . . .if confined to Wapping'. He admitted that 'It is an acknowledged fact that the Chinese empire is the most powerful on the face of the earth' and so could enforce its strict rules about the import of foreign goods, but he pointed out that Europe's weapons were far more advanced. China could, he implied, become just another eastern country, ready to be pounced on, a prophecy that was fulfilled only a few years later with the Opium Wars.

Walker produced figures to emphasise how tea, once a luxury, was now everybody's drink in England, 'the common people using it as a portion of food'. The government raised £4,000,000 annually in revenue from tea – a sign of how much was flowing out of China. Yet tea was known to grow in other places. He reminded the Governor-General of the reports from Buchanan Hamilton fifty years earlier from Burma, with the descriptions of a tribal people called the Singphos bringing tea down in baskets to the plains.

Tea, like all camellias, he pointed out, was happy on hillsides on gravelly soil, and India had plenty of these, 'of very little use to the East India Company'. Chinamen could be brought up from Calcutta or from the East Indies to oversee the process of growing and manufacturing it. Indians with their 'sedentary and tranquil habits' and their ability to live on two or three pence a day would make ideal labour. The East India Company wanted to provide 'some reasonable occupation' for natives. Also, most importantly, revenues for the Company would be increased if they no longer had to purchase tea from China.

This paper convinced Bentinck, and Dr Wallich drew up a report on the plant. He advised that it liked moist valleys and the banks of rivers, which was true, but also recommended the slopes of the Himalayan range, the Kumaon hills, Gurwhal, Dehra Dun and Kashmir, making sense of his advice by suggesting a warm nursery for a spell, and then somewhere with frost and snow for at least six weeks.

Without further ado, the Tea Committee decided to send one of its members, a Mr Gordon, to Penang and Singapore and if possible into China, to pick up information, plants and Chinamen. Gordon took with him a questionnaire for the Dutch to answer. How much did it rain in the tea districts of Java? Were there fogs? Snow? Were there trees for shelter? What about manure and irrigation? How much were the labourers paid? How were they fed? How were tea chests made?

The Dutch seemed happy to answer and Gordon sent back a report. The Dutch had more than 3,000,000 plants in Java, but they found it difficult to get Chinese to emigrate, because they were terrified of the sea. However, 'they have recourse to forced labour' and this would be no problem in India.

Yet the argument was also couched in grander, more altruistic, terms. Moving tea production from China to India would be of great benefit not only to the British, but also the Indians themselves. Samuel Ball, writing in the 1840s, gives a flavour of the arguments to hand.

The population of British India and its dependencies is computed at 114,430,000. Supposing these to become, like the Chinese, all consumers of tea, the impulse which this novel demand for labour would give to a country mainly dependent on its agricultural resources; the new, unprofitable and otherwise unoccupied mountain lands which would thereby be brought under cultivation; the industrial activity its manipulation and preparation would call forth; as well as the new and indirect demands on industry it would develop; and lastly, though least to be considered, but nevertheless of high importance, the new sources of revenue it would open to the government – are all considerations of such vast interest, that it ought not to be a matter of surprise, that the encouragement of the cultivation of tea on an extensive scale, is daily becoming more and more a subject of anxious solicitude on the part of the India Government.

He also suggested that if tea drinking became widespread in India,

. . . when we consider the abstinence from animal food, which is imposed on the Hindoo by his religion, we cannot but think that the introduction and adoption of the Mongolian method of using tea in its broth-like form, mixed with butter and meal, would furnish not only a refreshing, but a somewhat substantial adjunct to his meagre dietary; while the leaf used as an infusion . . .would administer greatly to his comfort, health, and sobriety.[84]

Others wrote in a similar vein, including the great tea explorer Robert Fortune.

In these days, when tea has become almost a necessary of life in England and her wide-spreading colonies, its production upon a large and cheap scale is an object of no ordinary importance. But to the natives of India themselves the production of this article would be of the greatest value. The poor paharie, or hill-peasant, at present has scarcely the common necessaries of life, and certainly none of its luxuries. The common sorts of grains which his lands produce will scarcely pay the carriage to the nearest market-town, far less yield such a profit as will enable him to purchase even a few of the necessary and simple luxuries of life . . . If part of these lands produced tea, he would then have a healthy beverage to drink, besides a commodity that would be of great value in the market. Being of small bulk compared with its value, the expense of carriage would be trifling, and he would have the means of making himself and his family more comfortable, and more happy.[85]

The only problem was where, exactly, the tea was to be grown and how the methods could be improved to make it profitable. Completely by chance a solution was found. A new location for the production of tea that they could control, which was soon to become the centre of world tea production, suddenly fell into the hands of the British.

Chapter Seven

Green Gold

On 13 March 1824 the British marched slowly up from Calcutta, guns mounted on elephants, to take Assam.

There was no hurry; this remote and unrewarding kingdom was to come to them as part of a package, when the Burmese were evicted. The East India Company troops had little trouble in accomplishing this task, the Burmese being decimated by cholera and with little in the way of an army to defend them. By the Treaty of Yandabo in 1826 the British took possession of all Burmese Indian possessions, and also a third of Burma itself, the first of 'three bites of the cherry' as Dalhousie jokingly referred to the conquest of the country completed sixty years later.

The newly appointed Commissioner David Scott was reassuring. 'We are not forced into your country by the thirst of conquest,' he told the Burmese king and his court, 'but are forced in our defence . . . to deprive our enemies of the means of attacking us.' Assam had long been recognised as unhealthy both physically and mentally (being known for fever and unpleasant religious practices). Walled in on three sides by mountain ranges harbouring Rude Savages, it did not come high on the East India

Company's list of countries to be conquered. Though a trading concern, the Company was *de facto* ruler of India, making treaties, organising military adventures, collecting revenue. It was only when the Burmese ran up against their borders in Bengal, thus threatening the most profitable jewel in the British crown, that the Company felt it was time to act.

The Burmese had been in Assam for three years, and its people were heartily glad to see the back of them. Like all mercenary armies in a defenceless land, they had raped and pillaged with unprecedented ferocity; stories circulated of flayings alive, of burnings in oil and setting fire to the prayer houses and incinerating everyone inside. They also neglected to build the vital banks and dykes needed to prevent the valley from flooding. Crops had been lost, cholera and other epidemics had taken their toll of both conquered and conquerors. Possibly the Burmese were not too sorry to leave. They reputedly took thirty thousand 'slaves' with them when they crossed the mountains back into their own country. Assam had never been populous; now it was even emptier.

The problem facing the new administration of Assam was how to administer; whether to keep the king in place (in which case which king) or simply annex the place as in other parts of India. They settled for a compromise; the young Purander Sing could have Upper Assam, which produced less revenue than Lower Assam, which the Company would take over. He was crowned in April 1833 and given a salute of nineteen guns, a ceremony watched in sullen silence by the part of the crowd who had backed his rival. He was to pay the Company 50,000 rupees a year for the privilege, the highest tribute in British India. He was also to give assistance when asked for, in road works or military adventures.

Presumably the Company had been aware of the situation during the previous years – indeed, it had been happy to supply arms to all sides in the dynastic struggles that had brought in the Burmese, and even a small contingent of sepoys at one point, but generally speaking it was busy elsewhere. Its only real interest in this north-eastern frontier was as a possible opening to China. Everyone was vague about Assam's boundaries, which had never been properly defined, but everyone had an idea that there were passes linking it with Tibet, and with China's southern corner, Yunnan.

Finding a north-east passage to the huge Chinese markets in Yunnan and beyond was something of an obsession with the British. Probes had also been made in the north-west via Ladakh but both Russia and France were obstacles here. The Governor-General of India, Warren Hastings, had been interested, and sent China tea seeds to his emissary, George Bogle, in Bhutan and told him to take these and other useful trading objects into Tibet, as another possible point of entry. In his progress Bogle skirted a corner of Assam and described its forests of sal trees, its rice, mustard seed, tobacco, opium and cotton.

He was enthusiastic and thought that any objections about the British moving in would be easily dealt with by an 'expedition'. Once in, things would be easy, 'a few months after entering Assam the troops might be paid and provisioned without making any demands on the Company treasury.' The King of Burma unfortunately claimed a lot of the mountains and passes leading into China. Even at this early stage it became part of the Secret and Political thinking that he would, sooner rather than later, be removed.

Assam had never been conquered before. In the thirteenth

century the same Hukawng Valley through which the Burmese had retreated, brought in some wandering Shans who, in waves and with little opposition, established a kingdom. They named it 'The Kingdom of Golden Gardens', so fruitful and lush was this land lying along the great Brahmaputra river, with a dozen lesser rivers feeding in and out. Another name, 'The Country of Cocoon Rearers', told of the vast forests with trees on which silkworms were reared. Every Assamese woman knew how to spin exquisite silk; it was a skill she needed in order to get a husband.

The rulers had introduced wet-rice cultivation to the valley and for five hundred years it prospered. As a dynasty the Ahoms were tolerant, and evolved a way of living in harmony with the hill tribes, distant cousins some of them. When the Mughals, lured on by stories of the rich timber and vast hordes of elephants of this remote kingdom, thought to invade, they were conquered by the weapons Assam always had at its disposal – jungles, quagmires and fever.

Self-sufficient, except in one commodity, salt, Assam wanted no foreigners; seeing what the British were doing in Bengal they especially suspected them. They set up a series of guarded customs posts along their boundary to prevent predatory merchants crossing. Traders camped with little armies of sepoys, quarrelling with each other and engaging in small enterprises. The Company held the salt contract, the only really valuable one.

Then things started to fall apart in the Golden Gardens. Dynastic squabbles weakened the centre, and there were revolts and incursions. When the British were asked to come in and help on one side, Lord Cornwallis, the Governor-General, saw this as an opportunity to enter forbidden territory. He sent up a Captain Welsh with three companies of sepoys, and instructions 'that no pains should be spared to avail ourselves of an opportunity to obtain good surveys and to acquire every information that may be possible both of the population and of the manners and customs of the inhabitants as well as the trade and manufactures and natural productions of countries with which it must ever be our interest to maintain the most friendly communications'.

Captain Welsh took with him a doctor as well as smiths, armourers, firemen, carpenters and some English privates. Doctors were always available for expeditions, their white patients being few. This one, John Peter Wade, had the usual rather chequered career of his kind, starting off with the army in the Maratha Wars, but his chief asset was his friendship with Francis Fowke, Resident at Benares, an enormously wealthy trader in opium and diamonds, his father a friend of Samuel Johnson with the ear of the Directors of the East India Company in London.

Wade's salary of 300 rupees was reasonably generous, and he was excited at the thought of what this unknown country would offer. He wrote to Fowkes, 'Assam is not a country for diamonds but it is for gold dust, and that is much better for industry and trade.' Moreover, 'Today we shall enter a kingdom scarcely ever trodden by Europeans before,' so there would be little competition. With Fowkes as a friend he would be aware of the enormous riches that lay about in India, ready to be picked up by even the least enterprising, and under the wing of the East India Company. Indeed the first thing Captain Welsh did when he had put the king back on the throne was to negotiate a commercial treaty giving the Company exclusive control of the salt trade. Wade told Fowkes that he hoped for a commission on this, and expected it to amount to one and a half lakhs.

There were other rich pickings. When Welsh had evicted the rebels from the king's palace he found within it bullion to the value of 105,000 rupees. Wade was appointed one of the Prize Agents and they divided this up between them all, 'according to the customary rules', without asking permission. They noted gold and opium poppies, and asked Calcutta to send up 'a few boatloads of salt and opium' as bribes. They missed the real green gold growing in the tangled forests. An unassuming tree, producing small white flowers, tea did not announce itself. There were more profitable trees it seemed – teak, sandalwood and aloes on which the silkworms fed. Yet quietly in their midst was the plant that would make the British rejoice in the Treaty of Yandabo.

Unfortunately for Welsh and Wade a new Governor-General, Sir John Shore, had replaced Lord Cornwallis. Shore recalled the expedition, disapproving of the looting which he said did not come within the discretion of a capture by storm. He wanted no further interference in the affairs of Assam: they must sort out their kings for themselves.

At this point a certain Robert Bruce emerged, one of the few traders who had set himself up in Assam. He was employed first by one side, then the other, and finally by the Burmese in their struggles. His brother, Charles, also appeared on the scene, in charge of a British gunboat. They were the kind of adventurers Conrad wrote about. They were also the discoverers of what was going to make the British rich for generations to come and change the physical, social, and economic face of Assam.

The Assamese themselves at first welcomed Yandabo and their new rulers. It was quite hard for the British not to be popular, seeing the mess they had inherited. However, it soon became apparent that it was out of the Burmese frying pan and into the British fire. Ten years later the Governor-General's office in Calcutta was sternly critical. 'We have hitherto governed Assam extremely ill . . . the country has been retrograding, its villages decaying and its revenue annually declining.' There was 'a direct tendency to reduce the *ryots* [cultivators] to a state of poverty and dejection, to cause a great decrease in population and to ruin those resources whence the Government might have somehow derived a handsome revenue . . . and to eradicate every feeling of gratitude towards their rulers.'

The 'handsome revenue' was the cause of the trouble. The relaxed Ahom methods of tax collection in service or produce was replaced by an army of revenue 'farmers' tramping the country bearing demand papers totally incomprehensible to the illiterate peasantry. They measured out areas that had previously been overlooked and taxed everything in sight – betel-nut trees, gold-washing, fishing, forests. These duties had to be paid in cash, something of a problem in a coinless country.

The Marwaris, the merchant moneylenders of Rajasthan, saw their chance to fish in these troubled financial waters. A system evolved by which the peasant gave his crop to the Marwari who would then produce the cash to pay the revenue. Scenes of desperate families selling their possessions at the collection points became common. The opportunities for blackmail and corruption, both by the tax collectors and the Marwaris, were many and seldom missed. There was a general exodus into Bhutan and Bengal, and only a great influx of Bengalis in the opposite direction prevented a total drain of population.

One of the few big landholders of Assam, Maniram Dewan, wrote an aggrieved letter describing the situation as 'living in the belly of a tiger'. He had at first supported the British, but became bitter and disillusioned when he found himself being excluded from the generous land deals offered to Europeans. The British had opened the borders, so carefully guarded before, and Bengalis came streaming in to settle on land that nobody seemed to own and this also annoyed Maniram. Bengalis, being desperate fleers from famine, worked harder than the Assamese. Their presence from the first was resented and the socio-economic and racial disruption caused by their arrival (exacerbated by the fact that they were Muslims) festered for years.

Nobody, according to the Company, owned the forests which it designated Waste Lands. The British were prepared to rent out the rainforest at very low rates, but only in blocks of a hundred acres, and no Assamese peasant could take up their generous offers. Nor could he explain that the lands were not waste and not without owners. They were held corporately by each village, well demarcated and a vital part of the economy. They provided bamboos for every possible use, timber for burning, medicines, grazing, elephants, burial grounds, dyes, lac, resin, honey, incense and food for silkworms.

Even when they didn't clear the forests the British made it illegal for villagers to collect firewood. Any pleas of poverty they dismissed as the result of the indolence and addiction to opium of most Assamese. They forbade the cultivation of poppies, except by themselves; large areas were laid out by the Company for the production of opium, fenced and guarded. Company men always carried opium as a bribe when they went into the hills on their many efforts to find that north-east passage.

The puppet king Purander Sing never had a chance, and when the tea plant was discovered the British found they had given him the wrong bit of the country, the region where tea grew. The Commissioner decided he was a 'rapacious miser' and dethroned him without further ado. His son joined Maniram Dewan's rebellion, and then no more was heard of the once strong and able dynasty. Even their graves were looted, probably by some of their own needy relations.

The valley having been dealt with, the Company then had to turn its attention to the hills which framed the country on three sides and were sparsely but fiercely inhabited. The attitude of nineteenth-century colonialists to tribal peoples was predictable. The clansmen of their own Scottish Highlands were generally described as barbarians. There were no Noble Savages among them, or in the East. The tribespeople were dirty, aggressive, cunning, pagan and childlike. 'Vile and barbarous and their persons filthy and squalid'; 'hideously wild and ugly visages'; 'discontented, restless and intriguing'; 'rude treacherous people' were some of the opinions of the first white men to meet the Tibeto-Burman races who fringed their new acquisition, Assam.

It was unfortunate that so many of the hill people were to be found in a part of the country important to the British – 'designed by nature as the great highway of commerce between the nations' was how a surveyor described it, 'allowed to lie profitless and in impenetrable jungle', alas, but 'its crystal streams abound in gold dust . . . its mountains are pregnant with precious stones and silver, its atmosphere is perfumed with tea growing wild and luxuriantly . . . and it might be converted into one continued garden of silk and cotton and coffee and sugar and tea over an extent of many hundreds of miles.' Nobody, it was decided, owned this Garden of Eden, its human inhabitants were regarded rather as a species of animal, who would either die out or find some other jungle to go to.

The hill people could not, however, be ignored, situated, as many of them were, on that route to China. Boundaries must be made between mountain and plain for a start, and for this purpose a Government Survey Department was used. These surveyors doubled as spies and were looked on with a great deal of suspicion by tribal peoples, sometimes to the extent of removing their heads. But apart from anything else, the raids of the hill men into the valley disturbed revenue collection, the main task of the new administration.

The new Commissioner and his assistants frowned on the relaxed attitude of the Ahoms towards raids. All along the border there had been a no man's land called *posa*, where tribesmen had yearly collected a form of blackmail – pieces of cloth from every house in return for which the tribesmen would refrain from raiding. Regular markets were held on *posa* land when cotton, honey, ivory were brought down, rice and salt taken up. On the whole, a harmonious balance was maintained. For different reasons the hills and plains people despised each other; the British despised them all but treated the hill peoples more warily. It was quite difficult lugging large guns up mountains and across rope bridges, and a problem to get coolies to carry stores and equipment, which meant that these people were harder to subdue. In fact, a plan was put forward for a permanent Coolie Corps. The British also considered using convicts as coolies, but in a country as free of serious crimes as Assam these were in short supply.

Apart from interfering with revenue collecting, the British didn't much care for the yearly arrival on *posa* land of hordes of

savages to claim their cloth. What was the answer? A whole row
of forts along the borders? Expensive and difficult even then to
stop Abors, Mishmis, Miris, Daflas, Nagas, and other tribal
peoples from slipping through. In their efforts to bring some sort
of order to the situation, and at the same time to show who was
master, lines were drawn, punitive expeditions sent up, treaties
offered to be signed. An Abor chief, presented with one of these,
ate it. Between 1835 and 1851 ten expeditions were sent up
against the Nagas alone; with tea gardens expanding along their
borders it became vital to keep them at bay.

These expeditions, however, were costly and Lord Dalhousie
decided they were also futile. He issued orders that 'we should
confine ourselves to our own ground and not meddle in the feuds
and fights of these savages . . . rigidly exclude them from all
communication either to sell what they have got or to buy what
they want if they should become turbulent or troublesome . . . far
better at less cost and with more justice than by annexing their
country openly by a declaration or virtually by a partial
occupation.' Dalhousie, a great annexer of territory, thought it
best to draw an imaginary line across the hills and leave all the
tribes behind it to their lawless ways. Others nearer the spot
planned for missionaries to join the trading caravans across the
hills into China, 'thus while the jealous mandarins were
excluding foreigners from their ports they might plant
Christianity in the heart of the Empire'.

For the first ten years the Commissioner, David Scott, was kept
busy collecting revenue and setting up the first hill station,
Cherrapunji, where he himself lived and died. His acquisition of
this, and other areas, was questionable but nobody questioned it,

except the small kings who were dispossessed.

Communications were wretched in Assam, its rivers capricious, its forests dangerous, but all these negative aspects were soon to be forgotten. The Bruce brothers, Charles and Robert, had settled, married local women and in their travels stumbled on the plant that was to transform Assam, India and in some senses the world. Yet for ten years after this discovery of wild tea growing in Assam, nothing further was done. The experts in the Botanical Gardens of Calcutta, who were sent specimens by David Scott (who had also found some in Manipur), said it was the same family — *Camellia* — but not the Chinese variety.

Meanwhile, the Bruce brothers were both discovering what they were sure was the real thing in their trading with the tribes on the fringes of the valley. Robert Bruce said he had made an agreement with a chieftain for some plants, and he gave these to his brother, who handed them on to David Scott. Scott planted some in his garden and sent some to Dr Wallich in Calcutta. He assured Wallich, 'the Burmese and Chinese in this place concur in stating it to be wild tea. I had a much more perfect seed than any of those sent but cannot now find it. It was of this shape agreeing with the plate in the Encyclopaedia.'

Then he found the elusive seed 'and forward it with the others in a tin box'. Seeds were vital in the identification of the plant, but these did not convince Wallich. Lieutenant Charlton of the Assam Light Infantry, however, became enthusiastic, and got in touch with the Agricultural and Horticultural Society. He described how 'the natives of Suddyah are in the habit of drinking an infusion of the dried leaves . . . they acquire the smell and taste of Chinese tea when dried.' Still no reactions came from the authorities.

In January 1835, while their Mr Gordon was still in China, electrifying news reached the Tea Committee from Assam. Major Jenkins, agent to the Governor-General, and Lieutenant Charlton sent reports, accompanied by samples of both leaves and fruit, of tea they had found growing in Upper Assam. This time, having fresh seeds to examine, Wallich was able to state that this was the genuine thing, *Camellia sinensis*. Jenkins said 'Camellias are to be found in every part of this hill country and within our jurisdiction in the Singpho district of Beesa a coarse variety is undoubtedly indigenous . . . It grows wild everywhere . . . all the way from this place about a month's journey to the Chinese province of Younnan where I am told it is extensively cultivated . . . I think there is no doubt of it being bona fide tea.' Tea all the way to Yunnan. What more could they ask for?

In fact Jenkins and Charlton had been fairly certain six months earlier that they had found 'a coarse variety' of the plant in the Singpho region on the Company's borders. Charlton had actually seen the Singphos preparing a basic kind of tea by pulling the leaves into pieces, boiling these bits and squeezing the result into balls. He even sent down a jar of the concoction to Calcutta, but it wasn't until the seeds arrived that Wallich was convinced.

Then there was euphoria, this discovery 'by far the most important and valuable that has ever been made in matters connected with the agricultural and communal resources of this empire' crowed the Committee, 'tea indigenous in Assam from Sadiya to Yunnan.' Yunnan was not exactly in their control, as yet. But a road towards it was to be started forthwith.

All came forward with wilder and wilder schemes. Jenkins suggested two or three 'able Chinamen' being sent up over the

Patkoi and into Yunnan, there to collect more of their countrymen to start cultivation in Assam. It seemed to be a common assumption that to be Chinese automatically conferred a skill in tea growing. Jenkins grew lyrical at the thought of all that 'unlimited waste' of jungle and mountainside that could support three or four million people. It was simply a matter of clearing it, but there were 'colonies of Shans' around for this job. What about taking over Ava (Burma) and then detaching Yunnan from China?

It was a heady vision and the rest of the world was dropped. Who now cared about Rio de Janeiro and where was St Helena? Gordon was recalled from his mission, and when a sample of made tea arrived on Wallich's desk in May, sent by Charlton, he pronounced it to be reasonably drinkable, though slightly mouldy. It was certainly better than a 'Burmese' brew sent by the Resident at the court, Colonel Burney.

Meanwhile three experts, Wallich and two doctors, Griffiths and Maclelland, set off in August to see how much more tea they could find in Assam. Charles Bruce was to meet them; they knew nothing of the country, the language, the protocol involved in dealing with the local rulers. It took them four months to meet up with Bruce; the Brahmaputra in flood slowed their progress, but at least they didn't get stuck on a sandbank, which was common in the cold weather. For all the difficulties of travel by elephant, bullock cart, canoe or on foot, it must have been a magical experience to the two botanists, and dozens of trees and plants labelled *Wallichi* or *Griffithi* testify to the delight of their discoveries.

Yet it was in the east, in Upper Assam, that they were most successful. Griffiths wrote a journal of this expedition, recalling their arrival in a Singpho village, whose men he described as 'a

stout rather fine race, free, easy and independent'. The Singphos
in eastern Assam were ready to show them round. On 16 January
'we gave up to the examination of the tea in its native place.'
They waded through jungle for some time, then suddenly came
on the tea. 'This plant is limited to a small extent, perhaps three
hundred yards square . . . We were fortunate enough to find it
both in flower and fruit owing to its site . . . its growth is tall and
slender and its crown, at least that of the smaller, very small and
ill developed. Large trees are rare, in fact they have been all cut
down by the Singphos who like all other natives are excessively
improvident.'

These natives were able, however, to show what they did with
the leaves, the first real information on tea manufacture that any
of them had had. 'I must premise that they use nothing but young
leaves,' Griffiths wrote. 'They roasted or rather semi roasted
these in a large iron vessel which must be quite clean, stirring
them up and rolling them in the hands during the roasting. When
duly roasted they expose them to the sun for three days, some
dew alternately with the sun, it is finally packed into bamboo
chungs into which it is tightly rammed.'

After some more exploring in thick jungle, they moved over
the river, where the abundance of the wild tea and its growing
'indiscriminately' spelt future doom for those living in the area. It
was in fact taken over as the location of the first experimental
garden, and when the time was right 'annexed'. Forty years later,
when the Political Officer of Manipur said he was going to grow
some tea for himself, the king pleaded with him to refrain,
because if it was found to be a success, his country, like that of
the Muttocks, would be promptly taken from him.

Wallich and Maclelland returned to Calcutta to report their

findings, while Griffiths set off towards Burma. When he met up with Dr Bayfield, the British Resident at the Burma Court, they found a different kind of tea again, 'the difference between this and the tea I have hitherto seen consists in the smallness and the finer texture of the leaves', but the drink produced was bitter. Local Chinese 'talk of the jungle tea and affirm that it cannot be manufactured into a good article. They talk of the valuable sorts as being very numerous.' Their intense interest in the plant was evident.

While Wallich and the Tea Committee made arrangements for Chinese men to be sent up to Assam, Charles Bruce continued to explore, and to let Jenkins know of his findings. In August 1837 he wrote of a particularly fruitful encounter. With one servant and two porters he entered a Singpho village and talked to the Gaum [headman]. This was a chief they had visited before, he and Wallich, and he assured Bruce there was no more tea than he had told them about then. He admitted there was 'a large patch not far from his house'. This proved to be true – but it was positively all, said the Gaum. Bruce, sitting cross-legged on the ground, smoking a Singpho pipe and calling the Gaum 'elder brother', had his gun beside him. 'The chief took up Mr Bruce's gun and begged him to ask the Commissioner to grant him one' as other Gaums had already been given them.[86] Bruce said he would give the gun if he got more information. So off they went to find more tea trees, and Bruce persuaded the Gaum to clear them of jungle and some tea was 'prepared'. Bruce thought it compared well with Chinese tea. Back in the village, more money and more opium and the Gaum's memory was jogged into further revelations.

Bruce's knowledge of language and etiquette was vital on this and all the other occasions when he was searching for tea. In the previous October he had ventured into Muttock land again, the country of the Moamarias across the river, a tribe whose revolts had contributed to the fall of the Ahoms. Here he found that 'kindness and a few presents' satisfied the ordinary tribesmen, and he was 'richly repaid . . . by being informed of one tea tract after another, although they had been strictly prohibited from giving me any information whatever.' He told them that he had come to 'do their country good ...but I do not think any of them believed me, so strongly had they been prejudiced and assured to the contrary.' He told the 'Rajah' he would be taught how to make tea and the Company would buy it from him and as 'he and his country were to reap all the benefit, he ought to go to the expense of clearing and manufacturing it'.

While in the area he made an interesting discovery. The villagers had been preparing land for rice, and in the process cut down tea trees level to the ground, hoed round them and cleared the weeds. Two months later when they cut their rice the mutilated tea trees were sprouting. By October they were three to ten feet high. Bruce pruned the ten-foot trees back to four feet, and shoots sprang up from below the cut. The first lesson in tea cultivation was learned, namely that tea grows faster when pruned. He also noted that tea grew best by water – it certainly didn't need gravelly hillsides.

This Muttock country seemed the most promising for the first experiments, and after explaining to its 'Rajah' that the British government was 'at a deal of trouble and great expense about the tea on his account' (thus making him feel they were doing him a great favour), he renewed his promise that when the Gaum had learnt how to manufacture tea, the Company would buy it off him.

The least he could do, Bruce repeated, was to clear the land at his own expense. He assured Jenkins, who passed on the news to the Committee, that if these Singphos were won round 'we would have all upper Assam a tea garden'.

That same October of 1836 the first Chinamen appeared in Assam, and a couple of months later six chests of made tea were ready to be sent to Calcutta. Charles Bruce told Jenkins that the Chinese were 'delighted and astonished at our tea trees', but only two of them were tea makers, and he wanted a dozen more to train. The Singphos, he found, soon lost interest; their job was to clear the jungle but 'they work how and when they please'.

The local tea bushes were not enough, Bruce had to send for others in the same area, and in the process found that the tea plant moved happily. About three thousand young plants were taken eight days' journey from their native soil and settled in happily. 'To show how hardy they are,' Bruce said in an account given of Assam tea manufacture,

I may mention that they were in the first instance plucked out by the roots by the village people who were sent to bring them from their native jungles, put upright into baskets without any earth, brought two days' journey on men's backs, put upright into canoes, a little common earth only being thrown amongst their roots, and were from seven to twenty days before they reached me; and then had to be carried half a day's journey to the intended new plantation, and were four or five days with only a little moist earth at their roots before they were finally put into the ground; and yet these plants are doing well, at least the greater part of them.[87]

Wallich and Jenkins envisaged that with 'a numerous colony of labourers' all would be well. The indolent Assamese and Singphos (all assumed to be opium addicts) ought to be replaced by 'industrious races' from Chota Nagpur. With these people Bruce's experimental garden could produce two hundred to three hundred chests of tea a year and then 'the great capitalists will move in'. They could then solve the labour problem, which became one of the industry's biggest headaches.

Stuck in the middle of nowhere, surrounded by jungles full of herds of wild elephants, tigers so plentiful they were referred to as pests like the leeches and rats, far from their families, without women or recreation, with only Singphos for company, Charles Bruce did well to keep his Chinamen from absconding or collapsing under the strain.

He wrote regularly, and Jenkins sent on the news to Calcutta, a journey of weeks with some uncertainty as to its arrival. However, the presence of the Brahmaputra was always immensely important to the tea industry; turbulent as it was in the monsoon, and vague in its changes of direction and its unexpected sandbanks in the winter, it was the great highway for landlocked Assam. In contrast, the Dutch in Java had to send their tea on ox carts over rough roads to reach a port.

Bruce sent to Jenkins a very detailed description of how the Chinese made the tea, the best and most accurate British account of the time. First, Bruce said, there was the plucking, four tender leaves being nipped off the bush with forefinger and thumb; such a delicate process that in Japan pluckers used gloves. These young leaves were scattered in baskets and dried in the sun, pushed up and down with long bamboos to help them wither. When ready they were brought inside to cool for half an hour and then put in smaller baskets and clapped in the hands for ten minutes, then back in the baskets, the process repeated three times until the leaves had the consistency of soft leather.

They were then put in hot cast-iron pans and heated on bamboo fires, taken out and spread carefully and briskly turned by hand, then back on the fire, this done three or four times. After that they were spread on a table and divided into heaps and, each dealt with separately, rolled to extract the juice. This rolling was a very delicate affair; the art lay in 'giving the ball a circular motion, and permitting it to turn under and in the hand, two or three whole revolutions before the arms are extended to their full extent, and drawing the ball of leaves quickly back without leaving a leaf behind, being rolled for five minutes in this way.' At every stage treatment should be gentle, leaves separated by lifting in both hands with fingers apart and allowed to fall very softly, and when taking the leaves out of the basket slapping these to loosen them. If any of them fell directly into the fire this might cause smoke. The baskets were never put on the ground.

When half dry they were laid on shelves, and next day fired again until they reached the right crispness, then put into larger baskets and over a 'lesser fire' with a basket on top and tested with the fingers, and when exactly the right crispness, taken out and trodden into boxes wearing clean stockings. Cleanliness, delicacy of handling, but most particularly the experience of fingers knowing exactly when to move on to the next stage, showed how important these first Chinamen were in the teaching process. Without knowing why, they had arrived at a method that scientists later pored over, examined, tested, experimented with and wrote books about. For many years the first planters used

Bruce's method; it became for a lot of them the only real information they had.

The Governor-General was very impressed by a large sample of tea made from the Assam plant in 1837; but in spite of Bruce's success and a 'very favourable report' on twelve boxes a year later, there were conflicting views about where and how to set up the first experimental gardens. It was still the general view that China bushes must be used, and Gordon was sent back to collect more of these to be planted in Calcutta and the seed sent to Assam. They argued about whether the plains or the hills were best. Dr Falconer from Kumaon insisted that 'the tea plant appears to require a greater cold to thrive in', the Himalayas in fact. So seeds and plants were sent in all directions.

By 1839 one hundred and twenty tracts of tea had been discovered growing wild, but still China tea plants were preferred and from the mixture an uninspiring hybrid was produced. It was not until 1888 that 'the miserable China variety, the pest of Assam' was finally abandoned. With all the mistakes and muddles, it was thought that the time had come to hand the enterprise over to private entrepreneurs.

Chapter Eight

Tea Mania: Assam 1839–1880

The people of Assam were not consulted and it might seem strange that none of them objected to the selling of their country to foreigners, to seeing its forests disappear under thousands of acres of spiky green tea bushes, the profits of which went to Calcutta and London. Their apparent acquiescence can be explained by the nature of the country, its people, and its landlocked state. The Assamese refused to help the tea industry as far as it was in their power. They would not work on the gardens. They would not have their women standing all day in the sun and rain to earn tiny amounts of money. They did not starve like the people of other parts of India in bad years. As these other desperate peoples flooded into the country, upsetting the balance of society, sending up the price of commodities, especially rice, they could have changed their minds. But they did not.

The strength of the Assamese was also their weakness when it came to putting up resistance to the newly arrived rulers. They had no strong caste allegiances; in a statistical account of the country there were castes, but these were better described as occupational divisions, some with a higher status than others. There were no outcastes, no women in purdah. There was no mechanism for corporate bargaining or setting up solid resistance to what was happening. Relatively crime-free, caste-free, self-sufficient in the basics of life, the Assamese saw themselves being pushed aside as Europeans, Bengalis, Marwaris, Sikhs poured in. There was little they could do, but for doing that little they were always described as spineless and lazy. From the administration's point of view this was fine; from the tea planter's angle it was irritating.

Surveyors and explorers with their measuring rods and bribes were sent up into the hills to draw imaginary lines behind which the hill people were to stay. Other intrepid men ventured into the mountains, carrying crosses and sustaining drugs. The hill tribes were animists whose aim was to propitiate evil spirits. Ill fortune, including sickness, came from these spirits and their only medicine was sacrifice. So missionaries – who had had little success with the Hindus of the plains – were encouraged as it was thought that the tribes would be made more civilised by conversion to Christianity.

In 1839 the way was clear to rent the whole of Assam out to the highest bidder, and one came forward, calling itself The Assam Company. A group of merchants met on 12 February 1839 in Great Winchester Street to discuss the matter. There was talk of the unpleasant Chinese 'ordering the Barbarians as Englishmen are still popularly and unofficially styled' to quit China, and hence the need for an alternative source of tea. The tea trade, they argued, was carried out 'in the most humiliating circumstances' as far as the British were concerned. In India the price of labour was low and the process of tea making 'peculiarly suited to the peaceful habits of the Assamese'. Tea to the merchants was 'a great source of profit and an object of great national importance'.

A provisional committee was set up to look into tea production, and asked the East India Company to supply information on methods. Applications for shares in the venture were far in excess of the number available, and it was launched with £125,000 of its capital subscribed or promised. A report Charles Bruce sent to the Tea Committee[88], which was read to the Agricultural and Horticultural Society in June 1839, and then distributed to other important journals, probably did something to advertise what was going on in Assam and generate enthusiasm. In it he described all the different tea areas he had found, and insisted that all that was needed was more labour: 'When we have a sufficient number of manufacturers so that we can afford to have some at each tract or garden, as they have in China, then we may hope to compare with that nation in cheapness of produce; nay we might, and ought, to undersell them.'

Bruce's report contained a lot of useful information on weather, shade, moisture, and how to line the boxes in which the tea was packed with lead. He described the burning of the jungle to clear it, the tea plants emerging happily from the ashes. He suggested that given the labour problem, the leaves should be sent to England to be processed. 'After a year's instruction under Chinamen, it might be left to the ingenuity of Englishmen to roll, sift and clean the Tea by machinery . . . and thus enable the poor to drink good unadulterated Green Tea . . .'

Bruce also presented the costs, and then the profits. On ten tracts of tea, annual profits would be Rs 23,266, so on one thousand tracts it would be Rs 23,266,000. Of course this depended on getting labour, but not to worry, 'the redundant population of Bengal will pour into Assam as soon as the people know that they will get a certain rate of pay, as well as lands, for the support of their families.' He put down the lack of enthusiasm shown by the Assamese to their addiction to opium, 'that dreadful plague which has depopulated this beautiful country, turned it into a land of wild beasts, with which it is over run and has degenerated the Assamese from a fine race of people, to the most abject, servile, crafty and demoralised race in India'.

Much encouraged surely by this positive prognosis, and ignoring the warnings about the labour problem, a Joint Stock Company was set up. It had a double board of directors, in London and in Calcutta; the one in Calcutta had to employ a superintendent and some junior staff, recruit labour, get Chinese tea makers, and build some boats. There were to be three divisions, one under Bruce, and two others. In the spring of 1840 two-thirds of the East India Company's experimental gardens were transferred to the Assam Company rent-free for ten years.

Despise them as they might, it was unfortunately true for the English that the Chinese were still the only people who knew how to make tea and they would have to be lured up to Assam. The Assam Company scoured Singapore, Batavia and Malaysia for Chinamen, the first batch arriving from Penang in November 1839. These and later batches were escorted up to Assam by young assistants, and from the first were always described as troublesome.

One lot were so difficult that they were sacked halfway up-river, simply abandoned to the charity of the nearest town. The Assam Company Board described the situation: 'They procured at great expense and at heavy wages several hundreds of Chinese whom they sent to Assam . . . These men turned out to be of very bad character. They were turbulent, obstinate and rapacious.' So injurious did they seem likely to prove to the other workmen employed by the Company that their contracts were cancelled and the whole gang, with the exception of the most experienced tea makers and the quietest men, were dismissed. Everyone still seemed to be labouring under the delusion that Chinamen, however poor, desperate or ignorant, knew how to grow tea. They did not seem to realise that the sort of people willing to be hired might not be the people who had any knowledge of tea growing.

Back in London, it soon became apparent to the Board there that things were not going according to plan. It took months to communicate with the men on the ground, and when the expected profits didn't arrive they were mystified. Money was being poured in – where was it going? In 1843 the Board put on a brave face in front of the shareholders and professed 'unabated confidence'; but, frustrated and anxious, they sent out J. M. Mackie, 'a gentleman of high standing and character', to investigate. It wasn't a great help. He had to cover the hundred miles of company territory on an elephant at three miles an hour, and when he got back to Calcutta was too ill to write a report.

A second investigator was dispatched from Calcutta. Henry Mornay, the Assam Company's Deputy Secretary, who had been in Calcutta for some years, was loud in his condemnation and fierce in his reforming zeal. He was appalled at the weeds, the uncleared land, and the miserable state of the bushes. He immediately reduced the wages of the labour force and laid them off when things were slack. What he did not report, since he and all the members of the Calcutta board were involved themselves, was that planters old and young were engaged in taking over cleared land and setting up their own gardens, using Tea Company labour, Company elephants and boats and time. No wonder the Assam Company tea gardens languished.

The situation continued to deteriorate and by 1847 the Company would have been glad to sell out if anyone had been ready to buy. Acres, indeed miles, of land had been cleared but much of it was unplanted and the tea there was half China and half indigenous, neglected and often unplucked for lack of labour. The Auditor's Report for 1845 read 'the Company do stand possessed of the following Assets in England, viz. Cash Balance at the Bank of England £100. Ditto at Messrs Williams and Co £624.6.3d. Ditto of Petty Cash £171.4.2d. Ditto of stamps £35'. These were tiny sums when compared to the assets of reasonable-sized concerns.

Later looking back on these first disastrous years, calm assessments were made of what went wrong. Small areas of wild tea were used to set up gardens, however remote and difficult to staff and to settle labour. Being in the thick of jungle they were full of mosquitoes and everyone suffered from malaria. It was always a pity that what suits tea – warmth, wetness and partial shade – also suits insects and germs, and patently did not suit Europeans and Indian and Chinese labour brought in from drier areas. The clearings in which the living quarters of both staff and workers were built were steamy, smelly, and waterlogged, without sanitation or clean water. Dysentery, cholera, typhoid, worms were unchecked. There was no doctor for miles.

Elephants also liked the climate, which was fortunate because it is hard to imagine that anything could have been done without them. They cleared the land, carried stores and planters, and were used almost exclusively at first to take tea chests to the river; six chests to an elephant, and later an elephant cart to take fifty-four. A pair of coolies could only carry one chest between them. Smaller gardens sent leaf to a central point where there was a factory to manufacture it, though this 'factory' was simply a series of sheds, since the processes were done by hand. At the nearest river it was loaded onto dug-out canoes, and then at the Brahmaputra into country boats. Attempting to improve matters, the Company bought a steamer, but this proved an expensive mistake since it couldn't cope with the vagaries of the great, wilful river.

The first tea assistants were young men culled from other stations in India. Much has been made of the courage and endurance of these pioneers and some accounts give them hero status. 'Here removed from all his friends, stripped of every luxury, he breathes a miasmatic air, is exhausted by a perpetual vapour bath, but bears it all,' wrote W. H. Ukers in *All About Tea*. But there were compensations. The shooting was magnificent, with big game, deer and wild pigs and every variety of pheasant, pigeon and peacock for the pot. The rivers were full of fish, and if any of the assistants had eyes for birds, butterflies or exuberant flowers and trees, they were living in a paradise.

A young Englishman would have been poorly paid, but still enjoyed a life style few would have known at home: a whole house, servants, women brought to their beds as and when required, paid for with bars of soap. Their private gardens made some quite wealthy; accidents and alcoholism cleared the more senior managers out of the way, to early retirement or the grave, so that promotion was swift. Tea planters, like their fellows in indigo, rubber, coffee, sugar and opium, retired with large fortunes.

That their fortunes recovered was due to the last Calcutta inspector, Burking Young, who turned round the Company, and the Board were able to face their shareholders with good news at last. In 1853 the Company paid its first dividend, the first of many. There were still anxieties: the Rude Savages were always a threat, ready to swoop down for slaves or waylay and rob the carriers of wages. And there was still the biggest problem. As the industry took off, and thousands of acres of tea were planted, thousands of hands were needed to pluck the bushes. Throughout the 1850s and 1860s, however, things steadily improved. By 1850 there were fifty private tea enterprises in Assam; and then, after 1861, when Lord Canning introduced a new law that land could be owned outright, the rush was on.

In 1866 two young brothers, Alick and John Carnegie, were on their way up to Assam to take part in the Tea Rush. John had come out the year before and spent a year in China, but apparently found Shanghai unsatisfactory. On 7 February 1866 he was writing to his parents from the boat to India: 'I hear queer accounts of my future abode from a chap who has just come from there, he says that my nearest abode will be about 50 miles away and can only be got at on the back of an elephant, pleasant prospect.'[89]

A week later he was sending his parents his address in Assam: Mazengah, Golaghat. He was staying in Wilson's Hotel in Calcutta, where he had been joined by his brother Alick freshly out from home. John had a job but was not over-enthusiastic about it, as he wrote to his mother on the 17th: 'I can't think this berth any great <u>catch</u> for it will cost me two months salary to reach our destination. We land at Koolook Mook where we are to be met by elephants.' From the Brahmaputra the view was dull: 'We are now in the Brahmaputra, there is nothing visible on either side but mud and jungle so the scenery is not much to talk about, we have seen large flocks of Pelicans and lots of alligators.

Two coolies died this morning of cholera, that's the obituary.'
Steamers to Assam towed flat-bottomed craft carrying coolies for
the tea estates; these men died in large numbers on the way up.

The boat was not very comfortable even for him. The cabin had
only a 'stretcher' without sheets or pillows and was full of
mosquitoes, so he had to sleep on deck in his clothes. He was not
encouraged by the Captain's stories of chaps he had landed on a
previous trip, dumping them on the riverbank with no one to meet
them. They had sat there for three days, without food, all got fever
and two died. But 'worse than all we have 500 coolies on board,
the dirtiest brutes in creation with lice and one had <u>cholera</u>
last night. What with coolies, mosquitoes and lice I shan't be
sorry when this is at an end.' And then, the last straw, 'there is no
blacking on board so we can't have our boots cleaned.' The
elderly servant he had engaged had left his family behind: 'Fancy
a man making all his family arrangements for 2 or 3 years in half
an hour.' From a later letter it seemed that the old man had
turned round and gone home quite quickly.

On the day John set sail Alick got a job as well, after much
driving around Calcutta to various agencies. He had been met
with the dispiriting news that 'the rush of young fellows to tea
plantations was tremendous and every situation was filled
up. . . I was awfully sick of the job after the first two days, at last
Duncan Macneil of Begg Dunlop said that although he had no
vacancy he would send me up to Cachar to take my chance of one
of the others getting ill or dying as fever is awfully bad there just
now, so I was to start in about a week. I was to get £116 a year.'

It was not an alluring prospect and he considered getting a job
as a clerk on a British steamer on a run to China and back,
hoping something might have turned up on his return. But then

'Macneil remembered he had heard of a fellow Douglas of Mair and Company say he needed an assistant on a plantation so he called on him and told him about me.'

Alick hurried to the offices of Mair and Company where he was told, 'You need not look on this (£150 a year) as a fixed salary, what we want is good men.' After three years he would get a commission on all the tea sent down by him. The garden to which he was posted was only a day's journey by river from John, and a fortnight by steamer from Calcutta. The coolies who accompanied them on the trip up-river, three hundred of them, had cholera and smallpox. Fifty-nine died before they reached their destination. 'Coolies die awfully fast here,' Alick wrote at the end of the voyage, 'there are three dead here since I arrived and that only four days.'

When they disembarked Alick was met by Mair's manager, twenty-five-year-old Mr Martin, with an elephant. The three Europeans on board spent the first night with a local native regiment, the coolies on the riverbank guarded to prevent them running off. Next day he was told to give three days' clothing and bedding to the *mahout* on the elephant, and was provided with a horse in order to help corral the coolies to their various destinations.

'We had awful work driving the coolies, we rode up and down the line and had to shove them on exactly as nigger drivers in America.' The picture is not a pretty one. Men and women, newly arrived in a strange country after an appalling journey, crowded onto a boat without sanitation, from which dead bodies were heaved overboard at the rate of twenty a week, now driven like cattle towards a miserable journey's end.

Alick landed up in a reasonably comfortable situation.

I live with a young chap Burt who is manager of this garden (there are ten different gardens on the estate). I will live with him till I know the language a little (very little will do) and know about the planting which is very simple, and then I will be sent to a garden as manager, they want one just now one of the assistants having died of fever 2 months ago. Burt is a very nice chap, a London fellow, he is only 19 and six foot 3.

The pair of them were 'quite contented and I am very jolly and like the life very much,' he wrote, even though he had already had fever on the boat and was to take the place of someone who had died of it. 'I suffered most awfully from mosquitoes the first two days I was on board,' he wrote, not knowing of the link between the mosquitoes and the fever. 'My curtains were not put up properly and my face, hands and feet were in an awful mess for a good long time afterwards, if the bites were scratched they fester and get into great sores, one of the civil service fellows up here has his arm cut off near the shoulder owing to mosquitoes, his arm festered and mortified . . . I got over mine pretty well but I have great big marks on my hands where the brutes have bitten me.'

As to practicalities, 'this place is very heavy on boots but on nothing else, we wear white trousers a shirt and jacket (no collar) and gaiters and big boots, in the wet weather we have to wear jack boots to prevent the leeches from getting in your boots.' The weather got very wet indeed: 'next month the rains begin and it rains without stopping for 5 months all the country is under water for about a foot in depth and the mud is awful, the heat is dreadful too at that time.'

On the bright side, although the servant he had engaged in

Calcutta never turned up, 'I have a very good little chap who does everything and waits at table, looks after my clothes . . . cuts tobacco and would put on all my clothes for me if I let him but all nigger servants do that.' There were unexpected events. 'I was surprised one day, I saw two coolies dragging a dead coolie over the ground by the heels, I asked Burt what they were going to do he said they would take it about a quarter of a mile into the jungle and leave it there and the jackals would have it away before morning.'

In a letter to his sister on 4 April Alick talked more about the coolies.

I am now alone in the jungle, a sort of small king among the niggers. Counting women and children I have charge of about 450 people, an awful queer lot the most of them are. They are always getting ill and I am doctor and have made some wonderful cures of dysentery and spleen, they all have more or less enlargement of the spleen. I have a large store of medicines here and some receipts and every morning I have to administer oil of castor to a lot of them. I have a splendid receipt for spleen and have cured a lot of chaps and dysentery too, two of them are dead but they die here very easily so they don't think much of that.

They not only died, they absconded in a tiresome way.

I was wakened at one o'clock in the morning three days ago by the news that 7 coolies had run off so the manager who was here at the time sent his servant on a horse to the station, he had to take my gun loaded with ball to keep off the tigers,

bears and leopards that come out of the thick jungle at night
and lie about the roads, or rather foot paths for there are no
roads up there except one and that one is fully ten miles away.
Four of the coolies were caught, and brought in this morning,
they got a great mauling from the overseers and are put to
double work for the next month, at least I said so today but in
about a week I will let them do the same as they rest, this is an
awful bore when they run away.

Alick was clearly not a harsh master and treated his coolies more
like naughty children than wrongdoers.

'There is no church here,' he wrote to his sister, 'except at the
station where there is a German parson, by all accounts he does a
deal of harm, spreading mischief among the inhabitants.' As for
Alick, he was not entirely successful either.

I have been rather unfortunate in my doctoring. This morning
an old man and a girl were carried to the door, they were both
very ill and I gave them doses which I suppose did them good,
they both died however, about an hour ago, and I have seen the
bodies carried into the jungle where the jackals will have a
feast on them tonight. The man was not worth much, but the
girl was a good leaf plucker, her mother and father died on the
river on the way up, she was an imported coolie.

On more cheerful subjects, he wrote:

This is rather a pretty place, it is always green as the trees are
never bare and away in the distance you can see very high
hills covered with trees up to the top and above them again on

a clear day you can see the snow covered tops of the Himalayas, the highest mountains in the world. I thought they were clouds when they were first pointed out to me, you could not believe that mountains could ever be so enormous.

. . . There are any amount of beautiful birds always flying about, jays with brilliant blue wings that look very pretty in the sun and great numbers of bright green parrots with long green tails and red beaks, I have shot two or three of them as their tail feathers make good things to clean pipes with.

His brother John was chirpy and positive too. He shared a bungalow with a Mr Stubbs and there was a small 'factory' where he was in charge of the Tea Room where the sorting and packing was done. He reckoned he had already made improvements in sorting methods. 'My gun is a great service and we have lived on the produce of my gun. Eleven and a half brace of doves, also a beefsteak bird.' A gamekeeper brought in pheasants and deer, the bungalow was full of skins and deers' antlers, which were used for pegs.

He had no money and no furniture, no tablecloths or sheets or blankets and he borrowed plates and pots from Stubbs. But he had a scheme. 'There are 2 or 3 planters who are rather hard up and will be glad to sell their teas to me for cash,' for which transaction he would use 'John Grant's £1000'. This plan was not referred to again.

Quite quickly John and Alick's jollity began to dissipate as fever got to them both. By the middle of May, Alick had been so ill that he had been moved to a less remote garden. 'If I was laid up here I could not be carried in as the road gets impassable,' so an acclimatised planter was to go to his garden and he to one only nine miles from the station. He was cheered, however, by a visit from the Chairman of the Calcutta Board of Mair and Company 'to see how things are getting on and he was very well pleased'. If things continued well he would get Rs100 a month more, about £12. 'I have got into a stunning company,' he reassured his parents.

If this letter comforted his parents, John's next one of 26 May must have depressed them. He was writing late 'because I had like my neighbours a beastly relapse this week and today is the first day I have been able to be up two hours on end. Yesterday I was very ill and I took at night some 20 drops of Laudanum. My fellow labourer Stubbs being also laid up with Ague and Fever and cramps in the stomach.'

More gloom, for he was still in debt by 1472 rupees to the Company, 'which hung upon me a good deal as I never knew how I could free myself from their <u>claws</u> they don't want the money they say only to stick to us. I am afraid one of the <u>stingiest</u> companies in Assam. Rs 1000 for passage out, that is utterly unprecedented, not even the Doctor who gets Rs 250 a month <u>had to do that</u>, an advance on our pay Rs 200 to pay our expenses up here also a swindle.' The list of grievances goes on. He had to pay his hotel bill in Calcutta and 'then the horse for my health in order to be able to go and see the Doctor who also has no horse and Mazengah is nine and a half miles from here now in the rains as short cuts are full of mud and also to be able to go about a little . . . Alick lucky man says he is not a farthing in debt.'

He was planning to visit Alick, 'but poor Stubbs is now so ill if he is not better tomorrow I wont go for it is fearful being left <u>alone</u> very ill 9 or 10 miles from a soul with a Doctor who comes about once a week if you're ill to see you, and no strength to write a note to him, he always comes when you write him a line. Stubbs was one year alone and is sort of used to it, besides knowing the different lingos he can wile away the time talking to the people, but I who am naturally fond of society (the Doctor says the want of which is one of my diseases) would very soon die if left alone, not only ill but I think even well.

. . . My head all this forenoon was in a whirl speaking Assamese to one, and Bengali to the next and knowing so little of course, having been out here 2 and a half months, five weeks laid up, I can just make myself understood. I took ill first on the 14th of April and now it is the 26th of May but at first I thought nothing of it. My little leopard panther, or whatever it is, is all alive and kicking and follows me all about the Bungalow. At first it bit and scratched frightfully, I cut all its claws close off and for biting sent him heels over head insensible on the floor, the only way to treat these savage beasts. It is not I think above a month old, for it wont as yet eat flesh, boiled hen of course, and would lick up milk. . . Atty would have laughed if she had seen my tiger feeding bottle . . . I lay him on his back and have a bottle of milk and a quill shoved through the cork. He sucks bravely at that and gets fat on it, but seldom unless the milk is turned knows when he has had enough, he is a jolly clever little beast . . . the tiger's skin is now finished, as hard as iron.'

It seems that the mother of the cub had been killed; tigers and leopards were often confused. They were then very common, but not so anteaters: 'the animal is very rare . . . it is of the Armadillo breed . . . Stubbs shot it, it would make a splendid footstool.'

This, John's last letter, ill, bitter about his treatment, but still able to get enjoyment from his little cub, would have worried his parents, but not so much as the next one, on 12 June from Alick.

My dear Mother, Please excuse my not writing before, as I have been down again with intermittent fever, I think I am well now as I have escaped today, which is one of the fever days, I get it every second day. What helped me to recovery was the long expected arrival of the steamer which brought John here this morning – such a dreadful change! He has had a jungle fever for the last six weeks and is now lying covered up with blankets in a dreadful fit of fever and ague, which comes on at four every afternoon, he was carried on board the steamer and was nine days on the way, he is made as comfortable as possible here but there is no disguising the fact that he is most seriously ill. The Doctor has just left him. He says he must go to Calcutta and get on board a vessel bound for some of the coast ports. His own doctor says he can't <u>live</u> here unless the fever is stopped now. There is no other way of curing it. It is all very well but he has no money, I have only as much as will take him to Calcutta, without paying for grub &c. I have about £10 which I can give him, but I will try to get the amount for him and even Martin who has seen lots of men die in this house of the very same fever says that his strength is almost gone and one night he'll go out like snuff of a candle, he said plainly that John could not live through the rains.

Alick continued, 'I am awfully sorry about it. He is in a most beastly seedy company. They would hardly allow him to go away, when it was <u>certain death </u>to have remained. I am very sorry to have to write such bad news, but I can't help it. Am alright now and will soon go back to the jungle again. My hand is not very firm yet so please excuse my writing.'

To get such a letter and not know for months what had happened to John must have put an enormous strain on his parents. The last letter from Alick is dated 17 October, when his father's, written in August, has just reached him. It seems that his wonderful company, Mair, is in trouble, but he has heard that they will continue for some months. He does not linger over this depressing prospect, but describes the big festival of the year, Durga Poojah: 'The coolies got liberty but none of them are allowed to leave the factory, if they did they would be very apt to run away and I have no men spare just now so I have forbidden any of the coolies to leave. I had a case of rum sent a few days ago and they got some bottles among them for nothing.'

This led to a drunken brawl:

They were going to thrash my cook who was perfectly sober himself but had got into a row with about 20 or 30 coolies all more or less screwed. I very soon put a stop to the row but could hardly get away from them, they all began salaaming and swearing they would always do as I told them and that I was a very good Sahib . . . the drunker they were, the lower the salutes and the greater the compliments. I hate the pooja days when there is always a row.

He also hates having to give money towards the celebration, as he has to do to parties of dancers and drummers in April.

I have still fever and ague every day but it is getting milder, I wish it would go away it is an awful bore three hours of illness every afternoon and not able to eat after it. I suppose what gives ague is sleeping during the rains so often on a damp bed, when it rains everything inside the bungalow gets as damp as if you were to put them out in the morning dew at home. I have often gone to bed with the mattress not only damp but wet, there is no fire place in my bungalow . . . My ague just begun to show signs of coming on so I must stop.

So on this note of hopeful pessimism the letters end. An enclosed note in this last one says that Alick is looking forward to a 'box', for 'it will be stunning opening it here.' He adds, 'Ask John please if he has any spare banyans, I am rather short of them.' This implies that John was still alive, perhaps moved to some other part of India. These fourteen letters written over a period of six months by two young men reveal a steamy, sickly world of isolation but also of many pleasures of killing animals, amazing scenery and the luxury of space and servants.

They also lay bare the whole structure of the plantation system, a pyramid with at the broad base the thousands and thousands of 'niggers' on whom the whole contraption rested and relied. The British government (now replacing the Company), was at the top and since it 'owned' Assam, it handed out land to anyone who wanted it, at this time almost exclusively Europeans.

Below the government were the tea firms who had agents in both London and Calcutta to direct young men towards vacancies. They arranged (but didn't pay for) passages to India and China, and seemed to have been employed by small and not very reputable tea companies. When the young men were taken on in Calcutta they signed contracts with specific companies that were hardly generous, but it was implied that there were 'perks' and quick promotion what with the death or early retirement of superiors. They were candid about the health risks but rather brutal in their unconcern at sending men, on very small salaries, to what was often an early death.

Beneath the Europeans a thin layer of native doctors, clerks and shopkeepers (also moneylenders) filled the gap between managers and the labour force, the latter referred to as coolies. They were all imported; in the year the Carnegies were writing forty thousand of them were shipped up to work on the gardens being slashed and hacked into existence by frantic speculators of the Tea Rush. Many of these gardens collapsed quite quickly but the labour force would be transferred to steadier concerns. They were always treated like working animals, presumed not to have choices or personal needs, or even the ordinary human desire for the comfort of a home that they could care for and to which they could become attached.

John and Alick neither loved nor hated their workers, they never questioned either the conditions under which the workers were collected and transported up-river, nor the flimsy barracks they lived in, their water supply a muddy stream or pond, their common end as food for jackals. 'They die very easily,' John wrote as if this was a genetic flaw, part of being a nigger. When they ran away it was appropriate to chase after them and then whip them for being naughty. This attitude changed little over the years. Even when 'coolie' became a rude word, the planters still assumed that their workers were inferior humans.

The Empire was a bran tub into which everyone plunged up to the elbows, assured of a reward, with any luck a rich one. The truth was harsher. Whether these two young planters lived to enjoy any future at all seems doubtful.

However, even before the Carnegies had arrived in India, the government in London was uneasy enough about the situation in Assam to set up a Committee 'to enquire into coolie emigration to Assam and Cachar'. They questioned firms, recruiting contractors, passengers on steamers, officers attached to regiments in Assam.

They asked about wages; there was no special contract which specified these in most cases, though one firm, Cachar and Equitable, wrote one to which a coolie put his thumb mark: 'I understand that my wages will be Rs 4 a month, but I agree to work a contract or system. I understand that although I can expect extra wages by working contract, I must work hard to do so.' A peasant from Chota Nagpur or Bihar or anywhere else could not 'understand' or 'agree' with anything written down, especially if it was in English, nor comprehend what was meant by *nereik*, a task set by the manager.

The system of engaging labour was for planters to send orders to contractors for so many bodies; these were then collected and the planter informed. His agent in Calcutta then visited the depot where the coolies were herded, and agreed with the contractor on their dispatch up-river. A lump sum was paid for each person landed in a tea district, and also for those who died on the voyage, though not for deserters. These were naturally written off by the contractor as deaths.

The Committee visited a depot in Calcutta; 'a square of ground was pointed out to us . . . a hut, a few feet square, and now in course of completion, was said to be the sole accommodation. This square resembled rather a half dried bed of a small tank, greatly defiled by the surrounding people. A spot more repulsive to sight and smell we could not imagine . . . we felt no surprise at the stories we heard of the numbers that yearly fall victim to disease in his hands.' This was a reference to a notorious contractor who had decamped before they arrived.

Against this there was a Mr Bennertz, a European, who had 'good and sufficient sheds', separate drinking and bathing water, 'well chosen diet and clothing' and a resident native doctor. He seems however to have been the exception to the general rule. Coolie Catchers came to be looked on as evil kidnappers whose name was invoked in native nurseries: 'Be good or the Coolie Catcher will get you and take you to Assam.'

The contractors sent provisions and clothes for the coolies on their journey up-river, and 'peons' or supervisors to look after them; the latter, however, entered the sordid scramble by selling the rice intended for the coolies to the steamer's crew. The clothes, warm shirts (perhaps unsaleable stock), were hot and uncomfortable. The Committee commented on the native subordinates who defrauded everyone; there were tales of coolies being fed raw rice because there were no cooks, of unqualified doctors, of unhealthy landing places, like one owned by the Assam Company – 'a locality of a very insalubrious character, low, damp and bounding in miasmata and no shelter'.

There were lists of failings: no inspections of boats; the more deaths the better since the contractor could claim on them and have less mouths to feed; stores meant to feed the coolies being landed and sold as soon as the boats were out of sight; the flats on which they were carried being lashed aside the steamer at night and being completely airless.

A doctor interviewed by the Committee was firmly ignorant of medical practice. Quarantine in cholera cases 'has never had any foundation but of the vaguest most hypothetical kind,' and the cause was 'noxious agencies and atmospheric ones'. In any case he asserted, with some reason, coolies would be landed all over the place to evade quarantine restrictions.

A planter whom the Committee put questions to 'ventured to dissent' from any new laws or regulations made by the government. He admitted that he had seen coolies being embarked in the last stages of emaciation and disease, and on board he and that his party did carry out 'the humane activity of ridding the vessel of the dying men'. The Committee advised reforms, but no action was taken.

Undeterred and still unsatisfied, another report six years later was as damning. Labourers were 'hawked about the country to be handed over to the highest bidder', like so many pigs or sheep. A Dr Macnamara described the depots as 'infectious localities' and the coolies had to be disinfected on leaving them. Before they even reached these they had endured a seven-hour train journey with only one break of a couple of minutes.

On-board sanitation consisted of '2 or more boxes attached to the sides of the vessel near the stern, with 2 seats in each with a loose purdah screen in front'. These privies for up to one thousand coolies on a three-week voyage were next to the cooking galleys and livestock enclosures. Orders to carry drinking water were 'systematically neglected' and the coolies had to drink from the river.

Witnesses were called: one from Begg Dunlop, a major company, said they had sent up 13,895 coolies in one year on three steamers, 586 of whom died. A Mr Williams admitted that mortality had increased in the last four years and said there should be compulsory medical inspection in districts where contractors 'engage coolies to transfer them to others at a profit'. Another witness talked of recruiters who 'wander over the country with the coolies endeavouring to dispose of them to the best advantage'. He was himself a contractor and confirmed that the demand was insatiable: ' I have an order now for 1000 men.' He was critical of conditions – coolies should be allowed to land every evening 'for exercise and other purposes', and get an ounce of rum twice a week.

Three doctors gave evidence of the filthy boats; the coolies 'eased themselves' on deck at night, but this was not surprising since there were no railings round the privies and people fell overboard in the dark. Those who arrived were 'in tatters without blankets and look objects of pity'. One planter, a Mr Forbes, admitted that of a hundred coolies he had recently imported, nearly every one died on the way up or on arrival: 'The up-country coolie travels well but sickens directly he gets to the Tea Garden. The Dhangar (tribal) sickens on the journey but on the garden flourishes,' he told the Committee, as if describing the movement of tea bushes.

Another of the doctors, Dr Allnutt, agreed that 'jungly' Dhangars were more unhealthy, and was disgusted at the way women and children 'are filthy in their habits, the children defecate on the deck continually'. If they were allowed to land they would run away so there was no alternative to keeping them on board, however filthy. The ship's commander was kinder – he thought there should be sheds at the landing places and a glass of rum for those who had survived the journey.

After this catalogue of incompetence, corruption and cruelty the Committee as usual made recommendations. Coolies should be sent on special trains on journeys of no more than four hours; contractors should be licensed, contracts countersigned by the District Magistrate of the area where they were collected; the

Civil Surgeon of the district should inspect the workers to see that they were in a condition to work and travel. Of course, only desperate men would want to leave their homes, as the result of poor harvests or visitations of cholera, so not too much could be expected of their health.

Each batch of coolies should be cared for by a responsible person sent down by a planter, not left to the mercy of contractors' peons. Commanders of steamers should be paid head money, as in Mauritius, to encourage them to keep their cargo alive. Steamer owners, not contractors, should supply food. Blankets used by cholera victims should be destroyed.

The Committee ended with some sharpish remarks on planters: 'Many men never give thought to their "lines" [living quarters] and to other sanitary conditions' and they weren't impressed by the ministrations of the Carnegies and their like. It would be easy to get qualified sub-assistant surgeons from Calcutta Medical School, who 'would be amply remunerated with half the salary usually offered to Europeans'.

Since all the recommendations would cost money, and planters were forever complaining about the 'burden' imported labour imposed on the industry, the system of contractual labour recruitment was not abolished until 1915.

A FRIEND IN NEED.

Chapter Nine

Empires of Tea

'The British have an umbilical cord that has never been cut and through which tea flows constantly. It is curious to watch them in times of sudden horror, tragedy or disaster. The pulse stops apparently and nothing can be done, and no move made, until "a nice cup of tea" is quickly made. There is no question that it brings solace and does steady the mind. What a pity all countries are not so tea-conscious. World-peace conferences would run more smoothly if "a nice cup of tea", or indeed, a samovar were available at the proper time.'

Marlene Dietrich, *Marlene Dietrich's A B C*

The rapid development of tea cultivation in Assam, and the pressures on Indian labourers to produce more, cannot be understood without returning to the wider role of tea in the development of civilisations. In China, Japan and then Assam, tea became much more than a luxury. It became a primary motor for the development of great empires whose health and strength could not have been sustained without tea, and who therefore put enormous pressures on those who produced it. In turn, it was this wealth that allowed, most dramatically in the British case, for investment in tea manufacturing. It is reasonable to argue that four of the greatest developments in world history over the last twelve hundred years could not have occurred without tea drinking, which in turn fed back into improved production and manufacturing of tea itself.

The great surge of population, economy and culture that occurred in China after about 700 AD, reaching its climax in the glories of the Sung dynasty, has never really been explained. Clearly, there was political unification and improved technology and communications. All this was important. Yet it is worth noting that however much economic and political efficiency was improved, it would have been of no avail if China had suffered the normal trap of rising death rates. If the people who lived very close together, whether in the growing cities, towns or crowded countryside, had grown rice and drunk unboiled water, they would increasingly have suffered from dysentery and other waterborne diseases. Their strength and their numbers would have dwindled, and large numbers of infants would have died from enteric diseases. The spreading far and wide of tea during the Tang dynasty 'may have had . . . far-reaching consequences: the hygienic benefits that resulted from boiling water for tea are believed to have played a major role in longevity and hence in China's rapid rise in population – from 41 to 53 million – during the first half of the eighth century.'[90]

Tea drinking may have made it possible to maintain, for the first time in history, a relatively healthy population on a huge scale, despite the dangers of water pollution. Furthermore, this very cheap, invigorating drink would have aided the immense labours that are famously associated with Chinese agriculture, with its intensive cultivation methods and relatively low use of machinery and non-human energy. Double-cropping rice on a minimal diet puts a huge strain on the human body. Tea probably helped to make the work possible. We know tea drinking became very widespread at exactly the time the Chinese took a great leap forward. It does not seem implausible to connect the two events through the strengthening effects of tea and the lowering of the dangers of waterborne disease.

In Japan, the development of tea drinking coincides with a notable period of expansion, both economic and political, during the fourteenth to seventeenth centuries. In this period when Japan first attempted to colonise mainland Asia (Korea), its population grew very rapidly and its agricultural production went through a period of considerable change. New varieties of fast-maturing rice, the claiming of new lands and the use of better implements increased productivity greatly. The amount of hard labour required to set up and continue this intensive agriculture was enormous.

Tea growing had a clear effect on the way in which people worked. Intense wet-rice cultivation is very hard work, especially on a relatively inhospitable and very limited area of suitable land, as in Japan. There was not much room for larger domestic animals to help in the task, which in any case largely relies on human labour and cannot make much use of wind- and waterpower. In the past, almost all of the processes in wet-rice cultivation required human energy, to prepare, plant, weed, harvest, carry and beat the rice. Even when the rice was ready, much further effort was needed to transport it, carrying huge loads by land or pushing it along the inland waterways. All this was achieved on a minimal, and mainly vegetarian, diet. The extra stimulant to maintain the immense toil was provided by tea.

The Western observer W.E. Griffis described how

> After a hard night's toil, poling and walking in a nipping frost, I wished to see the breakfast by which they laid the physical basis for another day's work. At the stern of the boat, resting on a little furnace, was the universal rice-pot, and beside it a small covered wooden tub, full of rice. Some pickled or boiled slices of the huge radish called dai-kon lay in another receptacle. The drink was the cheapest tea . . . The first course was a bowlful of rice and a pair of chop sticks. In the second course, history repeated itself. The third course was a dipperful of tea. . . The fourth course was a bowl of rice and two slices of radish; the fifth was the same. A dipperful of tea-liquor finished the meal, and the pole was resumed.[91]

Another American observer, Elizabeth Scidmore, noticed the same use of tea and the same enormous energy. 'The diet of these coolies seems wholly insufficient for the tremendous labor they perform – rice, pickled fish, fermented radish, and green tea affording the thin nutriment of working-days. Yet the most splendid specimens of physical health are reared and kept in prize-fighting condition on what would reduce a foreigner to invalidism in a week.'[92]

It seems conceivable that without the tea the whole delicate system would not have worked and much of the efficiency of bodily and mental movement behind the vast labour which sustained both China and Japan would not have been possible.

The famous agricultural revolutions in China and Japan, based on double- and triple-cropping new varieties of fast-maturing rice, might not have been possible without the simultaneous presence of this revitalising drink.

Alongside the introduction and spread of tea, Japan became the most urbanised and densely populated nation in the world. By 1720 it had the largest urban agglomeration on earth. In the small region containing Tokyo, Kyoto, Osaka and a number of smaller cities and towns there were more than two million people. Edo (Tokyo) became the largest city in the world and the proportion of people living in towns was greater than anywhere else on the planet by the middle of the eighteenth century.

Almost all of Japan was mountainous and reckoned to be uninhabitable. The usable area on the main islands (Hokkaido was as yet uncolonised) was tiny, the size of a small English county. This area supported up to twenty million people by the middle of the eighteenth century. They were packed together in hamlets, villages, small and large towns and cities in the flatter and more productive valleys.

This was a situation where one would have expected a rising rate of stomach diseases as the bacteria thrived in the increasingly crowded towns and countryside. Yet there is a great deal of evidence to suggest that infant mortality caused by waterborne diseases, especially dysentery, was low. Among the reasons for this surprising absence of dysentery is the strict attention to hygiene, the careful carrying away of human excrement for use in the fields and the unusually long suckling of children who were protected to some extent by the breast milk.[93]

An added reason may well have been the ubiquitous drinking of tea. However careful people in a city of half a million or more are, they are dependent on wells and sluices, and water is bound to become polluted. Yet in Japan, adults and children did not drink cold, unboiled, water. The infants drank their mother's milk, which would have contained high levels of bacteria-destroying phenolics from their mother's tea drinking. Adults and children once weaned just drank tea, which was made with boiled water.

Consequently Japan was largely free of amoebic and bacillary dysentery. It was also relatively free of those other scourges, typhoid and paratyphoid. As for cholera, the first world pandemic of cholera spreading from India in 1817 only affected western Japan and the second one, of 1831, did not reach the country. The third started in 1850 and only arrived in its last year, 1858. In the later nineteenth century when cholera was again prevalent, Edward Morse recounts how 'not a swallow of cold water could be drunk. Tea, tea, tea, morning, noon, and night, and on every possible occasion.'[94] The author, journalist and scholar, Sir Edwin Arnold, who in the late 1850s had seen the ravages of cholera in India, commented that 'I may add that the custom of perpetual tea-drinking greatly helps the Japanese in such a season as this. When they are thirsty they go to the tea-pot, and the boiled water makes them pretty safe against the perils of the neighbouring well.'[95]

The industrial revolution in eighteenth- and nineteenth-century Britain takes us to a period when there is much more evidence with which to examine the connection between tea drinking and economic and political power.

If people are successful in producing resources, in particular food, the population will almost inevitably grow. This can increase efficiency. People create demand for goods and services; with people closer together in cities, moving objects between them is less expensive. Additionally, the various production processes can be made more efficient through specialisation. So wealth increases and the population grows even more.

Yet, alongside the growing human population, the bacteria, amoeba and viruses, which have evolved to live off plants and animals, also thrive. Many are beneficial to man, but some cause sickness and death. Countless of these have adapted from their original animal hosts to invade human beings. So, when populations reach a certain critical threshold, the level of disease rises to a point where escalating mortality halts the population growth. The crowding in cities, in particular, leads to disease rates that not only stop the cities growing from internal surpluses, but destroy large numbers of country people who migrate into the urban conglomerations. Thus human civilisations reach an impasse or trap, famously described by the theorist Thomas Malthus in the later eighteenth century. Death rates rise to a point where further economic growth is halted.

One recent well-documented example occurred in fourteenth-century Europe. After the Black Death, populations of most countries began to recover in the later fifteenth century, the cities expanded again and great advances were made in the period of the Renaissance and early scientific revolution. But then, in the seventeenth century, much of Europe suffered a 'crisis', with rising death rates and economic stagnation. Diseases had risen to such a level that further growth of both the population and economy was halted. Likewise, in Islamic civilisations, the growing cities and more densely settled countryside were suffering from rising levels of disease, in particular bubonic plague.

In 1650 it looked as if any chance of an escape into a world of low mortality was impossible. Yet we know that something mysterious and unprecedented must then have happened. Furthermore, we know quite precisely where and when it happened – in Britain in the middle of the eighteenth century. We even know that the change was precisely in the incidence of waterborne disease.

In the middle of the eighteenth century a leading contemporary demographer, William Black, noted that 'dysentery and bloody flux' were beginning to decline in London.[96] Another demographer, William Heberden, provided a detailed analysis of the bills of mortality to show the decline of dysentery, which was particularly marked from the decade 1730–40.[97] In 1796 he wrote that several diseases, including 'dysentery . . . have so decreased, that their very name is almost unknown in London . . .' Writing in the early nineteenth century, the political reformer, Francis Place commented that 'In the latter half of the seventeenth century, the dysentery caused the death of 2000 persons annually in the metropolis; its prevalence gradually decreased during the last century, and the disease itself is now almost extinguished as a fatal disease. Only fifteen are stated to have died of it in the year 1820.'[98]

What could have caused this extraordinary and unprecedented change? One possibility is that there was a growing resistance or immunity among the population to the pathogens. This is always a possibility and may account for part of the fall. But it is unlikely, in such a short time, to be the major explanation. Another explanation lies in the change in drinking habits.

Several contemporaries guessed that there might be a possible link between tea drinking and the fall in mortality. In the middle of the eighteenth century the Scottish philosopher Lord Kames pondered on the question of why all types of mortality seemed to be falling. He noted that 'plague, pestilential fevers, and other putrid diseases, were more frequent in Europe formerly than at present, especially in great cities, where multitudes were crowded together in small houses, separated by narrow streets.' He suggested that this change was principally caused by greater cleanliness, but also that there was more fresh meat and 'the great consumption of tea and sugar, which I am told by physicians to be no inconsiderable antiseptics'.[99]

In the first decades of the nineteenth century, as the improvement in health became even more apparent, several authors suggested that perhaps the reason for this was tea drinking. The Scottish physician Sir Gilbert Blane wrote that '*Tea* is an article universally grateful to the British population and has to a certain extent supplanted intoxicating liquors in all ranks, to the great advantage of society . . . The modern use of tea has probably contributed to the longevity of the inhabitants of this country.' Even more interestingly, the founder of the modern census, the statistician John Rickman, wrote in 1827: 'It is not for Mr Rickman to assign causes of the decrease of mortality; if he might venture further than in the Preliminary Observations to the Census of 1811 and 1821 . . . he would ascribe it to the general use of tea and sugar . . .'[100] Neither of them was in a position to prove how tea, had this effect, apart from its well-known antiseptic qualities. Now, with our increased knowledge of the antibacterial properties of tea we can build on their insight.

Tea drinking helps to explain the paradox that the eighteenth century seems to have witnessed both a decline in the nutritional levels of the poor and an improvement in health. Tea may be less nutritionally useful than beer yet it led to a reduction in certain diseases. It also had other health effects in that it replaced less wholesome alternatives, such as gin, which, rough but cheap, was drunk extensively in the period 1720–50, particularly in London. There was a drop from 6–7 million gallons of gin consumed each year before 1751 to 1–3 million gallons a year in the period 1760–90, despite a rapid growth in London's population.[101] It seems unlikely that this rapid conversion from gin would have been possible without the sudden arrival of a cheap and stimulating substitute, which also avoided the necessity of drinking polluted water.

Furthermore, this worked not only for the tea-drinkers themselves, but also for those who lived with them. As in China and Japan, the widespread tradition of breast-feeding in Britain, usually lasting for up to a year, meant that infants were fed on relatively safe breast-milk. They may have been given added protection because most infections they picked up through food, through contact with soiled materials and so on, were killed off in their mouths and stomachs by the phenolics which pass so easily through mother's milk to their infants.

In eighteenth-century Britain, as in early China or late medieval Japan, a new drink permitted a new urban civilisation. The struggle between humans and micro-parasites was briefly tipped in favour of humans. By a giant set of accidents the spread of deadly water- and food-borne diseases of the digestive tract was minimised. Only from the middle of the nineteenth century, as public sanitation and safer water were introduced into European cities, did the need for tea become less pronounced.

Only then would the coffee-, wine- and water-drinking populations of much of continental Europe have their own urban and industrial revolutions without the benefit of tea.

Tea did not cause the industrial revolution, in the sense of making it inevitable. The Chinese and Japanese had long benefited from the healthful effects of tea and attained a very high level of commercial civilisation with few, if any, signs of industrialism. Yet, in Britain, a preceding growth of labour-saving mechanisation using wind, water and animals could now lead into a new era of steam power. This required an immense surge in the numbers and energy of the working population. It is not difficult to see how this may have been facilitated by the accident of widespread tea drinking. Before tea, beer was the universal drink and had taken the civilisation up to the high level of commercial wealth that we see also in Holland in the seventeenth century. Yet by the end of the seventeenth century, beer production was consuming half of the English grain harvest. When the population doubled and doubled again, all of the grain in England would have been needed, plus further imports, to make enough beer for the rapidly expanding populace.

Beer was given in large quantities to help revitalise agricultural workers and others engaged in heavy manual work. Yet drinking beer has its limitations. It is always mildly intoxicating. It stimulates the body for a short while, but it relaxes the mind and after an hour or so leads to drowsiness and sometimes very mild depression. On the other hand, the extra energy released by tea, which not only makes the muscles work more efficiently, but also helps mental concentration and reduces the effects of fatigue, usually starts a few minutes after the first drink. The positive effects last for an hour or two, reaching a peak about three-quarters of an hour after the first drink, making it ideal for industrial workers, which beer is not.

Working with fast-moving machines requires great skill and concentration. A hand-weaver could move at her own pace and take rests. Working with a machine loom, on the other hand, required constant, unremitting, attention. It seems unlikely that Lancashire cotton mill owners would have issued large rations of beer, or encouraged a 'beer break'. It is also unlikely that barrels of beer were to be found down coalmines for people to invigorate themselves with. So when muscles or minds were stretched to the limit, as they were in the first industrial revolution, tea was an invaluable background feature. The factory tea trolley was developed extensively in the First World War, while from the middle of the nineteenth century tea stalls for passengers were found on the new railway stations, and later on steam-ships.

Tea has continued to be an invaluable relaxant and stimulant for workers and it is often drunk in huge quantities. An industrialist friend of mine tells me that in the 1960s he questioned a worker at James Booth's, a large manufacturer of aluminium sheet and foil in Birmingham, as to how much tea he drank each day. The man worked it out at seventeen mugs, the stronger the better, always with milk and sugar. These were enamelled steel mugs, with about half a pint capacity. So he drank nearly nine pints of tea a day.

It is true that eighty years later, when the French and Germans had their industrial revolution, they managed to do this without tea. But by then conditions had changed. For one thing, the machinery was more efficient and needed less human muscle and less careful attention than the early pioneer devices.

So when tea became the centre of a new dietary regime for the working classes in the later eighteenth century, it was corresponding with labour needs. By the later eighteenth century labourers were spending ten per cent of their food budgets on tea and sugar, as compared to twelve per cent on meat and only two and a half per cent on beer. Tea with bread and cheese formed the heart of the diet. The white bread provided twice as many calories per penny as meat or sugar, so that the 'bread-and-tea diet was a rational choice for restricted incomes'.[102] Without this cheap and warming commodity that gave life to a meal, it is difficult to know what would have happened as the cost of meat and beer soared.

The effects of tea were greatly increased by the fact that it was drunk with energy-giving sugar. Britain had become the leading sugar importer in Europe and this gave an extra boost to millions of toiling people. The effects of tea are closely related in the West to the sugar story. Sweet, hot, relaxing and invigorating, the 'nice cup of tea' became a central motor for the human machine that was at the heart of industrialisation, perhaps as important as steam was for the non-human machines. Food, clothing, housing – all these might deteriorate and the poor live in abject poverty and terrible sanitary conditions as report after report described, but the 'good old British tea' helped to see them through the crisis and a new world was created.

Was there also a possible link between the rise of tea trading and tea drinking and the rapid growth and spread of the British Empire? Before tea, Britain had some colonies in America, the West Indies, and some trading posts in India and the Far East. This was the position in 1720 on the eve of the inward rush of cheap tea. A century and a half later, Britain controlled the largest Empire in world history, including Australasia, Canada, colonies in many parts of Africa, South America and elsewhere, and the massive jewel in the Crown, India.

The demand for tea had a great effect on the merchant navy and hence on the Royal Navy, on merchant capital and on banking and credit systems. It affected the rapid growth of British commerce and particularly the power of the trading networks to Asia. It encouraged the extension of the Empire outwards to places where tea could be grown, above all in the Himalayas and in South-East Asia. So tea bent the Empire in a certain direction, towards the east and south-east, both by the pull of China, and through the loss of North America after the Boston Tea Party. It also provided a central commodity for this trading nation.

The effect of tea on the East India Company is especially important. The company may have started with pepper and spices, but as the Dutch gained a strong hold on these commodities, the Company began to specialise in that other lightweight high-value commodity, tea. Tea took over as its most lucrative source of revenue, giving it the profits for an expansion that helped it to conquer and govern India and become one of the most powerful forces in the world. 'It was a formidable rival of states and empires, with power to acquire territory, coin money, command fortresses and troops, form alliances, make war or peace, and exercise both civil and criminal jurisdiction.'[103] In turn, this power and wealth was fed back into further pushing the fortunes of tea.

It is somewhat paradoxical that if it had not been for the Chinese tea trade, and hence the wealth and power of the East

India Company, the British would not have been able to take over India. The connection is less than obvious because tea was not grown commercially in India until just after the East India Company lost its tea monopoly in 1833.

Another indirect link worked through the effects of tea in boosting British industrialism, as discussed above. It is obvious that the Empire would not have been possible if Britain had not gone through an industrial revolution and developed, side by side, the weapons and productive technologies, based on iron and steam, which would give it an advantage over its rivals. It needed markets for its industrial goods, particularly cotton at first. The expansion would not have happened if it had remained an agrarian civilisation. Thus tea's role in allowing the growth of industry, cities and population had an interlocking effect on Empire, an empire which in turn would provide sugar, tea, rubber and other commodities for the industrial homeland.

One often-told part of this link between Empire, tea and the sea is the story of the tall ships which brought back the tea from China. The sleek clippers had originally been the invention of American shipbuilders in the 1820s and 1830s. In the 1850s the British built the new iron-framed ships that became the famous participants in the race to bring tea back to Britain. So the amazing tea clippers evolved with their new clean prows to cut through sea, and their less solid sterns, the ratio of width to length much reduced, and the amount of sail they carried greatly increased.

These new ships revolutionised long-distance sea travel in the decades before steam. If we compare the bulging East Indiamen of the early nineteenth century with the magnificent ships from the middle of the century, we see a vast difference. The tea ships, both of the earlier and the later kind, became the most effective sailing ships in the British fleets. Because the sailors were not pressed, or forced, onto them, and because a system was developed whereby the officers and ordinary sailors were given a share in the profits of the voyages by being allowed some 'stowage' to bring back goods for sale in Europe, the tea ships attracted the best seamen.

These clippers improved through competition with each other until they reached a construction which was, given the constraints of iron, wood, canvas and human ability, as near perfection as it was possible to be. This is shown by a tale of three ships, all built in the same Glasgow shipyard, that set off on the same tide from China. For many thousands of miles they were separated from each other. Yet they sailed so well and equally that, after many days at sea, they arrived off the Lizard in the English Channel within one hour of each other.

It was not only at sea that tea may have been of importance for British expansion. Much of the penetration and defence of this immense and rapidly expanding Empire depended on small numbers of British army officers and civilians, often living in hazardous health conditions. The world of Kipling and the Raj conjures up that small band. What could they drink as they sat in their bungalows and mansions around the world, or camped in desert, forest and mountain? If they drank the local water, they would have been very ill. Although there were local breweries in some of the places where British personnel were concentrated, on the whole beer was too bulky and unstable in very hot climates to send to all the far-flung corners of Empire. Were the merchants, captains and government officers who had been inculcated in the tea-drinking habits of their homeland from the 1740s onwards, and who ran the Empire from the 1760s, tea drinkers? If they were, did this make a significant difference?

We may also wonder about their native troops. When the British marched with their cannon and men in various parts of the globe, often defeating larger armies, what part did tea play? We know that by the later nineteenth century tea became an essential part of British and American army rations, precisely as a health measure. As a saying attributed to Napoleon puts it, 'an army marches on its stomach'. A soldier's ability to be at the right place at the right time, feeling relatively fit, and then to fight with energy and skill, depends very much on his health. An army or navy weakened by disease will lose the competitive edge and probably be defeated. Yet armies, great masses of people scouring the countryside for food and drink, packed together in temporary accommodation, under severe pressures of many kinds, are notoriously susceptible to illness, particularly the debilitating stomach disorders such as the dysenteries and typhoid and cholera. They are also particularly prone to other diseases, diseases associated with cold and crowding, in particular typhus.

In earlier phases of history, European armies had tried to protect themselves against contaminated water through drinking wine. But too much wine lessens efficiency, causing lethargy and depression. A shot of alcohol just before battle may help in the fight, but only for a very few minutes. Furthermore, wine being bulky and heavy to carry on long marches, tended to run out or to turn sour and undrinkable, after which many of the men collapsed with widespread enteric disease.

The Duke of Wellington was a strong advocate of the virtues of tea, carrying in his baggage a teapot designed by Flaxman and made by Wedgwood. He told his generals at Waterloo that tea cleared his head and left him with no misapprehensions. In the Crimean War, during the horrors of the cold and mud, Garnet Wolseley 'saw to it that his hungry men at least got plenty of tea' and likewise during the Red River expedition in Canada he issued tea to his soldiers and instructed them on how to make it and to drink it hot or cold. Florence Nightingale noted the beneficial effects of tea on the wounded and demoralised soldiers who flooded into her field hospitals, where 'there is nothing yet discovered which is a substitute to the English patient for his cup of tea'.[104]

Tea was certainly important in the First and Second World Wars, when the troops were issued standard tea rations. In relation to the stimulating effects of tea, an American professor of neurology M. A. Starr, MD, noted in 1921 that 'During the [First World] war the English troops were freely supplied with tea and carried it instead of water in their canteens. . . .'[105] Indeed, Anthony Burgess asserts that 'without tea Britain could not have fought the war'.[106]

Surgeon-General de Renzy of the British Army wrote that 'All I can say is that on a long march, and where troops are exposed to great hardships, a cup of Assam tea is one of the most sustaining and invigorating beverages a soldier could have. '[107] He had put his views into practice in many parts of the world. One in particular is interesting, for it is the very area where tea first originated, the borderlands of Assam and Burma. Previous to the Naga Hills expedition of 1879, de Renzy 'pointed out that an immense amount of sickness is everywhere due to the use of impure water, and from his knowledge of the country he recommended that all troops sent into the hills should receive a daily ration of tea, which not only assuages thirst, but is also valuable as a stimulant and restorative. Drinking rainwater, says Dr de Renzy, should be strictly forbidden.' [108]

Captain Carl Reichmann of the Seventh Infantry, the United States Army, gives a particularly poignant account of the value of tea from another war area.

> In the war, which I witnessed in Manchuria, two nations were engaged which are known as tea drinkers. The exertions they put forth no one can appreciate who has not seen them. In the summer the heat was humid and stifling, and alternated with torrential rains, so that the roads were always muddy and marching became a painful fatigue. In the great battles the troops marched and fought day after day, night after night, were always under fire, had little sleep and little food; they were terribly fatigued, but never collapsed; they brewed a cup of tea and on they went . . . Nothing quite so satisfied thirst on a hot day as a glass of tea. Nothing quite so well stifled a growling stomach, so quickly warmed up a frame stiffened with cold as a glass of tea; when in the saddle without food for thirty-six hours or more nothing so restored the physical balance as a glass of tea, and my first care in getting into camp was to have my canteen filled with weak tea.[109]

All this suggests that the likely effects of tea on military and naval strength lie in one of the main constituents of tea. The caffeine stimulates and relaxes both mind and body, adds to the confidence of the drinker, and so makes him more efficient as a fighter. The caffeine also combats stress and injury; hence the immediate response of most British people after any accident is to offer or drink a hot cup of sweet tea. The sugar helps as well. The caffeine in the tea also protects against cold. Since tiny advantages make a huge difference in war, tea drinking may have been one of the vital factors that turned the tide in many encounters.

Thus it may well emerge that right along the Himalayan frontier, through the great plains, up into Burma, across Africa, as the map of the world turned red, one reason for the success was the relative health of the forces led by tea-drinking and tea-promoting British officers. The muscles and the minds, as well as the stomachs, of the troops would have been much improved and in war, as in any competition, a consistent small advantage at crucial moments can lead to huge long-term gains. An edge in one battle can have vast consequences.

Tea and the British have become almost synonymous. This is not just a matter of noting that far more tea was drunk in Britain than anywhere else in Europe almost from the beginning of its importation from the East. Tea also became associated with the wider Britain, namely the British Empire. Just as the British exported their other institutions as their Empire increased, their language, law, political system, games (cricket, football and many others) and associations (clubs, trusts etc.), so they spread tea.

In the first wave, tea became the imperial drink of the white colonies. The Canadians and the New England colonists drank tea. At the Boston Tea Party of 1773 the Americans rejected both tea and British rule, emphasising that the two were a 'package'. Most of this was at the symbolic level, for in practice the Americans continued to drink huge quantities of tea; but they pretended that they were exclusively coffee drinkers.

Yet as one part of the Empire was lost, another was opening up. As mentioned earlier, the greatest tea drinkers in the world (outside China and Japan) have long been the Australians. They drink more tea per head than even the British. New Zealand is not far behind. The most famous Australian song, 'Waltzing Matilda', has in its central refrain the 'billycan' in which tea was boiled and carried.

So, at first, tea was the white person's drink in the British Empire. But with the development of the tea industry in Assam and then Ceylon in the second half of the nineteenth century a vast new market opened up on the Indian sub-continent. Until the late nineteenth century hardly any Indian drank tea. By 1959 India was the second largest consumer of tea in the world.[111] It was a vast growth, and now the country consumes about three-quarters of the tea it produces. So, just as the Portuguese, Spanish and French Empires spread their own drinks, wine and coffee, so the British spread and heavily depended on tea. As Dr Sigmond wrote in 1839, a book on tea would prove that our national importance has been intimately connected with it, and that much of our present greatness and even the happiness of our social system springs from this unexpected source. It would show us that our mighty empire in the east, that our maritime superiority, and that our progressive advancement in the arts and sciences have materially depended upon it ... [it is] an incentive to industry, contributes to health, to national riches, and to domestic happiness. [112]

Chapter Ten

Industrial Tea

Without tea, the British Empire and British industrialism could not have emerged. Without a regular supply, the British enterprise would collapse. Great hopes were placed on Assam. Yet as late as the 1860s the situation was uncertain. A crash in the Assam tea industry in 1867 marked the low point of the British attempt to undercut and replace Chinese tea production. From optimistic beginnings, it now looked a hopeless task. Investor confidence was gone, demand was sluggish, and the tea labour was dying in droves. To turn round the situation, something drastic would have to be done.

The method was to turn the tea plantations into outdoor factories, to 'industrialise' every stage of the production as far as possible and by this method to reduce costs. The aim was to apply science and management skills to the production of tea in the way which had brought success in other British ventures. What made tea plantations special was that they took the process from start to finish; from the clearing of the land, through planting and picking, all the way to the finished product of boxed tea.

The plantation combined the capitalist financing, labour

organisation and mechanisation as used in industrial production in a normal factory, but applied this not only to the manufacture of raw materials into a finished product (as with cotton factories), but to the production of the raw material as well. It is thus a combination of the British developments of the eighteenth century, namely the agricultural and the industrial, or factory, revolutions. In all of its parts, it applied a regimented, military, and precise way of using human labour and other energy sources.

In Britain, success had been achieved by dissecting work processes and making them more efficient. In particular, manufacture was divided into small parts and each worker specialised in one operation. Uniformity, standardised parts, the sub-division of tasks and the application of a trained and highly disciplined work force, regulated by the clock and capable of endlessly repeating monotonous single actions whose sum would be a desired product – the forerunner of the conveyor belt, indeed – these were the lessons of early British industrialism. Could they also be applied with benefit to equatorial crops such as cotton, coffee and, above all, to the great British commodity, tea? The lessons of the improvements in British agriculture suggested that these improved methods could certainly be extended beyond factories and workshops, and that animals and crops could also be treated as machine products.

There were, of course, problems. One was that the Indian tea workers would have to compete with extremely cheap labour. Chinese and Japanese tea growers were paid almost nothing for their work and only survived because tea was often produced by women and children alongside the major crops that formed their livelihood. Whatever methods were adopted would have to be awfully efficient to compete with these minimal labour costs.

The problem had already been outlined and solved (as he claimed) by Samuel Ball in 1848. He pointed out that 'The prominent argument put forth against a successful cultivation of the tea tree in our colonies, has chiefly been the great cheapness of labour in China; its dearness in our colonies, and an erroneous supposition that the process of manipulation was a laborious and expensive art.' He proceeded to show that this was untrue. The Indians were even poorer than the Chinese, and hence their labour was cheaper. 'Thus, it appears, that so far as the wants of the two people, and wages of labour are concerned, India possesses no small advantage over China for the successful cultivation of tea.'

He worked out that 'under the most favourable circumstances, the Chinese are not able to furnish good teas, suitable to general consumption, at a less cost than from 10d. to 11d. the pound; and, from the present state of our commercial relations with China, it seems probable that the cost may continue so high as from 1s. 2d. to 1s. 4d. the pound.' Meanwhile in India, the 'wages paid to the manipulators of tea are 5 rupees, to their assistant coolies 3 rupees, and, to the labourers, from 3 to 4 rupees the month; and the chests cost only 1 rupee each.' So he believed that 'With so low a rate of wages can there be any doubt that, under a suitable and inexpensive system of management, Assam ought to be able to compete with China in the cultivation of tea . . .'

That this was the case could be seen from the Dutch success in Java. 'The quantity of tea manufactured at Java from 1839 to 1844, exhibits an annual average of 218,000 lbs., so far as the contents of each package can be established.' (From the amount sold in Holland.) Ball found that 'tea may be shipped from that island at eight pence the pound . . . and there can be no reason why tea should not be produced in India at the same cost as at Java. Indeed, if tea can be manipulated and packed in China at its seat of growth, for seven or eight pence the pound, as now shown, it may fairly be assumed, so far as the price of labour is concerned, that the same quality of tea ought to be shipped from India at four or five pence the pound.' So there was no doubt that India could undercut China. Given the mark-up of about 120 per cent on the raw product that he had observed as being normal in Britain, this would mean a vast profit for the British.[113]

The normal solution in such a situation would be to mechanise – to replace humans by machines as had been done in British agriculture. Yet planting, growing and picking tea is, in fact, impossible to mechanise to any extent. It was difficult enough to replicate the work of a handloom weaver or thresher with machines. The mechanisation of the early stages of tea production – that is, the steps up to the production of the raw leaf – has not been achieved to this day. Clearing the jungle and planting tea on steep slopes, hoeing and weeding, picking the top shoots (the most intensive stage), carrying the tea to the collection points, machines could do none of this. Yet the early stages could certainly be made much more efficient, the British argued, than the haphazard methods to be found in China.

The process started with the clearing of the jungle, followed by the planting of the tea bushes and the shade trees to protect them from too much sun. Already a great deal of care and 'science' was to be applied. Exactly how much space should be allowed between each bush; what land was best; how carefully must the rows be planted for optimum picking; how many shade trees and of what kind; what were the best seeds and how were the nurseries to be tended – all these had to be carefully planned. Once the bushes were planted, a further set of experiments and instructions related to the frequency and the nature of the pruning, the application of fertilisers and the use of sprays and pesticides to protect the plants against various diseases. Tea research stations, such as that at Toklai in Assam, were later set up to investigate the best methods. This constant experimentation with and application of ever-improving methods could not be achieved by the Chinese small peasant. Considerable investments in larger-production sites and the avowed intention of maximising the returns on that investment made efficiency possible.

So, as the tea bushes were planted in Assam, they were arranged carefully, not dotted around as in the semi-wild state in China or the hedgerows of Japan, but in systematic plantations. The application of chemistry and knowledge of economic botany, the constant experimentation with soils and pesticides, as well as the best methods of planting, pruning and drying were combined in an almost military operation.

The tea workers were assembled in the lines, tiny huts similar to tents or barracks. They were subjected to an absolutely rigid time discipline. The long, unrelieved, hours of work that had been pioneered in organising labour in the mines, factories and workshops of industrial Britain, were applied to them. They were ordered to undertake methodically a set of carefully devised and sub-divided jobs, in particular the picking of the tea. They had become part of a huge machine, and within it were themselves machines gathering up the tea. The only real difference from factory work was that instead of workers remaining rooted in one spot and the materials rolling towards them on conveyor belts, the tea bushes remained stationary and the pickers moved across the exactly spaced lines of tea endlessly picking just the delicate top bud and two fresh leaves from plant after plant.

Under the hot sun, the pickers stood for hour after hour and concentrated on the exact work of picking the appropriate leaf. The process was described in an article in a special issue of the *Daily Telegraph* in 1938. 'Using both hands, women can pluck as many as 30,000 shoots in a day. In view of the care that has to be exercised in examining every shoot before plucking and in seeing that no stalk or coarse material reaches the factory, this is a commendable figure. Plucking takes place about every ten days, and 3,200 shoots are needed to make a pound of tea.'[114] This means that, assuming a person in the nineteenth century picked for ten hours a day, he or she would need to pick about 3000 shoots an hour, or fifty a minute.

Allowing for movement between bushes, unloading the baskets and so on, this would mean that the brain, arms, back, legs and hands, would have to be co-ordinated into a reaching-plucking-and-depositing set of movements every second or less for many hours a day, six days a week. Other estimates put the amount plucked much higher. Writing in the 1950s, the authority on tea C. R. Harler claimed that 'A woman can pluck 60 to 80 lb. of leaf a day, and it takes a half to three-quarters of a minute to pluck a bush.'[115] The human cost in boredom and mindless activity, let alone the physical cost of standing and plucking for hour after hour, is difficult to contemplate. It continues to this day.

So the tea gardens became intensive nursery gardens. Roads,

paths, bushes, the factory, the tiny one-roomed houses, and the disciplined movement of the labourers through the system were all minutely regulated. The green world was an extended factory, roofed only by the shade trees.

The British could, however, apply their industrial techniques even more directly in the processing of the raw material, the green leaf, into the final black, fired and boxed tea. Once they had gained control of tea making on their own plantations in Assam and, later, Ceylon (Sri Lanka), they began to apply machinery to the second half of the process. Tea became an industrial product. The raw material was fed into a factory whose machines were powered by steam or water and, with little human intervention, out came the chests filled with black tea. It was one of the reasons why tea in Assam began to cost less to produce than even the very cheap Chinese tea. The story of what happened can be told through the activities of one extraordinary inventor, William Jackson (1850–1915).[116]

In the early 1870s the young William Jackson and his brother John were travelling down the Brahmaputra on their way back from a visit to a tea estate. The ship ran aground and while waiting for repairs they wandered around the surrounding country. They came upon a Marshall portable steam engine, which had been used in India for some ten years. Jackson returned to England and formed an association with the Britannia Iron Works, out of which the extensive tea machinery business of Messrs Marshall Sons & Co., Ltd (then of Gainsborough) developed. Jackson set up his first tea roller on the Heeleakah garden in Assam in 1872. Although based on earlier ideas, his roller was far more efficient and soon replaced the enormously time-consuming business of hand-rolling tea. His many inventions included the Jackson 'Cross Action', 'Excelsior' and 'Hand Power' rollers, complicated machines with heavy castings. In 1877 he invented the 'Rapid' roller which dominated the industry for twenty years. In 1899 alone, some 250 of these machines were sold.

Jackson produced his first mechanical hot-air driers in 1884 and their names, we are told, are still known today: the 'Victoria', 'Venetian', 'Paragon'. (Certainly, when I visited a tea estate in Assam in 2001, they were still using Britannia machines.) These machines used a suction fan to help draw the hot air upwards through leaf trays to speed up the drying process. In 1887 he brought out his first roll breaker, the following year a tea sorter and in 1898 a tea packer. Marshall's produced the improved machines as he evolved them and they were shipped to almost every tea country.

An indication of the effects of Jackson's machines can be seen in the price of tea production. In 1872 when he began his work, the cost of production was 11d a pound, roughly in line with Chinese costs. By 1913 the improved machinery had cut the cost to threepence a pound. Some eight thousand rolling machines now did the work that would have needed one and a half million labourers. Previously some eight pounds of good timber had to be converted into charcoal to dry one pound of tea, but Jackson's machines produced the same results using any wood, grass or refuse. A quarter of a pound of Assam coal produced a pound of dry tea. Jackson also understood that better tea was produced if the fermentation was stopped as soon as the leaf entered the drying chamber and that tea should be cooled down as soon as possible after drying. This improved the quality of the tea by conserving the essential oils in the leaf. Jackson died in 1915 and left half his estate (£20,000 – then a very considerable sum) to charities linked to tea.

In the Chinese case approximately a third of the cost of tea before it reached the British ships lay in transportation from the growing areas and payments to middlemen on the way, including the merchants at the ports. In the Assamese tea gardens two strategies eliminated much of this cost. The middlemen and corruption were sidelined by British power. No one had to be paid off, no tolls and taxes were extracted as the tea headed down to Calcutta. Secondly, the tea was not carried on the back of endless coolies or even animals. The steam revolution had given the British the two great devices for carrying tea at a minimal cost, by way of steamship down the Brahmaputra river, or using the rapidly expanding network of railways which arrived in central Assam by the later nineteenth century.

All of this was underpinned by British political and military control of India and Ceylon, which provided the peaceful administration, and judicial security that was an essential foundation for prosperous development. It was also supported by the huge capital financing, ever searching for new profitable investment, which brought together the land, labour and the tea bush in a new combination. This would soon provide enough tea to give the whole world as much tea as people could drink at a very cheap price. So machines, labour organisation, steam and capital created new Manchesters and Birminghams on the banks of the Brahmaputra. The green and pleasant lands of this eastern Eden became ghostly reflections of the dark Satanic Mills of the metropolitan country.

As befits a regimental-style organisation there was a strict hierarchy or chain of command in the plantation. Under the Manager and his European assistant work was divided amongst native staff; the Head Mohurer, responsible for all work done and accounts rendered, cash being in his special charge, was the most senior. A Land Mohurer went out to the garden with the coolies and stayed with them all day, seeing that they and the sirdars did the tasks allotted to them.

The sirdars were coolies who were deemed more intelligent than average, and each was responsible for his 'gang' of workers, turning them out in the morning and giving a daily account of each man's or woman's work to the Land Mohurer to be entered into books. They also had to present themselves to the manager in his office and give a report of the day's work, mention defaulters, and get orders for next day. An English writer was in charge of accounts, sitting in his office all day, and in the factory there were Tea and Leafhouse Sirdars, on whose skill and knowledge the quality of the tea depended.

There was a native doctor who looked after the coolies, and they were visited occasionally by a European who kept a record of births and deaths. There were chowkidars, or watchmen, one who looked after the lines, reported sick coolies to the doctor, and saw that there was no pilfering of property. One man was deputed to accompany coolies on all excursions, perhaps to stop them running away. There were keepers of elephants used in clearing and transport, delicate animals requiring great care and a lot of uncooked rice. Bullocks for transport were given boiled rice in the evening, consuming more than the average family.

Planters' manuals record how, in spite of this network of overseers and watchmen, the manager and his assistant had to be on constant guard against the ways the coolies tried to cheat them. The women stuffed other plants into the bottoms of their baskets to make them weigh more, and men pruned slowly so as to be paid overtime rates for an unfinished task. Even children could not be trusted: one of their jobs was to collect caterpillars, twenty pounds a day was a *nereik* or 'task', and some would present the previous day's haul as a new one.

The disciplined flood of bonded labour, paid minimal wages, provided the inner engine for the plantations. When combined with the machines in the factory and the efficient transport, they provided standardised and high-quality tea. The winners were British merchants, investors and the tea-drinking public in many parts of the world. The costs were born by the workers in China and Assam.

The cheap, strong Assamese teas destroyed the Chinese export market. The industrial revolution had won again. This time not by destroying the livelihood of the cotton workers of India, as the Lancashire mills had done, but by undermining the export trade and hence a good deal of the work of the Chinese tea workers. The figures were indeed bleak as far as the Chinese were concerned.

J. Dyer Ball, author of *Things Chinese*, published at the beginning of the twentieth century, gives the figures. 'In 1859 there was no Indian tea trade, and China sent 70,303,664 lbs to England . . . By 1899 China had fallen to the figure of 15,677,835 lbs, and India had risen to the enormous figure – a figure never attained by China – of 219,136,185 lbs.'[117]

Two sets of regional figures and reports flesh out these amazing figures and give hints as to their local impact. In 1882 over 60 million pounds of tea left Fuzhou for Great Britain, nearly 70 per cent of the port's foreign exports in that year. Australia took another 18 million pounds, another 20 per cent of the exports. Only eight years later, this had dropped to less than half, with 23 million pounds going to Britain and 14 million to Australia. In his 1994 book on the tea trade, Robert Gardella quotes an anonymous Chinese.

Those who relied on tea-farming for a living were not few in number: those who clear the mountains, the tea pickers, those who open *chazhuang* to process and package tea, tea sellers and tea experts and selectors. After 1881 tea prices were very low... Those who opened *chazhuang* and the tea-chest makers went broke, and many producers could no longer rely on tea [for income]. Those with fields recultivated them, and the ones without land cut brushwood for a living. How lamentable those peoples who laboured to plant tea received so much bitterness from it! Only those cultivating land for food can continue to have tea gardens.... People without food let the tea mountains return to wasteland – they cannot [afford] to look after them.[118]

The Customs Annual Reports for Amoy in 1896 reported:

The annual value of the trade has fallen from Hk. Taels 2,000,000 a quarter of a century ago to less than Hk. Taels 100,000 to-day, and the cultivator, whose plantation formerly supplied him with a comfortable income, is now compelled to plant rows of sweet potatoes between the tea-bushes to keep body and soul together.

The following year the report read:

> In all probability this trade report will be the last in which
> reference will be made to Amoy tea as an important factor in
> our trade. Twenty-five years ago, 65,800 piculs [one picul is
> approximately 60 kg] were exported; this year the total is 12,[127]
> piculs . . . It is now too late to propose remedial measures
> which would resuscitate the already moribund leaf, formerly
> the leading article of export.

Four or five years later it was noted that 'Tea has now
disappeared from Amoy. There were no shipments to London
direct from Hankow in 1900, for the first time on record.' [119]

Many hundreds of thousands of Chinese peasants and
middlemen, already living in great hardship, were suddenly
deprived of their supplementary cash income. All along the
supply line, from the tiny growers, through those who ground the
tea in the factories, the toilers on the tea trails, the workers and
merchants at the ports, people were thrown out of work. The
effects were catastrophic and added to the instability of China in
the later nineteenth century with its widespread political and
religious turbulence.

Chapter Eleven

Tea Labour

With success in Assam assured by the collapse of the Chinese trade, the lot of the Assamese worker should have improved. As the chaotic conditions of the tea mania period gave way to a more orderly world, with very large profits being made and a greater knowledge of preventive medicine and diet, the theory of enlightened capitalism suggested that the workers would benefit. The 'invisible hand' of the market would ensure that all would share in the bonanza. All that one had to ensure was that government did not interfere. The rest could be left to self-interest. After all, healthy workers were more efficient.

This was the philosophy expounded by a Colonel Edward Money in his widely read text book on the tea industry, published at the end of the nineteenth century.

All evidence collected, all enquiries made, tend to show that coolies are well treated on Tea estates. It is the interest of the proprietors and managers to do so, and self-interest is a far more powerful inducement than any the Government can devise. The meddling caused by the visits of the 'Protector of

Coolies' to a garden conduces to destroy the kind feelings
which should (and in spite of these hindrances often do) exist
between the proprietor or manager and his men. I do not
hesitate in my belief that imported coolies on Tea plantations
would be better off in many ways were all Government
interference abolished.[120]

To protect the tea plantations from this 'interference', a
management organisation was set up. The Indian Tea Association
(ITA) was established in 1888 as a sort of miniature East India
Company focused solely on tea. Its functions were much the same
– to support the trading community, to regulate wages, working
conditions, and recruiting. Ninety per cent of Assam's companies
were members, and stood shoulder to shoulder with their
representatives in London and Calcutta in their dogged
insistence on arguing against almost every move to improve the
conditions of tea garden labour. They stood between the
managers and the government, and, as a Committee of 1901 put
it, 'Commission follows Commission, Act follows Act, with
wearisome iteration . . . each one has been a greater failure than
the last.'

The Association members were particularly incensed when
Henry Cotton was made Chief Commissioner of Assam in 1896,
and saw it as part of his job to inspect personally many of the tea
estates, and send round officials at regular intervals to look at
others. He also got a Surgeon-Major Campbell to make a report
on the conditions aboard the ships that brought up recruits. The
inspectors, Campbell's suggestions, and Cotton's final report led
to a flurry of ITA meetings condemning the 'absolutely insupport-
able interference in the matter of inspection of gardens and the

trouble and worry planters have been put to . . . systematic bullying, for I can call it nothing else . . .' Cotton even had the effrontery to 'flourish his penal weapon in our faces' shouted the Chairman at one of the ITA meetings, to loud and prolonged applause.

After a brilliant career in Bengal in the judicial department, and having written a book, *New India*, sympathising with the independence movement, Henry Cotton's reputation was that of a man deeply committed to helping the average Indian and of righting wrongs that most of his colleagues did not even recognise. His idol and role model was the last Viceroy, Lord Ripon. Both of them were looked on with suspicion, distaste, and even loathing by many.

The Bengalis of course adored him. The Indian press expressed their feelings.

The people of India have not had a truer friend or more disinterested well wisher . . . The educated natives of this province idolise him as they do few Englishmen . . . when the majority of Englishmen are sneering at native pretensions . . . Mr Cotton's sympathy for the people of this country presents a most pleasing contrast, a contrast that is doubly appreciated in that it is so rare . . . Many of the educated natives of Bengal owe their positions entirely to his discriminating kindness.[121]

When he left to go on leave, hundreds of his admirers saw him off on the train: in so doing, 'They paid him an honour that, except for one exception, they had never before paid to any official,' reported the *Indian Mirror*. As for his book, the press was surprised and shocked. The *Sidney Morning Herald* said, 'It is not pleasant to hear that the English in India are as scornful and as arrogant as they were when the East India Company administered the affairs of the country . . . the people are not attached to English rule.' The Tory press demanded to know whether someone who owed his position to the government should be allowed to preach revolution.

Set such a man down among the tea planters of Assam, have him look at the way the workers on their estates were paid, housed, doctored, recruited, and it was no wonder that he was soon being described as a 'malicious slanderer' who questioned and publicly denounced practically everything he saw. His views got into the papers. They also filtered down to the workforces, 'weakening the authority of planters over their labourers'. Cotton was certainly brutally frank. 'The condition of labour is very scandalous. Coolies are practically bond slaves . . . the period of bondage may be interminable,' he wrote in his report.

He looked at repatriation, and the fact that there were 'many waifs and strays wandering about in the bazaars, who often perished in the vain attempt to return to their country'. He recommended that there should be a Central Board of Management that would acquire lands and buildings in which coolies could stay on their way home, with provisions made for their travelling. The ITA claimed that they got land on which to retire, but Cotton noted that 'Coolies coming out of the gardens are in most cases so sickly and so penniless that they are the last persons to undertake any reclamation of waste land . . . which requires labour and capital.' A magistrate confirmed that in his area only seven coolies had in fact managed this.

Before they even reached the gardens a great deal was wrong, and an Assam Labour Emigration Bill actually became law in 1901 with regulations that the ITA described as 'extraordinary provisions' and deplored 'the stringency by which these provisions have been enforced'. They comforted themselves by being sure that the sirdars who collected the coolies 'won't insist upon the *absolute* letter of the law and the *absurd* rules'.

The Act tried to prevent coolies from being recruited without their understanding the terms of their contracts, or even what a contract was. It decreed that there must be a magistrate present at the recruiting centre to witness the signing. Quite unnecessary, the ITA had maintained, the Magistrate often couldn't be reached easily. He should accept the written statement from the employer – after all, the illiterate coolies couldn't even put their names to the piece of paper. The ITA was frustrated when the authorities in both the Central Provinces and Madras forbade further recruitment there. Mr Taylor, later Collector in Madras, 'strongly urging the closing of the hill tracts to recruitment . . . these men being for the most part ignorant and having no ideas as to where they were being taken until they were at a considerable distance from their native districts.'

The two surgeons who reported on the conditions of the coolies as they travelled up country wanted compulsory inoculation at recruiting stations, with thirty-six hours' rest afterwards. The centres should employ an Assistant Surgeon, two hospital assistants, a clerk, bearer, water carrier, and sweeper, whose wages should be paid by the companies involved. Not surprisingly the companies did not think they should be 'saddled' with these expenses – a nominal fee for each body should suffice.

It was on the question of wages that Cotton caused the most resentment amongst the planters. Reading their denials, evasions and half-truths, one pauses to wonder why they seemed to have been so resistant to the idea of having a well-fed, well-housed, contented labour force; why for the next seventy years they resisted many measures to bring this about. One of the problems was that managers received yearly commissions based on the profits of their gardens, so that money spent on welfare would be deducted from their own pay packets.

Their own houses and clubs became ever grander, and, fifty years after Cotton's report, a similar report noted that labourers were suffering from severe anaemia, mothers died far too often, children worked instead of going to school . . . the dreary catalogue of inadequacies went on.

Cotton demanded from each tea estate a monthly statement of the actual wages received by active men and women, including overtime. He wanted the value of rations given in lieu of wages to be entered, but 'the charges of hospital accommodation, medicines, medical attendance, house accommodation, water supply or sanitary arrangements . . . are *not* wages and are *not* to be included'. All the usual excuses about the coolies getting 'perks' were to be dismissed. And as for the system of deducting from deserters' wages the rewards paid for catching them, he called this an 'outrageous custom'.

'Rather strong language,' the ITA complained and said that this monthly statement, to be sent to the Deputy Commissioner, 'would impose an excessive amount of clerical work on gardens'. Rubbish, said Cotton, 'a clerk of average intelligence would not take more than an hour to prepare it each month.' He was equally dismissive of their other complaint – that the industry was going through hard times – and maintained that the present slight dip in profits was simply due to overproduction and the situation would right itself; which it did.

In response to Cotton's figures – which demonstrated that tea garden labourers only received half as much pay as other workers – the ITA pointed out that those were employed on temporary projects so would naturally get more. And what about the figures for births and deaths? Why did women fail to produce healthy children, or fail to produce at all when 'they are people who in their own homes are as prolific as any in India?' The ITA refused to put this down to overwork and anaemia as Cotton suggested, and produced one of their feeblest excuses: it was due 'to the weakness of the marriage tie among coolie emigrants'. As for the death rate – of 43.5 per thousand, twice as high as among the general population – this Cotton claimed was a direct result of wages too low 'for health and comfort', and because the atrocious conditions in Assam failed to attract healthy coolies in the first place.

A George Dickson of the ITA seemed to be one of the exceptions to the general run of members. In his description of the death rate at an Association meeting he set out an interesting set of figures. Viewing the statistics he said: 'Take a garden with a population of some 700 or so. This would make a fair-sized village at home. With a death-rate a shade under 7 per cent this would mean a funeral every week, for every week of the year, or two funerals a week for six months of the year, or, if it were an epidemic, a funeral every other day, for nearly four months in the year.' In fact in 1892, 57,000 people, or more than one-eighth of the garden population of Assam died.

In spite of these alarming figures the ITA remained unmoved. Its members countered Cotton's criticisms by saying that out of 605,000 coolies they had only received twenty-six complaints. This argument would not have impressed Cotton and his inspectors, who had visited the gardens and seen the vigilant watch that was kept on 'troublesome' or absconding coolies. To Cotton's idea of pinning up notices about their rights, wages and so on, where the labour could read them, the ITA wanted to know who would be able to read these amongst a totally illiterate workforce.

The Association members were mollified when the new Viceroy, Lord Curzon, paid a visit 'and will see his way to withdraw the wages proposal' of an extra rupee a month. All Acts landed up finally on the Viceroy's desk, and this man was going to be a strong supporter of all British interests in India it appeared, of which the tea trade was one of the most vital.

Over and over the dreary figures are repeated, and the ignorance as well as callousness in the system revealed. In 1892, according to an ITA spokesman,

> Sixty-four coolies were sent up after registration in Calcutta and after executing contracts . . . they were described in their contracts as Ghasi by caste, and as coming from the Santhal Pargannas, a district in which recruits are ordinarily obtained. Seven months later only 16 were left in the garden; 26 had deserted, 16 had died, the contracts of 6 were cancelled for permanent physical incapacity; the remainder were a sickly and feeble set. It was found when they reached the garden that they were not Santhals at all, but coolies from the North West Provinces, of a low and sickly type.[122]

It is only fair to include an extract of a letter from a missionary who took up a party of Christians from Orissa to Assam in 1889; a letter proudly produced for the doubters of the ITA:

I found that the conditions of the coolies was better than that of the great majority of ordinary labourers in Orissa . . . who live on the merest pittance, and are often in great straits . . . the coolies earn more, wear better clothes and have better food than tens of thousands in these parts. House accommodation is provided for them, they have medical aid in case of illness, and while sick and unable to work are entitled to receive half pay . . . They can all save money and buy cows (great numbers of them do) . . . The tasks exacted from the coolies are such as ordinary able bodied men and women can accomplish without distress and hard working individuals can do more, up to the extent of doubling their wages. Riding out one day between 1 and 2 o clock to visit my men where they were at work, I met a coolie returning to the lines who had finished his task and was free to do as he liked for the rest of the day . . . My men agreed that the work was not hard, though harder to their unaccustomed hands than the experienced ones. The wives of these men, who were picking tea leaf, also asserted that their work was not laborious, though it would require practice before they would make up the required quantity.[123]

Orissa was the poorest state in India, prone to devastating famines, so bad that almost anywhere was going to be an improvement. Over the years the Orissa workers turned out to be the most anaemic and sickly of the workforce, because their Christian pastors forbade them to go to the drink shops where they would be supplied with extra calories. Henry Cotton was critical of these shops, which were situated at the gates of every tea garden, run by Bengalis but licensed by the government.

They may have provided calories for the coolies and revenue for the government, but they produced raw liquor that was often contaminated, rough on the stomach and even rougher on the purses of men and women who did not have even enough for food.

So the century ended with a flourishing industry, now mechanised and powerfully protected by its own Association from any whimsical do-gooders like Henry Cotton. There were no more crises, though profits rose and fell slightly, overproduction one year corrected the next. Railways had started to crawl rather slowly across the country. The problem of getting coolies to build them over malarial swamps and through thick jungle hampered their progress. The tiresome tribals were kept at bay by military police; the Assamese were the same, as always keeping to themselves. For the tea industry it was a happy outlook that allowed them to proceed, comfortable in the knowledge that things would forever remain the same.

The Great War of 1914–18 produced the largest crop and the highest profits yet achieved. The troops in the trenches needed tea and they were not too bothered about quality, so that it could be plucked coarse and the government ensured its steady sale at fixed prices. Few planters 'joined up' and the war did not touch India geographically, although there were a good number of Indians who went in the native labour corps to the various fronts.

After the war, things became uncomfortable quite quickly. First there was the influenza epidemic of 1919, which sent the mortality rates among the labour force soaring even higher. Then there was a steep rise in prices, which made the workers restless for a share in the profits, their own wages being at a pitiful pre-war level and quite insufficient. Then there was Mahatma

Gandhi and his Congress Party, visiting Assam and stirring up unrest.

Three years after the end of the war, destitute coolies from Sadiya (which had been visited by Gandhi's men) were arriving in Chandpur (the nearest station, and with a jetty) at the rate of two hundred a day, leaving their gardens and heading home on any train or boat that would take them. Some of them stormed onto the trains and steamers, the rest camped on a football field near the station, using temporary shelters erected by a compassionate Mr De, who also provided medical help.

The workers were scared to leave the station for fear of being sent back to their gardens, and the situation became dangerous when 'troublemakers' from the town joined them shouting 'Gandhi *Maharaj ki jai*'. Neither the government nor the ITA were prepared to 'create a precedent' by helping them, and in the end the police and Gurkhas moved in. The newspapers took up the case and one of Gandhi's right-hand men visited the scene and described the coolies as being destitute and half-starved. Soon cholera broke out and sixty-five of them died.

Questions were raised in the British Parliament about the incident. The ITA offered a rise of two annas (less than a penny) and called on an Act that would prohibit meetings on gardens. There were some more Reports; one from 1931 said there 'should' be free access to workers' houses; there 'should' be land given for allotments; there 'should' be free feeding for children under five, and a welfare officer to see things were carried out. There even 'should' be a Board of Health and Welfare, Sanitary Inspectors and vaccinators. And yet still, in Assam, little changed.

In 1927 A. A. Purcell, MP and J. Haldsworth, delegates from the British Trades Union Council, made a four-month tour of India.

They visited textile mills, railway workshops, engineering works, hydroelectric plants, water and irrigation schemes, printing offices, coalmines, gold and oilfields, rubber plantations and tea estates. They published their findings on their return with predictable results: astonishment and shame from the liberal press, anger and repudiation from the rest.

The practice of building workers' houses in lines for all Indian employees they found repugnant. 'They are all unutterably bad and cannot in any decent sense be regarded as homes. We visited the workers' quarters wherever we stayed and had we not seen them we would not have believed that such evil places existed.'

On tea gardens, families had one dark room, 'used for all purposes, living, cooking, sleeping, nine foot by nine foot with mud walls and loose tiled roof'. There was a small open space in front, a corner of which was used as a latrine. The only ventilation in the living room came from a broken tile in the roof. In this dark, airless space four to eight people, including children, ate and slept.

By this time Assam had 420,000 acres under tea, employing 463,847 permanent workers. In the year of Purcell and Haldsworth's visit, 1927, 41,176 were 'imported', though they were not now employed under the old bondage system. They described the process:

Large numbers of recruits for the most part primitive and illiterate, are lured from their villages, situated hundreds of miles away, in the belief that in the tea gardens the struggle for a living will be less grim. Once in the gardens however their freedom is severely restricted and although some of the legislation invoked . . . preventing the labourers leaving the gardens has been repealed, there are still sufficient punitive regulations to make it exceedingly difficult for the labourers to give up the work if they so desire.

'It is undeniable,' they wrote 'that Indian workers are half starved, badly clothed as well as horribly housed.' The average daily earnings on a tea estate were 6d, 5d and 4d a day, depending on the worker – 'Combined labour of man, woman and child brings this human trilogy to 1/3d per day.' And then the statement that really angered the planter community: 'We witnessed a group of men women and children working away – while about 5 yards away was a planter's young assistant proudly hugging a whip. This we regarded as proof of the contentment prevailing among the tea garden population.'

They finished their tour by trying to rouse Assamese students to change the exploitative capitalist system that had started one hundred and fifty years ago in their country. 'The general condition of the coolie is a positive menace to civilisation,' they boomed at a public meeting in Gauhati. 'During the one hundred and fifty years of British rule between three hundred and four hundred millions of pounds have been drained out without any return. Time is ripe that you should demand of your masters to spend this amount for the improvement of health and sanitation . . . Organise, and organise, agitate and agitate . . .' They could start right in their own back yard. Of tea gardens, they said 'the conditions there are the nearest approach to slavery . . .'[124]

Among the members of the public most outraged by this TUC report were the Board of the Indian Tea Association. They sent affronted denials to all the leading newspapers, nineteen of them, including *The Times*, the *Morning Post*, the *Daily Telegraph*; to journals such as *The Tea and Coffee Trade Magazine*, to Reuters' head office and to Lord Birkenhead, Lord Winterton and Ramsay MacDonald. Some of these papers were sympathetic; the magazine of the Anti-Socialist Anti-Communist Union could not have agreed with them more when they described the tea industry as a kind and caring concern. The press was not so sure. In fact they were horrified: 'That such a state of affairs should exist in the twentieth century after one hundred and fifty years of British rule is a serious reflection upon everybody concerned.'

The Second World War was different, and for a couple of years Assam was the centre of attention. The roads out of Assam that had been part of the Great Game with China now became part of the Great Escape from the Japanese. Bulldozers smashing through rock faces in a desperate hurry to rescue the defeated British Brigade that was being chased up Burma by the Japanese, and as a secondary objective to rescue the thousands of Europeans, Chinese, and Indians who were fleeing from the wrath of the Burmese when the British were no longer there to protect them.

Rangoon in Burma fell to the Japanese on 2 February 1942 and it soon became obvious that India was to be the next target and the best way to enter would be through Assam. This tea-rich, oil-rich, rice-rich province could be entered over two passes from Burma. The Japanese were pleased when the roads over these mountains started to be repaired from the Assam side. They bombed a little but avoided damaging what was going to be very useful to them in their final push.

The speed of the Japanese advance, its obvious target, and the fear that another Singapore tragedy was to be enacted on the banks of the Chindwin, had the planners in Delhi sending telegrams and urgent commands to this eastern frontier. The story as then told in history books is one of noble selflessness on the part of the ITA and the plantation industry, allowing their labour to go off and make roads (voluntarily, it was stressed) and themselves struggling on as best they could. Planters were heroes, their wives angels of mercy, greeting the refugees with many a cheery smile and endless cups of tea. This was before the documents of the ITA, all highly confidential and some in code, were released and came to rest in the India Office Library. These tell a different story, which is as follows.

A month after the fall of Rangoon (Burma), on 1 March 1942, the Chairman of the Indian Tea Association and a committee member were asked to attend a conference in Delhi. Here they were ordered to supply twenty thousand labourers to build a road through Manipur up to the Burmese town of Tammu, and another seventy-five thousand from Ledo, to connect with the Americans in China. The arrival of the monsoon, as well as the Japanese, meant it must be a rushed job. The road to Tammu was to be finished by 7 May, a matter of nine weeks to turn a mule track of 260 miles into a highway for lorries and heavy artillery.

As soon as the ITA pair got back to Calcutta, telegrams went flying, and four days after the Delhi meeting a planter with a hundred labourers was on his way up to Dimapur, the starting point of the Manipur road, to prepare bivouac camps for the thousands who would follow. Labourers were to live in bamboo and grass huts, and these were ready in a few days. A week later every wayside station on the way up to Dimapur was crowded with men carrying hoes, blankets, and enough food for a fortnight.

How fortunate the army was to be able to commandeer this huge resource so close at hand. How would they have managed without them? It is safe to say that the blood and sweat of these coolies saved the British Brigade coming out of Burma; they and the hill men who were porters and guides and carried up the supplies to keep the labourers alive as they headed up towards Burma. A. H. Pilcher, a tea planter who was Liaison Officer in charge of the Manipur road operation, described the extraordinary task.[125] One hundred and sixty-four miles up, the track petered out and the last fifty miles to Tammu had to be scratched out of barren waterless mountains rising to six thousand feet, one portion a thousand feet in ten miles. Twenty-eight thousand labourers were scattered over an area of two hundred miles, ponies, bullocks and mules slogging with them, water having to be carried in bottles. The work had to be done with hoes, hacking on the edge of precipices, carting enormous boulders, all at a furious rate to meet the army's deadline.

And then there was the steady stream of refugees coming the opposite way, out of Burma. This was a tiresome complication for the army, but, while it was not too difficult, they lorried them in the vehicles that had brought the labour up. They were not Burmans, they were British, Indians, Chinese and a mixture of these races, and they were not just fleeing from the Japanese but from the wrath of the Burmese, who would turn on them once their protectors had gone. Since the final annexation of Burma in 1885 its own people had been turned into dependent second-class citizens, all the wealth and power in the hands of outsiders.

The refugees lucky enough to be lorried down were nursed in the Dimapur hospital, cheered with tea and biscuits from Lady Reid, the Governor's wife, and taken on to centres in India. These were the lucky ones, because five days after the Manipur road was completed on 7 May, General Wood closed it to the forty-five thousand still trying to escape. They were directed to the other pass, the Pan San, and the Hukawng Valley, to a track used by opium traders. General Wood ordered the ITA to set up posts as far up as they could along this track, where the refugees could get food and basic medical treatment.

With the monsoon approaching it was a curious decision by the General. It seems that the army was prepared to sacrifice this polyglot riff-raff, many of mixed race, to the malarial jungles, the raging rivers of the dreaded Hukawng Valley, and to the ravages of dysentery, sores and starvation, in the interests of keeping the new road free for the troops. This decision led to four thousand deaths, but nobody was censured and the historians of the episode have accepted the decision without comment.

A diary written by a reconnaissance officer at the time shows the appalling conditions these people faced: '. . . stiff marches in rain over muddy paths, hundreds of leeches, evacuees arriving tired and then having to build shelters for the night, sleeping with wet blankets if they can sleep when there are so many sand flies and other insects that bite, trying to light a fire and cook a breakfast in the rain . . .'[126] The mud was so deep that many who fell into it didn't have the strength to climb out. The RAF dropped supplies when the weather permitted, tea garden doctors did their best for those who reached the camps. Women, children and the old died and had to be left for the animals.

There was one other escape route, further north, 'a more exclusive clubbable route,' said Tyson, in fact just a path. The little party who followed it got hopelessly lost and were finally rescued by the elephants of a certain Gyles Mackrell, a Calcutta businessman who had rented large areas of the country for big-game shooting. They were also helped by some local hill men – as porters, bridge builders, fishermen and mappers these hill peoples played a role almost as vital as the tea garden labour in keeping India safe. They died in large numbers, many from meningitis, many as the result of accidents.

Meanwhile the Japanese paused, not only for the monsoon of 1942 but for the next year as well. They too could have used the Tammu road, neatly completed to time with their arrival, but perhaps they just preferred to watch other roads being made ready, widened and kept clear of landslides. They flew over, dropped a few bombs, and watched airports being made ready for the Americans and for Wingate's Chindits. These airports too would be useful for them in due course.

By September 1942 it became clear that tea garden labour was going to be needed on a regular and long-term basis, and it was given a name, Shadow Force, and an exact quota for each garden was set out – ten men per hundred acres. Their pay was raised from 12 annas to 1 rupee a week and their living quarters slightly improved. Rice to feed them was brought up through a Bengal suffering another fearful famine. Steaks and ice cream were airlifted up for the Americans. A certain orderliness, a sort of settling-in was apparent. A planter was put in charge of a very large vegetable garden.

This peace was shattered in April 1944 when the Japanese approached on both sides of the Manipur road and attacked Kohima. A famous battle was fought, decided by air superiority, the Japanese became the pursued and then subject to atomic bombs. The Americans went home and so did the tea garden labour. Assam was left with a few airports, quite a few planes

(Dakotas), a great many jeeps, and an indefinite number of half-caste children. The heady days of the war were long remembered and regretted by planters' wives.

General Wavell's voice was one of many congratulating the ITA and the tea plantations for their wonderful, unselfish, contribution to the final victory. The ITA's secret files reveal that right from the start it was less selfless patriotism than necessity that dictated their actions. It was well put in a circular of 1944. They had given labour to protect the industry from indiscriminate commandeering by the army and their agents. Contractors were poaching from the estates offering higher wages, and they were getting nothing from this steady absenteeism. They circulated in a highly secret document their views 'that there must at all costs be avoided the possibility of the humiliating experience of a great industry having its role changed'; more succinctly it must avoid the stigma of being seen to be unwilling, from selfish motives, to help the war effort.

In fact it was clear from the start that the industry was going to do very well out of the war. The British government was going to pay for replacements being brought up to the gardens. Compensation forms for loss of crops were filled in, though in 1942, the year of crisis, 470 million pounds of tea were plucked, the largest crop on record. Twenty-one million cups of tea were sold on the carts that circulated among the troops. By 1945 profits were up 200 per cent. A correspondence, growing more acerbic over the years, rumbled on about compensation. The 6884 deaths of tea garden labourers on the roads was described as 'gratifyingly low'. One planter died.

When the medals were handed out at the end of the war did it never occur to anyone to ask who had actually won the war? Or why tea garden labourers and Nagas, Abors, Khasis, Mishmis and others did not dangle MBEs on their chests? Without them and their work, both in the construction of the road and in supplying the troops in the battle at Kohima, the Japanese would have reached India.

As well as dealing with the Japanese threat during those three and a half years the industry had other jobs. In January 1943 the ITA were advised by the government that an Indian Tea Control Bill was proposed, in which the central government would set up wage-fixing mechanisms. This was strongly opposed and the government was persuaded to postpone the bill, and instead hold an immediate enquiry: another enquiry, another report.

Price rises and a shortage of rice, since Burma's borders were closed, were causing hardship to the labour left on the gardens. They would be given extra work and extra concession rice, but on no account were their wages to be raised. In the Surma Valley they had some cloth allowances too, but the Assam branch of the ITA refused even this. They also protested at an injunction to give four days' notice of a lock-out of labour in the event of a strike, or wages in lieu to workers who were not striking. They protested loudly against compulsory recognition of trade unions. The Trades Dispute Act, they said, was not applicable to tea garden labour; they pressed for 'specific exclusion of plantation labour from the scope of the legislation'.

The Defence of India Act was very useful to the industry since it prohibited public meetings on tea gardens, or anywhere else. When Mr Rege of the Civil Service was asked to head the new enquiry, his report of 1944 revealed a state of near siege on the estates. 'The plantation labour is absolutely unorganised and helpless, the planters are extremely well organised and powerful,' he wrote, saying nothing new.

Rege found it difficult to investigate because the ITA said such visits would unsettle labour. Access to the labourers' houses was only granted to relatives, and only religious and social meetings were allowed. Planters said the gardens were private property and they had the right to keep people out. The result, said Rege, 'is that we find a mass of illiterate people living far away from their homes in settlements scattered all over Assam practically segregated from outside influences, unorganised and unable to protect themselves while the employers have formed themselves into one of the most powerful and well organised associations in the country.'

The inspectors who visited every two years 'hardly have a talk with the labourers privately i.e. without the presence of the manager or the supervisor, and . . . they collect the necessary information from the managers themselves.' He put aside the pleas that low wages were compensated by perks such as free housing: 'The houses provided for the labourers are mostly *katcha* structures with split bamboo walls and thatched roof . . . the rental value per month of these huts would be a negligible amount.' So what then of their free medical attendance: 'It would be as reasonable to expect policemen, or sepoys to regard money spent on medicines, doctors and hospitals as part of his pay.'

'Their houses present pictures of stark poverty,' Rege said of the few he could enter; the women had no jewellery, a sure sign of absolutely nothing saved. Lack of schools, said the ITA, was because of 'apathy of parents who prefer them to work'. There were no welfare activities, no pensions; open drains, stamped through by cattle, led to 'highly polluted and dangerous' water supplies. The so-called hospitals were 'most uninviting' with a few iron or wooden cots. Rege reported and advised changes, but two years later Colonel Lloyd Jones of the Indian Medical Association found that nothing had changed. Practically all the labour force was anaemic, mortality was high, illiteracy taken for granted.

So much for the 'invisible hand' of self-interest in a situation of such glaring power inequality. The managers were maximising as they should, and there was very little bargaining power among sets of illiterate workers, unorganised, many far from their homes, always aware that if they were sacked they would be destitute. It seemed that in Assam nothing would ever change.

Part III
Embodied

Chapter Twelve

Tea Today

The previous chapters on tea in Assam paint a very negative picture. Further evidence on the negative side is provided by a recent book about tea labour in the 1990s by Piya Chatterjee, an American anthropologist who lived and worked in the Dooars for several seasons.[127] The book describes memories of neglect, arrogance, aggressive behaviour in the past, and of continued deference up to the present. Chatterjee found women labourers often overworked, consistently underpaid, sometimes sexually harassed and bullied. She followed them out to the gardens during the plucking season, leaving their homes after the first siren at 6 a.m., having cooked rice, vegetables and lentils for their families. They plucked for several hours and at 11 a.m. walked with their sack of leaves the two miles to the weighing shed: 'in full harvest the bundles of leaves overwhelmed the small and bent-over bodies.' An average plucker carried 54 kilos, though some managed 100.

There was a short break after the weighing and then back for another four or five hours. For this exhausting labour they were paid Rs32 to Rs40 a day, about sixty pence or a dollar. A very capable woman working during the peak time could earn a little over double this. The smiling seductive women on posters and packets bore little resemblance to the tired, often pregnant, poorly nourished reality. Chatterjee described the teaching at the garden school as 'desultory' and illiteracy as the norm. Children were employed as soon as they were legally old enough, the manager checking their teeth like horses to calculate their ages. This is the Dooars in 1990, which is likely to be very similar to nearby Assam. Conditions in other tea plantation areas may be even worse, with sexual harassment carried to far greater lengths. For example, there are rumours of systematic rape of new girls arriving to work on the estates in parts of East Africa, and their consequent infection with HIV AIDS.

What we have not heard much about is the other side of the story, the defence of the planters and their associations, their justification for their huge profits and the plantation system. There is a danger of being wise after the event and forgetting the general state of the world within which tea was situated in the hundred years after 1868. So it is important to hear something about what has happened in Assam since Iris left in 1966. How have tea and Assam changed since then? How is the whole British episode in tea regarded by those Indians who followed them?[128]

In England, Mr Smo Das described his time in tea.[129] He was born in Bombay in 1951 and joined the tea industry in 1972. One of the new, highly educated (Doon school) brand of Indian tea planters who replaced the British, he worked as a 'box wallah' in Calcutta, but spent two years from 1975 as a temporary assistant manager on a tea plantation. He left India in 1981 to become a management consultant in Britain.

When Das became an assistant manager in Assam in 1975 there were still several British managers left, as well as senior British administrators in Calcutta. All the senior positions were still held by the British and Das's Manager was British. There had been the big exodus post-devaluation in the early 1970s but some remained as managers for about another ten years. The ghosts of the ones who had left were still there, most of the stories were about 'old so and so'. What sort of 'ghosts' were they – old ruthless imperial horrors or eccentric Englishmen?

Much nearer the eccentric Englishmen than the ruthless Attila the Hun character. Most stories concerned people who had become part of the landscape, it was their home. When they came back to England they were a misery. No, they had given their best and certainly the tea garden staff I spoke to really looked up to these people. I can talk about 'Jones' as he was my boss; he had been thirty years in tea. Most of the people on that estate, even if you go back now, will look back with warmth and they loved having them in charge. And I think the main reason why the British were liked so much, whether it was in Calcutta or in tea was because of fairness, perceived fairness. In fact the bad ones we heard about were normally guys who were stealing things, smuggling out tea etc., they were just crooks, if you like. There weren't horror stories about mistreatment of people, which is interesting. In fact I can tell you that the feeling in India for people who were caught in this transition between having English bosses and Indian bosses, nine out of ten would have voted to have a British boss. And I can say that as an Indian. And that is whether they were a domestic servant; even to this day I know of domestic servants who manage to avoid working for an Indian family if they could help it. It is partly because they feel they are treated better and they are treated fairly.

Many of the Indians who took over from the British were just brown versions, just as many people would accuse me of being . . . I don't consider it an insult at all. They were brown sahibs and they did perhaps inherit how to look after people in a firm but fair way. No. Very few horror stories. If there have been unpleasant people in tea, most of them have not been from the ex-pat[riate] community, strangely enough. This is surprising in a way, since some who went into tea may have had reasons for getting away from Britain – criminals, economic migrants and so on. Yet, despite that, you may have got eccentricity, but inhumanity, beastliness, that sort of thing, very little, very little of that. I can't remember many stories, I would really have to hunt to find an example. The British provided leadership. Those who remained were there because they were very good at what they were doing.

As to aloofness, Das believed that the British were indeed aloof,

though not so much by the time I arrived. Certainly in the tea context there was lots of fraternising with the natives, but it was nearly always done on the quiet, there was definitely a barrier – their defence mechanism, I suspect – and they stayed behind it; children were sent to school to England, to make sure they did not get contaminated I suppose. I had, of course, seen this in Calcutta earlier on. The Calcutta swimming club did not let Indians in until the mid 1950s, until there was a Communist government. But the division was less pronounced up in Assam.

In fact, I believe that it is as much about class as about caste. There is a big class issue here. If you are from a particular 'class' and are brown, green or yellow, you have more in common with an Englishman from that background, than they would ever have with someone they think is from the lower class, even if they were English.

There was even more of a barrier between the upper middle class, say the burra sahibs and a possible tea planter who may have come from an entirely different class from over here, that barrier was probably much greater than that between two middle-class people of different races.

I think most of the individuals in tea were out there to earn enough money to live, they were economic migrants, most of them, they must have been. It was like the opposite of today. Britain did not have enough wealth to employ the people in it, so far as I can tell, so they had to go all over the world to try to make a living . . . It will always happen.

The British were certainly there for economic reasons, they saved up what they could . . . spent as little as they could, which we saw signs of, definitely, they did not spend much money, which would be putting it mildly . . . a bit tight-fisted perhaps. There were some who were terribly generous . . . there were no polo matches going on at that stage, though there was a vast amount of drinking. They worked hard and played hard. I was surprised when I got up there to find out how hard the work was actually. As a box wallah we had been told a little – all we saw when we went up for a short visit was the club. But when you got there you found these guys had to work pretty hard.

As for the wives, there were some famous memsahibs, but

again most of the burra mems were – it was maternalism . . . it was done for the best, there were some very tough ones and there were some less tough ones, but my burra memsahib was very kind-hearted. You can tell from the bungalow servants, they are the ones who will tell you. We knew because one of their main bearers came to work for us – so we knew what it was like to work inside their house. She was the one they would go to if they had a problem. She was seen as compassionate. So I have very fond memories. It was still very much British dominated when I arrived, and it changed while I was still in tea.

The second set of interviews comes from a brief visit to Assam and Calcutta, specifically to study tea in November 2001. On the tea garden in Assam there are some 1,500 permanent and 500 temporary workers.

Altogether there are 6,000 persons, counting families of workers in about 700 houses. The Estate was established in the late nineteenth century. The 'bungalow' was quite palatial, with extensive, carefully tended gardens, and a tennis court. Surprisingly, one could see no tea bushes from the first-floor veranda. The factory was built in 1926 and the coal-fired dryers still used to this day were installed then; their trade name is 'Britannia'.

Mr and Mrs Singha, the Manager and his wife, talked about the old days. Mrs Singha said 'It depends on the individual. People think we are living in these huge bungalows and we have an attitude problem. Some do behave like a memsahib – keep their distance. The one or two I met were all very nice. Not too many are remembered. They were very soft and caring ladies.' Her husband added: 'When the situation turned up they were far more friendly and advised you to your benefit, which is not so today. Today people are not giving advice, or willing to accept it.'

'I have happy memories of interaction with the Sahibs. Very few had that interaction,' Mr Singha told me.

People have the wrong concepts. Many comments are by people who never met them. Because we have huge places to live in, plus servants, there is a wrong concept that we are not accessible to the normal person. The British tea-planters never had the time for interaction with others, and who was the person they could inter-act with? A very limited number. The top of the local administration were all British.

The [Indian] people who came into tea were from army or feudal backgrounds, who had seen this kind of life in their childhoods. The selection of planters was based on their family backgrounds, sport, etc. Play hard and work hard, and enjoy life to the full. That is what the British did at that time, and we were told to do so.

There were hard tasks at that time, we felt miserable and angry at times, but there was very little you could do about it. But you took it in your stride. It was never done with a personal motive, always to educate you to withstand the hardships of tea life. You cannot be very soft in tea. The older generation taught you this, including the ladies who to some people appeared to be very strict. Their noses turned up – but this is not true. The older people who are still in tea, they definitely have very happy memories of the old days.

Fairness of play was there. Strictness is OK. It was never partial treatment. No brutality. Though the workers do mention things where they were scared of the British. Because the punishment was given out on the spot – not referred to a departmental enquiry. The local administration at that time totally backed the gardens. Because the garden management took action based on fairness. You took responsibility for your decisions. The action was never taken with the intention of being unfair. You might make mistakes, but it was not done with a bad motive. In fact, the interaction between workers and management was much closer than you find today. The youngster today is not as close to his worker as he was because we knew what was happening in the mind of the worker. Now there are the pressures of work and time. In the past you went out twice a week to the club and thoroughly enjoyed yourself. There was no other entertainment, so the rest of the time you got involved with the workers. You got to know them better.

We also spent several days in Calcutta and visited a tea auctioning company and watched tea testing and selling. We talked to Mr Gupta, a senior administrator in a tea auctioning company in Calcutta, who had joined a tea company in Assam in 1963 and remained there until 1997. He commented that 'The British do not have anything to be ashamed of. The British were very fair. They started the roads, they started the railways. It was all jungle.'

As for the quality of their business and administrative ability, he said that 'They were very good administrators. They made something where there was nothing.' He agreed that it is 'true that the planters were not interested in local culture' and gave an example of a wife who had tried to learn the language with a local tutor and had been told that it was 'not done' by a superior burra memsahib. He thought that the pressure not to get involved with local culture and people went back to the Mutiny. 'Before that they mixed a lot – after that you have to divide. The British were indeed aloof.' His relations with his British superiors were obviously very warm, since he still visits his 'first burra mem and second burra mem' from time to time in Scotland.

As for the manager's life today, all were agreed that there had been a great decline since the days of the British. Mr and Mrs Singha said:

The standard of living for the managers has definitely come down, though it should have gone up. For the labourers it has definitely gone up in that period. The club life has deteriorated – less interaction, because of TV, etc. There is increased danger and insecurity. People are hesitant to move about at night. The games and fun are gone. Younger ones have their children with them. Family life is much stronger. Younger children are around – mothers and families are tied down. In the past, the children, as in the days of the Raj, were often sent away to school. Now the situation has changed. There is quite a lot of isolation. People have become materialistic – thinking about the future, saving money etc. This is robbing the charm of tea life. In the past you did everything on the spur of the moment – what would you do this weekend was the biggest plan . . .

Now there are increasing pressures of work. Today a tea planter spends some sixty per cent of his time on labour management, there is a huge increase in paper work (for repetitive government form filling, etc.). Also, club life has declined because a lot of local boys are joining tea, so they have local attachments; before people came from far away, hence there was a need for clubs.

One particular added reason for the dramatic change in the pace of work for managers was well described by Mr Das.

> Thirty or forty years ago you just pruned the tea right down. So basically you did not pluck between October and March. By the time I got up there in the mid seventies, three-quarters of the garden would be skiffed – a light pruning, just the top of the bushes. One year I remember we stopped plucking on Christmas Eve, and we got going again by the middle of January. We only had two weeks or so of not working tea, but in the old days tea planters really did have a nice time, they had a six months' season . . . You just went shooting and fishing and what you wanted to do. The factory side was even worse, they were mostly under-machined factories, so they could not cope with the peak days so you ran continuously for up to a week.

Mr Das described his experiences of the conditions of tea labourers as follows.

> By 1975 things had moved on dramatically I can say. I can talk about my experiences in one tea company. I don't believe you can compare the workers on any tea estate in Assam with the inhabitants of Tunbridge Wells. But you can compare the lot of the people living next door to the estates, Assamese

people tilling their fields, living on the land. What have the government been able to provide for them in terms of medical care, schools etc? That is a fair comparison . . .

In terms of medical care, it was excellent. Really very good. Superb hospitals. And we had private aircraft for emergencies to fly people out – I know staff members did. Medical care was very good comparatively, for instance hospitals in nearby parts of India today are much worse.

Schooling was not bad, a big minus was putting economic pressure on people to come out and pluck, but I think that has moved on a bit. Most families would send their kids out to work rather than to school because they needed their money. There were vast amounts of legislation to protect the labourers, they had unions, but the soft things that cannot be legislated are what is important.

I'll give you an example where the Company were not proud, and I was not proud, and that was the housing. Half the houses on the estate were pukka (proper), they were still pretty awful, but they were pukka. And the other half were *katcha* houses which had to be re-thatched every year at vast expense and we would have been much better off building the houses. Cement was in short supply and all housing programmes subject to availability of cement. But if you needed cement to extend the factory, that took priority. This meant that the labour houses did not get done. You would supply water pumps – just hand pumps – bits would not be available. So they packed up. They tried to improve things. People were beginning to pay more attention to the labour line.

So housing was mixed, medical was good, education OK, but subject to pressures (as in England in the industrial revolution). In terms of wages, because that is all collectively bargained, the average wage levels were *way* above the unorganised sector. . . Assamese landlords paid wages that would have been a fraction of that paid to tea workers. Their workers would have killed to get a job on the tea estate.

Moneylenders lent money for marriages and many other emergencies. And the other was alcohol. I remember throwing out Nepali drinks traders. The bondage had changed to that of being in debt and a feeling of hopelessness.

As for the conditions, I have to say that though they were still much better than next door, they were still such that the houses were places where you would prefer to keep a goat, you wouldn't as a human being really want to live in those conditions. Unfortunately this was and is typical of most of India.

As for the circumstances of tea labourers after companies became Indian concerns, Mr Das believed that

it probably went backwards, actually. I think the progressive British firms were ahead of the Indian ones. Speaking freely, the Indian entrepreneur has not been the best, the most responsible corporate citizen. The average Indian business-man is a marwari, the average marwari is not interested in things like this. He is interested in money. To me in India the only people I would hold up as being good citizens are the Tatas. They are not the majority, unfortunately. Certainly the privately owned Indian estates have bad conditions. They are not good: rotten housing, ancient machinery, poor practices. Constantly in trouble for not complying with various things. Not good, no.

As for health:

There was no malaria problem by the time I got there. There was widespread spraying. It was originally sorted out with DDT. Stagnant water was cleared up. Air conditioners were installed in the bungalows. Originally it was a horrendous problem – but by my time a past issue. In fact alcoholism was the main health worry. It was serious, hundreds of workers were to be seen lying by the side of the road in a drunken state after a visit to the cinema and the drinks halls. They drank deadly stuff. I was told that they drank this because there was a calorie shortfall and they needed the energy. But the drink does not have nutritional value, which is why they were so thin. They were very thin – as was everybody else in India. Also they worked from dawn to dusk. But alcoholism amongst tea estate labour was much higher than in rural India.

On the hours and nature of work:

A lot of work was done by women. They were better at it, basically. It was generally based on *tika*, that is, incentive-based. People were paid on output, rather than input. People worked through the daylight hours. Machine work with spraying consisted of two six-hour shifts: twelve hours. People on plucking could work ten or twelve hours a day. Quite a lot of the time was also spent gossiping, chatting.

I seem to remember top pickers achieved figures as high as 20 and 30 kilograms. But it is not the tip of the tea, it is not the two leaves and a bud. That is the fine plucking. A lot of what was actually picked was good heavy stuff, getting down to branches. This coarser tea would be ten or twenty times the weight of the tea tips. If the garden got out of control and the bushes put on a spurt of growth, which happened in the monsoons, then you would get a lot of twigs. You could not just pluck the very light tips. So those who wanted to make money, could do so. Those who couldn't work that hard, ended up in the bungalows – as servants.

I asked Mr Das, who had left India in 1981, what his impression was as to whether things have been on a level, improving or declining since his departure.

I have visited and kept in touch and I get the impression that certainly as far as a life up in Assam it has lost all its nice bits. Because of terrorism in Assam and people being kidnapped on tea estates it has become a pretty horrible environment. How much worse or better off the labourer is today, against his local counterpart, I don't know. But I suspect it has not changed a huge deal. Again it is difficult to tell because there is a whole new middle class in India, and I don't think the tea garden labour have got into that. But maybe the staff have.

Mr and Mrs Singha described education on the tea gardens today.

There are considerable problems with education, many young are disaffected, the state government has taken over the company schools, there is a high drop-out rate, many study up to grade 6 or 7 and they are frustrated and causing anxiety to the tea management. They feel that working in the fields is below their level, a menial job and they become frustrated –

they don't want to work on a tea garden. We want the workers to be educated because an educated worker will work better – those to class 9 or 10 can understand. They live better and habits are changed.

I asked how wages compared to someone working outside the tea garden.

The money that is given may be a little less than a worker outside, but the facilities and privileges are tremendous. He has free housing, free medical care and protective clothing. There is virtually free food, people paying only half a rupee per kilogram of rice or wheat – that is the price it was in 1952. There is a provident fund scheme into which the employer pays twelve per cent of the worker's salary every day and he has a pension scheme, a gratuity scheme, an insurance scheme. His future is well provided. His replacement is more or less guaranteed because we don't have to look outside when he retires or expires, his family is considered first as a custom, a replacement in the same family.

Wage rates for women and men are exactly the same; except tasks for women workers are lower. The international concern that tea employs child labour is absolutely wrong. We do not employ any child labour. They start at fifteen years. From fifteen to eighteen they are adolescent workers, they virtually get the same wages, but their tasks and time of work is only five hours, not eight hours, and if there is task work, they only do half the task.

People work six days a week. There is annual leave – for every fourteen days of work they get one day of annual leave.

And festivals and holidays – a fair amount of these. Normally there are about 300 or 302 working days and about twelve days, paid holidays.

Some jobs are task work, they have incentive tasks such as plucking. The minimum task is 21 kilogram of tea, green leaf. For this they get their full wages. Any leaf more than this, they get another 27 pice for a kilogram. There is pregnancy leave of three months, paid leave with all facilities, with childcare, there are no expenses for them.

The medical facilities are a hundred per cent free; for whatever is curable or treatable on the garden we have a fifty-two-bed hospital, which can take care of minor surgery as well. What cannot be handled there is referred to the civil hospital and their expenses of treatment, checks etc. are all paid by the Company. Not only the worker, but his dependants also are covered. Dependants are children up to school age.

The wages at the moment for men and woken are 43 rupees a day (approximately 70pence or one dollar a day), while adolescents get 17 pice less than this for a daily waged worker.

Things have definitely improved. When I joined tea, we had small children of the age of ten or eleven working in the fields, which is not so now. Now nobody aged under fifteen works on a tea garden. Remember that any developed nation today used to use child labour in the past; even in America now children distribute newspapers etc. A mother can take a daughter to help her if she is fourteen or fifteen, to add onto the mother's extra leaf – we don't encourage it, but don't stop it. A little extra money is earned, but this is not child labour.

The early labour was not bonded, but contracted, though it is true that there was no way in which he or she could get away. Nowadays there is no contract, they are all on permanent service. The Industrial Act of 1952 is there and they have their rules and regulations. They are better protected than the employer.

We are not bringing in labour from other parts of India. We have enough and in fact many are looking for work outside tea. I have a workforce of 1500 permanent persons. And another 500 in the peak season. Another 500 or so of those who live on the estate go outside for work. We don't mind that.

The way a person is working in a tea garden is far better than a lot of the people who are working in the villages. The tea management has to provide a lot of things under the plantation management act. What the government is supposed to do in the villages, but fails to do, is definitely done in the tea gardens . . .

Take our water supply. In the villages they are still drinking water from open wells etc. We have a filtration plant, water is filtered, chlorinated etc. and brought by pipelines. Maybe each house does not have a tap, but they have a common tap to eight to ten houses, they have a bathing enclosure, and they have hygienic toilets. Now whether they use it properly is something it is very difficult to calculate – we try our best. In the small government schools on the estates that have no toilets from the government, we provide the toilets. A healthier worker is a better worker for us – it is costly to treat them.

The main diseases are basically a bit of stomach ailments, seasonal-change epidemics of viral fever. There is no malaria, scientific spraying every six months has seen to that. Inoculation and vaccination against common diseases is enforced one hundred per cent.

There is no malnutrition on tea gardens, because they are given subsidised rations. They have enough land to grow vegetables and they have their own livestock. They eat meat about three times a week. They have goats and pigs. People are not very fond of milk, though many cows are used for tilling and manure. So the mortality rates [infant] are about half of the national average. Statistics are available if you would like to have them.

Mrs Singha spoke about women's lives.

Women are participating more, more earning members. There is equal pay and reasonable maternity leave. There are good doctors on most gardens. As for the education of girls, girls are studying better. The drop-out rate for girls is lower and girls do better in examinations. The normal marriage age for girls is sixteen to eighteen, though the official age is eighteen.

There are health camps, some contraception and family planning and the birth rate is definitely much lower than the national average. This is in our interests; a smaller population allows better facilities. Before, there were large families. Today, life expectancy has gone up with better standards, so now the workers realise that a smaller family is desirable. Workers notice that those who have restricted their families are living a little better. We have records of the size of families; today, the average is three or four children per family. The educated worker who has reached eighth or ninth class is restricting his or her family to no more than three children, though the male child is still preferred. People realise that only one of their children will get a job on the tea garden – and the gardens are not growing.

Mr Singha concluded that 'on my garden most people have electricity in their houses, they have TV sets and so are aware of what is happening in the world. Video films are very popular. Today the worker is more aware of his rights. Not someone who can be bluffed, you can't bluff them today, the union leaders are there. The worker is no longer a thumb-impression-type man. He can read, argue.'

He had just resolved a thirteen-day dispute with workers over the reduced yearly bonus payment. During this they had locked him up for several hours. He had been offered protection, and a number of managers have used guards. But he has turned down this offer. The cost would be the equivalent of his salary, about £5000 a year.

Mr and Mrs Singha admitted that the tea plantation industry is very conservative.

A lot of traditions are still being maintained. The machines are old and they have not been changed. The working standards . . . We are very conservative in introducing anything new. At one point we employed the best brains from the Indian Institute of Technology, when I joined, they did not last more than a year or two. Their brain power was not used. The managers are not qualified in that, so he could not understand them.

In many ways the charm and beauty of tea has remained because we have not changed that much. One factory in South India is totally computerised, but it doesn't produce excellent teas – likewise Japan. We want slow change. Old machines work well – just improvement on the old machines. Tea is basically a food product, it is something you cannot make by machines only. The human touch is essential.

One reason for the slowness of the change has been how difficult it is to improve the efficiency of tea production. It works well enough – why change it? Indeed, some would argue that it works very well indeed – at least in terms of an efficient machine for producing a product. This is well summarised by Mr Das, with his wide range of experience as a management consultant across the world. Looked at from a global perspective, the tea industry is very well organised.

Certain parts of the world, like Calcutta and Assam, are enormously dependent on tea. Hundreds of thousands of people's jobs are dependent on it. What struck me in defence of tea, is this difference: India, which is supposed to know all about growing rice, came fifty-second in the world league tables of yield per acre. In tea we were first by miles. And that I find very encouraging. That to me was the effect of having companies, large holdings, professionalism, even with all the profits coming out, the end result was more productivity.

I believe you don't worry about distributing wealth until you know about how to create it. If you create it, you can raise people's living standards. You can't otherwise. As an efficient enterprise to employ lots of people and give India the position that it still enjoys, I believe that if we had not had the British and the plantation type industry, we would have had thousands of smallholdings like Turkey and places – which is appalling. Just contrast Turkey and India, on how to do it and how not to do it. I have been to Turkey – I brought tea samples back. A broker said the stuff brought back was unsaleable at any price. It is just done like a back-garden hobby, or used to be anyhow.

So the private sector is well organised; capitalism, which people are so quick to criticise, actually employs people. If we had had a socialistic sort of commune way of doing it, I can assure you half the people would be out of work and the standards would be appalling in the hospitals, etc. So I have to say, of the models that we have had, this one worked. And to this day, anything in India which came from that sort of background outperforms the small kibbutz-type thought process.

This does not, however, justify the slowness in the amelioration of the conditions of labour. The benign capitalist model put forward by Adam Smith which believes that a 'hidden hand' of demand and supply will ensure that the workers participate in the gains made by an industry has not tended to work. This was also forcibly recognised by Mr Das. The British may have been reasonably fair and efficient, but, like their *marwari* successors, almost all of them were out to make as much money as possible – and there were few countervailing forces, as all the evidence in earlier chapters shows. This explains his harsh assessment.

In fact, this is how I would sum up the British tea system. The whole British in India thing to me was much more an efficient machine for wealth transfers, if you like. An Englishman told me that twenty-five per cent of the UK's income in 1900 came from India alone, which tells you something.

We should remember that the profits that were made

between 1870 and 1970 beggar belief. I mean, some of these profits were embarrassing. It was not uncommon for a company to make two and a half times its issued capital in a single year. All right, it went on taxes and other things, but tea was a money-spinner – still is. As far as I can tell with the tea industry, when they are having a 'down' they are better off than most industries I have since worked in here.

So if you balance the enormous profits by the owners of these companies over these years against how much they put back into these things, then it is not a terribly good story and I think people would be right to challenge it. But that could be the same in many industries.

The gap between the high life and huge profits of the British and the squalor and misery of the labourers was most obscene in the nineteenth century, but it only really began to be closed in the last quarter of the twentieth century, linked to wider political events.

In April 1979 a few young men met in the ruined palace of the Ahom kings to talk of a free Assam in which the natural resources would be exploited for the benefit of its own people. There had been secessionist movements in the hills around the Assam valley from the 1940s, but it was only in the 1980s that the desire to create a separate Assamese state exploded into a violent secessionist struggle.[130]

The UFLA (United Liberation Front of Assam) 'virtually dismantled the administration and ran a parallel government'. The frustration caused by a hundred years of exploitation exploded into armed revolt, with intimidation, blackmail, robbery and extortion in the name of patriotism, and of claiming for the country rights so long denied.

Links were soon set up with the other insurgent groups – the mujahedin Afghans and Pakistani Intelligence. Pakistan had already put money behind the Nagas and Mizos in their struggles for independent status and now UFLA leaders went off there for intensive training in tactics, counter-intelligence and the use of weapons. Darrah in the North-West Frontier Provinces was the biggest arms market in the world.

The Pakistani intelligence service was encouraging and advised on a large-scale operation in Assam. Disrupt communications they said, attack economic targets like oil fields and blow them up, create chaos and then the whole country will rise. The UFLA leaders were more cautious. They knew how many people relied on government jobs. Dependent on a government they disapproved of, fed up with annual floods, unkept promises, rising unemployment, they could still be wary of a void. At first the UFLA took on a Robin Hood role, robbing banks and businessmen in order to fund road building and dyke making. They were middle-class Assamese and uneasy about violence.

However, they wanted still more training and weapons like the Naga Independence fighters before them and they made use of the Kachin connection. The Kachins over the border in Myanmar (Burma) had been waging a long guerrilla war against their own corrupt government. They were happy to help, but at a price: sixty thousand dollars for arms and training.

The young men who returned to Assam from their camps were harder and more confident. For the next four years Assam was virtually at their mercy. They raided, blackmailed and threatened, and the money poured in. They grew ever bolder and harsher, including kidnap and murder in their methods.

Fake UFLA gangs started to roam about, although if caught their leaders were summarily executed. Tea gardens paid up, few giving less than fifty thousand rupees. In 1990 when the UFLA was at the peak of its power the police were in its pay and a climate of fear spread across the country. The peasantry was quietly 'ignorant' of the insurgent camps near their villages – they were not targets. The state administration seemed unable to act.

In May 1990 the UFLA summoned executives of four big tea companies to a meeting in one of the elegant managers' bungalows. The chief planter spokesman offered to donate a hundred tractors to set up a sunflower seed farm. Thank you no, we want three million rupees, said the UFLA. Some of the companies paid up, but the giant international company Unilever refused. It was this refusal that set in motion a chain of events that brought down the rebels and ended their dream of an independent Assam.

Unilever contacted the Indian High Commission in London and the Disturbed Areas Act was promulgated. On 7 November 1990 a Boeing 737 flew the senior business executives and families out of Assam and the next day General Ajar Singh was summoned. He went back to organise one of the largest peacetime military operations ever seen in India, calling up thirty thousand soldiers in ten days.

At 4 a.m. on 28 November heavily armed troops swept out of barracks in armoured personnel carriers, and helicopters took off to drop paratroops. The UFLA was declared a terrorist organisation and to be a member was a treasonable act meriting the death penalty.

The Indian army, wading in Assam's mud and jungle, did not

find the experience pleasant. Their methods, later exposed by human rights groups, were alleged to include rape and torture. After a prolonged struggle lasting several years, the UFLA melted away, they too leaving behind mass graves to show that that their own behaviour had been questionable to say the least. They had not victimised the villagers, however, who were now terrified by the dawn raids, the harsh questions, the throwing into vehicles and carting away of their menfolk.

In 1992 there were talks in Delhi that rather inconclusively ended the affair. But though Assamese Independence was not gained, the conditions on the tea plantations were finally changed. At last there was real political leverage against the tea organisations. 'These days, large and small companies vie with each other in the setting up of schools for their workers and neighbouring villages, good roads, medical facilities and special training centres for promising athletes, especially footballers,' wrote the journalist, author and film-maker Sanjoy Hazarika in his book *Strangers of the Mist*. 'But much of this has been forced out of the companies at the point of a gun or a veiled written or telephoned threat.'[131] It is well to remember the word 'much'. Clearly there had been a slow, conservative, drift towards improvement as India's economy and society changed. A combination of the Indian economic progress of the 1990s and the threats of political reprisals suddenly spurred further action and the situation for tea labour has changed quite dramatically for the better in the last fifteen years.

As for Assam as whole, it has suffered at a higher level exactly the same fate as the tea labour. That is to say, it has been exploited mercilessly, with relatively little returned investment from its huge resources. Throughout the nineteenth century the wealth from tea exports went mainly to Calcutta and Britain. Then oil was discovered to add to its riches. But little good did this do this distant area. Almost all the profits on the export and use of tea and oil went to the central government. Today, Assam is still one of the most backward and poor states, with literacy and power-availability rates below the national average. It is still mainly growing rice and there is a very poor transportation and industrial infrastructure.[132]

Tea has been an enormous boon for many countries in the world. It should not be beyond the wit of richer nations, and India herself, to ensure that a fairer amount of the profits made from it, as well as from oil and gas, be returned to the people who work in Assam. Extreme actions and boycotting would put the jobs of hundreds of thousands of very poor people at risk. Yet fair trade, with profits going to the producers, should be examined closely in relation to this plantation commodity. Just as it is being examined as a way of improving conditions in the production of cocoa, coffee, rubber, cotton, sugar and other tropical plantation crops, so the considerable profits in tea, and the pleasures of the drinker, should be benefiting the tea labourers much more. It would only seem fair that some of the wealth generated by green gold, which has hitherto flowed elsewhere, should help the people of Assam.

The reasonable conditions which Iris Macfarlane witnessed on the Tata tea estates in Kerala could act as a model for what could be done throughout the tea estates of India and in other tea producing countries.

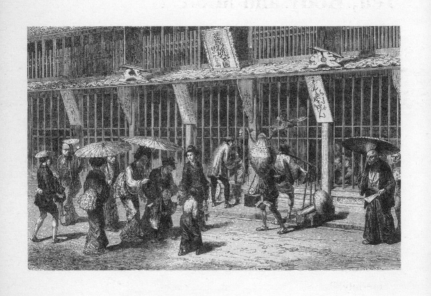

Chapter Thirteen

Tea, Body and Mind

'It is very strange, this domination of our intellect by our digestive organs. We cannot work, we cannot think, unless our stomach wills so. It dictates to us our emotions, our passions. After eggs and bacon it says, "Work!" After beefsteak and porter, it says, "Sleep!" After a cup of tea (two spoonfuls for each cup, and don't let it stand for more than three minutes), it says to the brain, "Now rise, and show your strength. Be eloquent, and deep, and tender; see, with a clear eye, into Nature, and into life: spread your white wings of quivering thought, and soar, a god-like spirit, over the whirling world beneath you, up through long lanes of flaming stars to the gates of eternity!"'

Jerome K. Jerome, *Three Men in a Boat*

The extraordinary fact about tea is that it turns out to be the most important and powerful medical substance on earth. The more than five hundred chemicals a tea leaf contains alter the human body and mind in many ways. And because tea is drunk by over half of the world's inhabitants this effect is widely spread. The effects of tea drinking on the human brain and body, half recognised before the nineteenth century in Asia and Europe, began to be seriously documented from the 1870s onwards.

Western observers in China and Japan during the nineteenth century were well aware of some of the medical benefits of tea. One who understood the role of tea in China better than most was the great American historian of China, S. Wells Williams, who spent forty-three years in the country as a teacher and later became a professor at Yale. In his two-volume *The Middle Kingdom* (1883) he speculated on the substances in the tea that made it attractive and medically beneficial. He did this specifically in a comparative way, placing tea alongside the other stimulating non-alcoholic drinks. 'The chemical analyses which have made known to us the components of the four or five substances used as warm beverages, viz., tea, coffee, maté, cocoa, guarana, and kola, indicate three constituents found in them, to which, no doubt, their virtues are owing.' One of these was a 'volatile oil' that gave tea a particular taste. A second was what he called theine, which we would now call caffeine, which he considered to be 'the chief inducement and reward in its effect on the system'.

If a few finely powdered leaves are placed on a watch-glass, covered with a paper cap and placed on a hot plate, a white vapor slowly rises and condenses in the cap in the form of colorless crystals. They exist in different proportions in the different kinds of tea, from one and one-half to five or six per cent in green tea. Theine has no smell and a slightly bitter taste, and does not therefore attract us to drink the infusion; but the chemists tell us that it contains nearly thirty per cent of nitrogen. The salts in other beverages, as coffee and cocoa, likewise contain much nitrogen, and all tend to repair the waste going on in the human system, reduce the amount of solid food necessary, diminish too the wear and tear of the body and consequent lassitude of the mind, and maintain the vigor of both upon a smaller amount of food. Tea does this more pleasantly, perhaps, than any of the others; but it does more than they do for old people in supplementing the impaired powers of digestion, and helping them to maintain their flesh and uphold the system in health longer than they otherwise would.

Commenting as a Westerner, he added, 'It is no wonder, therefore, that tea has become one of the necessaries of life; and the sexagenarian invalid, too poor to buy a bit of meat for her meal, takes her pot of tea with what she has, and knows that she feels lighter, happier, and better fitted for her toil, and enjoys life more than if she had no tea. Unconsciously she echoes what the Chinese said centuries ago, "Drink it, and the animal spirits will be lively and clear."'

Williams then described what we call phenolics.

The third substance (which is contained in tea more than in the other beverages mentioned) forms also an important ingredient in betel-nut and gambier, so extensively chewed in Southern Asia, viz., tannin or tannic acid. This gives the astringent taste to tea-leaves and their infusion, and is found to amount to seventeen per cent in well-dried black tea, and much more than that in green tea, especially the Japan leaf. The effects of tannin are not clearly ascertained as apart from the oil and the theine, but Johnston considers them as conducing to the exhilarating, satisfying, and narcotic action of the beverage.[133]

In nearby Japan, other observations were made. In the last third of the nineteenth century, the zoologist Edward Morse stated that 'For centuries the Japanese have realized the danger of drinking water in a country where the sewage is saved and utilized on the farms and rice-fields.'[134] He comments that 'experience has taught the Japanese to drink the water boiled or in the form of tea.'[135] This knowledge may explain the fact that even if the few tea leaves were for some reason not available, then water was still boiled.

The medical benefits of tea were particularly stressed in Japan with the dramatic events of the later nineteenth century when cholera entered the country. 'Cholera was very prevalent . . . not a swallow of cold water could be drunk. Tea, tea, tea, morning, noon, and night, and on every possible occasion.'[136] Sir Edwin Arnold wrote during a cholera outbreak in the 1890s, 'I may add that the custom of perpetual tea-drinking greatly helps the Japanese in such a season as this. When they are thirsty they go to the tea-pot, and the boiled water makes them pretty safe against the perils of the neighbouring well.' He had come from India where people were not yet drinking tea except in very restricted circles. The connection between tea drinking and cholera had already been noted in the early nineteenth century in China, where a French factory in Canton 'gets going again when the French decide that tea is a cure for cholera . . .'[137]

The head of the Government Agricultural Bureau of the United States, F. H. King, pointed out at the start of the twentieth century the link between population density and the boiling of water in China and Japan: 'The drinking of boiled water is universally adopted in these countries as an individually available and thoroughly efficient safeguard against that class of deadly disease germs which thus far it has been impossible to exclude from the drinking water of any densely peopled country.' He believed 'boiled water, as tea, is the universal drink, adopted no doubt as a preventive measure against typhoid fever and allied diseases.'[138]

King was writing explicitly in order to influence policy in the United States. He saw that America and Europe might well have to emulate Japan and China in this respect, given the difficulties of supplying safe water. 'So far as may be judged from the success of the most thorough sanitary measures thus far instituted, and taking into consideration the inherent difficulties which must increase enormously with increasing populations, it appears inevitable that modern methods must ultimately fail in sanitary efficiency.' He believed that 'it must not be overlooked that the boiling of drinking water in China and Japan has been demanded quite as much because of congested rural populations as to guard against such dangers in large cities, while as yet our sanitary engineers have dealt only with the urban phases of this most vital problem . . .'[139]

The links between tea and various ailments described above were based largely on observed associations. For most of history, it was impossible to test the connections since the primary micro-organisms and other causal agents were invisible until the age of powerful microscopes. So it is really only after the time of Koch and Pasteur in the later nineteenth century that it became possible to demonstrate how tea might be affecting health. The advent of more powerful laboratory technologies and the discovery of bacteria opened up new possibilities.

In 1911 tannic acid (phenolics), which is the central substance in tea, was 'official in both the British and United States Pharmacopoeias', so it was used in various medical preparations. Its medical value is described thus:

When applied to broken skin or exposed surfaces it . . . [forms] a protecting layer or coat. It is moreover an astringent to the tissues, hindering the further discharge of fluid. It . . . checks haemorrhage when brought directly in contact with the bleeding point . . . In the intestine tannic acid controls intestinal bleeding, acting as a powerful astringent and causing constipation; for this reason it has been recommended to check diarrhoea. Tannic acid is largely used in the treatment of various ulcers, sores and moist eruptions.[140]

The state of research by the 1930s is conveniently shown in the compendium of W. H. Ukers' history of tea, *All About Tea* (1935). There are detailed treatments of the chemistry and pharmacology of tea, but surprisingly little on its possible health benefits. In relation to health, he noted that Major J. G. McNaught, a United States Army Surgeon, had reported that 'The typhoid germ, in pure culture, becomes greatly diminished in numbers by an exposure of four hours to tea. After 20 hours it was impossible to recover it at all from the cold tea.'[141] This is one of the first references to the experimental proof of the antibacterial properties of the phenolics in tea. Otherwise, Ukers merely referred to some possible nutritional benefits. He noted that a Japanese tea advertisement of 1927 claimed that Japanese green tea contains a lot of vitamin C.[142] This might have been based on work done by two Japanese chemists in 1924 where they claimed to have found water-soluble vitamin C, the anti-scorbutic (relieving and preventing scurvy), in quite high quantities in green tea – but absent in black tea. He also referred to unconfirmed work in 1922 to show that tea contained water-soluble vitamin B, the vitamin that prevents beri-beri. But in general the understanding of the reasons for the development and the properties of the phenolics in tea was hardly understood.[143]

What was of more interest to Ukers, since he rightly considered it the main reason for the attractiveness of tea, was the question of caffeine. 'Caffeine is a powerful alkaloid, acting as a stimulant to the human system, and both tea and coffee are drunk largely because of the caffeine they contain.' Ukers discusses the effect of caffeine on heart action and his book contains numerous quotations on the effects of caffeine on human efficiency.[144] Since this is so important, a few of the many observations he makes are worth quoting.

Firstly there is the question as to what extent and how tea made physical effort more effective.

Caffeine acts as a stimulant to the reflex centers in the spinal cord; it enables the muscles to contract more vigorously without producing a secondary depression, so that the sum total of muscular work which can be done by a man under caffeine is greater than that done without it. I cannot resist pointing out how confirmatory of this conclusion is the universal experience of mankind with caffeine beverages-tea, coffee, etc.[145]

Or again:

It has been the custom of athletic trainers in many colleges to give strong tea before contests in tennis or ball or rowing. It is well known that Swiss Alpine guides carry tea and urge its use in climbing mountains. In Russia, where tea is drunk more generally as a beverage than in any other country, those who are called upon to make muscular efforts are given tea in large quantity . . .[146]

Secondly there is the mental effect.

A half-litre of Munich beer containing 15 grams of alcohol brought about an acceleration of mental action for twenty minutes, followed by a period of noticeable depression lasting twice as long. A cup of tea, on the other hand, drove the mental capacity higher by about 10 per cent for three-quarters of an hour, after which the subject of the experiment returned to normal without experiencing the ill-effects that followed the alcoholic stimulant.[147]

One account of how tea strengthens both mind and body is described in the British Pharmaceutical Codex of 1923 when describing the action of caffeine.

The action on the central nervous system is mainly on that part of the brain connected with physical functions. It produces a condition of wakefulness and increased mental activity. The interpretation of sensory impressions is more perfect and correct, and thought becomes clearer and quicker . . . Caffeine facilitates the performance of all kinds of physical work, and actually increases the total work which can be obtained from a muscle.[148]

Early studies showed that subjects who were tested for steadiness, tapping, co-ordination, typewriting, colour-naming, calculations and other tests showed a marked improvement when given caffeine.[149] Recent tests in the late 1990s confirm these findings and show that concentration, discrimination, memory and movement are all markedly improved with the use of tea. This may also be seen in relation to wider discussions of the effects of caffeine in improving thought, learning and 'emotional well-being'.[150]

After the Second World War attention for a time turned elsewhere. The new range of 'wonder drugs', from penicillin onwards, and the receding Western interest in Third World ailments such as typhoid, cholera, dysentery and so on, generally combined to turn research money in other directions. Yet even by 1975 in an important survey of research to that date, Geoffrey Stagg and David Millin were able to show how very widespread the possible effects of tea were. At the end of the article the authors summarise some of the findings, showing the disease or condition, the active principle and the proposed mode of action in relation to tea. Some of the diseases and conditions they list as being affected by tea are as follows: anaemia; dental caries; hypertension and depression; atherosclerosis, angina pectoris, myocardial infarction (heart disease); some forms of hepatitis and nephritis (liver); scurvy and other manifestations of vitamin C deficiency; radiation damage, prevention of leukaemia; bacterial infections (especially typhoid, paratyphoid, cholera and dysentery); toxic goitre, hyperthyroidism; bronchial asthma, gout, vomiting and diarrhoea; indigestion and other stomach disorders; senile capillary fragility, inflammatory conditions, haemorrhagic diseases. They show that polyphenols, vitamins, and caffeine, often working in combinations, could well have beneficial effects in all these areas.[151]

Then, in the 1980s, partly because of the growing realisation that the effectiveness of Western drugs was diminishing rapidly, partly because of an attempt to deal with the growing scourges of old age (cancers, strokes, heart attacks), attention reverted to many herbal and plant remedies in the Third World, among them tea. Much of this research in Western laboratories was confined to the 'Western industrial' diseases, but alongside it, though largely ignored, research was being conducted in Russia, Japan, India and elsewhere into some of the nutritional and epidemiological aspects of tea.

Japanese researchers have been at the forefront of the work. They suggest that the incidence of the succumbing to various cancers (skin, digestive tract, colon, lung, liver and pancreatic among them) is dramatically reduced, and the spread of the cancers often inhibited, by tea drinking.[152] Tea drinking lowers cholesterol levels, reduces blood pressure, helps strengthen the walls of the arteries, and consequently reduces the level of strokes and the incidence of heart disease. Furthermore, tea drinking lowers blood glucose levels and helps to control obesity and diabetes. It has been shown under electron microscopes to kill influenza viruses, as well as a number of harmful bacteria that are carried in water and food. For example, the bacteria which cause cholera, typhoid, paratyphoid and both amoebic and bacillary dysentery are destroyed by the chemicals in tea. Research in the last three years has begun to explain how these results are achieved, for instance by isolating the chemicals (catechins) that inhibit the multiplication of cancer cells.

These and other results, first established in research laboratories, have been increasingly reported by science correspondents in journals and newspapers. At about this time the newspapers also began to report exciting new findings about the possible health benefits of various tannins present in red wine, chocolate and tea. Here are just a few of the examples that have appeared in the British broadsheet press since 1995.

On 24 January 1995 in the *Independent*, under the heading 'Tea may prevent disease, says the latest research', Alex Molloy reported on various studies. 'Recent research from Holland has shown that the death rate from heart attacks among regular tea drinkers is half that of people who never drink tea. A Norwegian study showed decreased death rates from all causes, including coronary heart disease, among those who drank more tea than average.' Furthermore, 'Tea supplies nearly half the average person's intake of manganese, a mineral necessary for healthy joints. Tea is also very rich in fluorides that help prevent tooth decay.'[153] Nor is this all. 'Studies at New Jersey's Rutgers University and the American Health Foundation have linked tea consumption with decreased rates of cancer of the lung, colon, and particularly the skin.'

On 17 May 1995 the medical editor of the *Independent*, Celia Hall, under the heading 'Green tea helps to cut cancer risk', reported on a paper published in the *British Medical Journal*. She wrote that 'Green tea can protect against heart and liver disease and possibly cancer, Japanese researchers say today. They found that the more tea you drink the more you reduce your risk.' The study was on men living in Yoshimi, near Tokyo.

Nigel Hawkes, Science Editor of *The Times*, reported on 20 April 1996 that 'Drinking tea can protect against strokes, a study of the Netherlands has shown. In a 15-year survey of more than 550 men, those who drank the most tea reduced their risk of a stroke by two-thirds compared with those who drank the least.' He comments that 'Earlier studies have shown that flavonoids reduced the risk of heart disease. This is the first to show a protective effect against strokes.'

A small item in the *Sunday Times* on 12 January 1997 reported that 'Drinking tea may help to keep skin cancer at bay, according to a report released last week by Australia's Commonwealth Scientific and Industrial Research Organisation (CSIRO). Mice given black tea developed 54% fewer cancers and skin lesions than those given water and significantly fewer cancers than those given green tea.'

Alec Marsh in the *Sunday Telegraph* on 3 January 1999 reported under the headline 'Tea – the drink that really does make you think'. He wrote that 'Drinking a cup of tea increases concentration and the ability to learn, a study has found. It is especially beneficial to people when they are doing two things at once and also helps them concentrate when they are performing one task after another.' One interesting aspect of this was that 'caffeine was not responsible because those drinking tea out-performed those given a caffeine-only drink.' The experiments consisted of volunteers picking out letters in a long stream, which were flashed onto a screen every half-second. 'Those who did the test after drinking two cups of sugarless tea performed far better than those who drank nothing.'

Cherry Norton reported in the *Independent* on 21 September 2000 under the heading 'What you need is a nice cup of tea', suggesting that tea has real benefits 'such as reducing heart disease by 44 per cent and diminishing the risk of pancreatic, prostate, stomach and lung cancer. The benefits are believed to derive from a range of vitamins, minerals and antioxidants that lead to good nutrition balance and have anti-ageing properties.' Added to this is that 'drinking a lot of tea increases fluid intake, combating conditions, such as constipation and cystitis, caused or exacerbated by low fluid intake.'

The report adds that tea contains a range of important vitamins, such as vitamin A, vitamins B1, B2 and B6. It also is 'a rich source of potassium and manganese. Potassium is vital for maintaining a normal heartbeat, enables nerves and muscles to function, and regulates fluid levels within cells. Manganese is essential for bone growth and overall body development, and five to six cups of tea produce 45 per cent of our daily requirement.'

She refers to Japanese studies which show that 'Japanese men drinking more than 10 cups of green tea a day are less likely to get lung, liver, colon and stomach cancer.' A Chinese study 'found that both black and green tea restricted the development of lung tumours and colon cancer, as well as decreasing the risk of digestive-tract cancer. Furthermore, 'A large number of studies have provided evidence that tea may also help to cut the risk of heart disease, as it reduces cholesterol levels and high blood pressure. '

A report on 22 May 2001 in the *Independent* 'found that the bacteria present in dental plaque stopped growing when people rinsed their mouths with black tea five times for 30 seconds over a 15-minute period'. John von Radowitz in the *Independent* on 23 July 2001 reports that an American study shows that 'Drinking tea combats heart disease by improving the function of artery walls . . . The finding adds weight to previous studies which have concluded that antioxidants called flavonoids, contained in tea, may help prevent cholesterol damaging arteries.'

Lorna Duckworth, in the *Independent* of 9 April 2002, under the heading 'Tea drinkers "have lower risk of cancer"', describes a project undertaken by scientists from the United States and Shanghai Cancer Institute. Starting in 1986, some 18,244 men were monitored for signs of cancer. The researchers found 190 men with stomach cancer and 42 with oesophagus cancer and compared them with 772 similar men without cancer. Of the urine samples, those that indicated the presence of the polyphenol epigallocatechin gallate (EGCG) showed that it was associated with a lower risk of these cancers – and this substance was found to be contained in tea. The study concluded that 'tea drinkers were about half as likely to develop cancer of the stomach or oesophagus as people who were not regular consumers of the beverage.'

Sarah Cassidy in the *Independent* on 7 May 2002 reports, under the heading 'Drinking tea may boost survival rate for heart attack patients', on a study published in the *Journal of the American Health Association*. A study of 1900 American patients in the four years after a heart attack showed that 'Heavy tea drinkers were most likely to have survived while the death rate among moderate tea drinkers was nearly one-third lower than that of those who did not drink tea.' The researchers suggested that the flavonoids in the tea may have stopped the degeneration of the arterial wall and also may have had anti-clotting and relaxing effects.

These are just summaries of the hundreds of scientific papers a year that are now being published to report on the possible health benefits of tea. In 1991 only 153 green tea research reports were published in the entire world. During 1998 the number had reached 625.[154] In 2000, Cherry Norton noted that more than 700 studies of the link between tea and health had been published in the previous year. Not only is the quantity rising very fast, but also much of this work is made available to the layman for the first time through the World Wide Web. Until recently, research results were inaccessible to most people, locked away in learned and difficult to obtain articles. Now the results are available at the touch of a button. They include important recent work that suggests the actual mechanism whereby an enzyme in the tea may prevent the growth of cancer cells.[155]

Comparing older beliefs with this very recent research shows ways in which some of the older benefits have been forgotten. Many supposed benefits of tea – that it is good for eyesight, digestion, menstrual problems, coughs, asthma and ulcers – have faded from the research agenda. Modern research has tended to concentrate on cancers, heart disease, strokes and obesity. In particular, four of the major killers in history, bubonic plague, malaria, influenza and waterborne diseases (cholera, typhoid, dysentery), which earlier writers and doctors thought could be affected by tea drinking, are no longer of much interest to Western research laboratories.

It should be stressed that the research is still, after two thousand years, in its early stages. As they put it in the journals, 'the jury is still out' on many of the supposed connections between tea and health. Some things are definite, for example the effect of tea on concentration, memory, discrimination and the efficient functioning of both mind and body. Or again, there is now no doubt that the phenolics in tea will kill many of the major waterborne bacteria, including typhoid, cholera and dysentery. This must have had an enormous effect in the past.

Less certain is the link in relation to bodily diseases such as cancers, strokes, and heart attacks. Here the research is in a preliminary stage. Experiments with mice have suggested a correlation. Longitudinal studies on human groups have often shown a correlation. The way in which the inhibitions work is beginning to be understood. But large-scale tests on human subjects are only just being carried out.

In relation to other possible associations that would be extremely important, namely with bubonic plague, influenza, malaria and even AIDS, the research has hardly begun. There are suggestions of an association, and in the case of influenza we know that tea kills the virus. But the mechanism and the possible wider effects have not been investigated in relation to the other three diseases. In view of the increasing ineffectiveness of many modern drugs against malaria, the diversity and power of influenza, the possible outbreaks of new pandemics of bubonic plague and the massive tragedy of the AIDS epidemic, it would seem worthwhile for there to be more research in this area.

At this stage it is impossible to be certain as to what the health properties of tea really are. There is a growing body of well-substantiated evidence that tea has a positive effect on the reduction of some diseases, with correspondingly small adverse effects. It would be foolish to be either too confident and proclaim tea as a miracle medicine, or to be so cautious and sceptical that we stopped investigating its properties. At the very least it has had an extraordinarily powerful effect by persuading millions of people to take the trouble to boil the water that they drink. The effort, fuel, time and unpleasant taste of hot water on its own meant that this was an unlikely outcome. Millions have been made healthier just because of this. We also know that applied externally tea acts as an antiseptic. Unlike most other antiseptics, however, it may deal with some dangerous internal bacteria, as well as many other balances in the body. The numerous diseases that are now possibly linked negatively to the chemicals in tea are a potential bonus on top of the hot-water effect.

What, in fact, may be important is the simple fact that over two-thirds of the world's population drink tea regularly every day. It may not be more miraculous than many other plants that have adapted substances in their leaves to protect them against bacteria and viruses – for example the cinchona bark that gave us quinine. As any herbal will indicate, there are numerous plants that contain healthful properties. For example there is a description by the seventeenth-century herbalist Culpeper of the bay tree.

> The berries are very effectual against all poisons of venomous creatures, and the sting of wasps and bees, as also against the pestilence [plague], or other infectious diseases . . . A bath of a decoction of the leaves and berries, is singular good for women to sit in that are troubled with the mother [uterine problems] . . . or the stoppings of their courses [menstrual problems], or of the diseases of the bladder, pains in the bowels by wind and stopping of urine.[156]

The difference is that only a few people drink bay-leaf decoctions, while millions daily drink tea. Because of the caffeine and for political, economic and social reasons, whole civilisations have taken to tea and drink almost nothing else. If it does contain antibacterial and other agents among the more than 500 chemical compounds which have been found in the most recent tabulation of its properties (and many of whose effects are still little understood), then it could indeed be having a very great impact on world health.[157]

Chapter Fourteen

Bewitched Water

"No," he said, "look, it's very, very simple . . . all I want . . . is a cup of tea. You are going to make one for me. Keep quiet and listen." And he sat. He told the Nutri-Matic about India, he told it about China, he told it about Ceylon. He told it about broad leaves drying in the sun. He told it about silver teapots. He told it about summer afternoons on the lawn. He told it about putting in the milk before the tea so it wouldn't get scalded. He even told it (briefly) about the history of the East India Company.

"So that's it, is it?" said the Nutri-Matic when he had finished.

"Yes," said Arthur, "that is what I want."

"You want the taste of dried leaves in boiled water?"

"Er, yes. With milk."

"Squirted out of a cow?"

"Well, in a manner of speaking I suppose . . ."

Douglas Adams, *Hitchiker's Guide to the Galaxy*

The two main strands in this history of tea and its influence, the positive and the negative, are constantly intertwined. The global story of the way in which tea spread and was consumed saw some of the extraordinary successes and effects of tea. This success stems back to its earliest origins. In order to survive in the hothouse of the eastern Himalayas, the most plant-rich and contested eco-system in the world, a plant had to evolve very superior weapons of 'offence' and 'defence'. If it was a species that propagated itself by means of nuts or berries, it had to be attractive to birds or mammals such as monkeys, so that they would spread its seeds by eating them. Since there were so many edible leaves and berries available, if the plant was to survive the rigours of evolution, it was not good enough just to be tasty. An added attractor was needed. In the case of the tea camellia, the main attractor may have been caffeine. This would have the unusual double effect of pleasing both the body and the brain of many species that ate it.

The caffeine attractor had been used successfully in the wet and competitive jungles of another continent by the cocoa and maté plants of South America and in the difficult ecologies of the deserts of the Middle East by the coffee plant. That caffeine may have been developed in a wide range of plants as an attractor does not, of course, mean that it does not have other uses in the development of the plant. It may also be that the alkaloid was useful in helping to build up the protein molecules necessary for the plant's growth. Others argue that it is caused by the decomposition of molecules. Yet the very fact that many are still puzzled as to the exact biological role of so much caffeine in the tea leaf lends support to the idea that it was selected for a number of reasons.

In its fight for survival, the camellia faced another problem, how to improve its defences against predatory micro-organisms, fungi, bacteria of various kinds, particularly when it has been damaged. Trees develop antibacterial and fungal chemicals in their bark, various tannins including 'oak gall', which are often used by humans as medicines. Coffee and cocoa beans used the protection of their tough shells. The beans inside do not need to incorporate elaborate defences of this kind. Camellia and grapevines did not take this route, but instead, through millions of years, evolved another solution. They generated certain substances in their coating, in the skin of the grape or the shiny surface of the green leaf that could act as a shield against marauding micro-organisms.

These chemicals would kill off some of the predatory bacteria, amoeba, rusts, moulds and other parasites. Although some penetrated the defences, and tea is still a prey to many pests, fungi, rusts, and moulds, on the whole, it was very successful. It has been noted that unlike, say, coffee or the potato or vines, 'no serious disease has yet devastated the tea industry'. Later, humans were accidentally to add to its antibacterial strength, for when leaf is rolled, there is an immediate decrease in the number of micro-organisms due to the antiseptic properties of the chemicals released from the crushed tea leaves.[158]

Some 40 per cent of the solid weight of tea is taken up by the tannins (phenolics) and similar chemicals in the leaf. Phenolics are among the most powerful, broad-ranging, set of antibacterial substances ever discovered by man. For example, they were the antiseptic substance which Joseph Lister, among others, used to help make the later nineteenth-century hospitals sterile and operations safe. So the camellia (and also the grape) developed an enormously powerful defensive system in its skin.

As well as being a defensive mechanism, the powerful antiseptic feature of the tea leaf may also have been useful as an attractor. It has long been observed that monkeys are able to make an association between their health and certain plants. They have learned that if they have a wound or infection, they can chew a tea leaf and spread the saliva with the chewed leaf on the wound and it would be more likely to heal. We may also suggest that evolution worked through this more indirect method. Those monkeys that fed off the camellia would be fitter and survive better since the leaf would kill off harmful bacteria in their mouths and stomachs, and they would be more agile and successful from the stimulant effect of the caffeine. So a symbiosis between monkeys and tea may have been established well before man appeared on the scene.

First, monkeys spread tea through the Assam-Burma-South West China jungles. Then tribal peoples and traders discovered its uses. They brought it to the attention of inhabitants of the greatest empire on earth, in China. Tea colonised an area of East Asia that comprised over half the population of the world and altered religion, economy, aesthetics, crafts and society, accompanying the flowering of Chinese and Japanese civilisation. It may also have brought destruction and invasion. In Mongolian and Manchurian hands it may have contributed to the conquests of much of Russia, of the Islamic Empires and of China itself. Yet until the seventeenth century it was still almost exclusively used in the Mongolian-dominated parts of the world. The New World, Africa, India and Western Europe did not drink tea.

Between 1600 and 1900 it spread first to western Europe, the Middle East and Russia and, principally through the British Empire, began to be planted in many parts of the equatorial belt. It began to be drunk by the Indo-European peoples of western Asia (India, Islamic societies, Russia and Europe) and by the Empire's new offshoots (Canada, Australia, United States).

Against what may be considered positive effects have to be set the immense environmental and human costs. In the West, tea and sugar were accompanied by a form of sweated labour in factories and mines. Even more appalling was the exploitation of hundreds of thousands of workers on the tea estates, made more obscene by the huge profits of the tea garden managers and shareholders.

Likewise the accounting in relation to its effect on the rise and fall of empires is complex. It played an important part in the rise of China, Japan and Britain. But each of these new empires extorted a heavy price from its neighbours, as well as its own citizens and colonial dependants. In the case of China, for example, while it probably helped promote the glories of the Tang and the Sung civilisations, later it brought nemesis in the conquests by the British. Likewise in relation to Britain, the beneficial effects have to be set against the negative effects of the industrialism which tea encouraged, and the empire that it helped to create in India, including the ravaging of Assam.

Over the last twenty years, conditions on at least some of the tea plantations have improved. Furthermore, the gross exploitation, whereby all the profits left the country and went to Britain or other Western countries, is now less pronounced. After Independence, the gardens in Assam were handed over to Indian managers and mainly owned by Indian tea companies.

Human beings are the most successful large predators in history. They have munched their way through almost all the other species on earth, or enslaved them to their use. Yet they have one deadly competitor, which, in terms of evolutionary fitness, is their superior. Micro-organisms are too small for the human eye to see and capable of multiplying enormously fast.

Protozoa, amoeba, viruses and above all bacteria, pack the
human body and the surface of the earth.

Throughout human history, until the last one hundred and forty
years, humans were only aware of their effects. Apart from
limited sightings with early microscopes from the second half of
the seventeenth century, people could not see or understand the
workings of this invisible kingdom. Consequently, the efforts to
counter the dangerous micro-organisms were largely ineffective.
The problem was compounded by the fact that any economic and
productive success by a society, allowing denser and more
concentrated populations, also improved the chance that
microbes would replicate faster. It made the bacteria, which
could be transmitted in many ways, an ever-greater menace.

Evolving so slowly and being so relatively large and open to
attack, humans rely for their defence on several things, including
the immune systems that they share with other mammals. What
differentiates them from other animals, however, are two special
capabilities. One is their ability to generate, store and
communicate large amounts of reliable knowledge about the
world. The other is that they can use this knowledge in either
shaping existing resources or inventing new tools.

Yet in the struggle against bacteria, until the 1870s, when
Pasteur, Koch and others established their presence, there was
no way in which the enemy could be seen. So the techniques for
overcoming disease were hit and miss. In order to reach the level
which would produce sufficient knowledge and technology to
combat these diseases, a previous scientific and industrial
civilisation was a pre-requisite. Such a revolution could only
have happened if the normal spread of bacteria was held at bay.
How was this to occur if the enemy was invisible and little

understood? There seemed to be a vicious circle, with no way out.

For millions of years the world had witnessed similar struggles between plants, animals and bacteria. Through blind or random variation and then selective retention of successful strategies, certain plants and animals had thrived. When *homo sapiens* emerged, the species was heir to this vast set of experiments and fruitful outcomes. Men and women used various species that had already evolved to build a way of life, domesticating the wide range of plants and animals around them in order to build their civilisations.

The domestication of most plants and animals which serve as foods was largely undertaken with practical goals in mind and the benefits were usually obvious and immediate. A person was hungry, weak, tired. He or she ate and enjoyed the taste of a grass, fruit and leaf, and felt full and strong. All this was apparent and perceptible to humans. But in the war with microbes it was never certain as to where the enemy might be lurking. Perhaps illness and death were sent by spirits, witches, ancestors, gods or written in the stars. The world of thronging minute objects was not visible.

Any technology to combat microbial diseases would have to rest on blind variation and selective retention by human beings who began to notice an association between some actions, such as eating a plant or instituting quarantine, and better health. At a larger level, a population which made a correct connection by chance and then by choice would thrive and win out in the long struggle.

In this way, many useful plants and substances were noted.

Recent work has shown that many of those included in the herbal pharmacopoeias of Eastern and Western medicine were genuinely effective. Some, like quinine, quickly became famous. Most, like dock leaves to soothe nettle stings or St John's wort to relieve depression, or ginseng for many diseases, evolved over the ages. While many of them healed, hardly any of the herbal remedies provided protection against the disease in the first place. Some kind of powerful bactericide was needed, evolved by nature and then adopted and domesticated so that it could be produced in vast quantities.

There has only been one such plant in history, at least one which has become almost universally consumed. Tea not only contains an appropriate mix of antibacterials, but also contains other attractors that make it the most popular and widely distributed health-giving plant in history. Discovered by accident and used for all sorts of reasons, only now are we beginning to understand a little of how it has provided humans with one of their most important defences against disease.

The problem of polluted drinking water was solved in the developing societies in the century or so after 1870, when it became possible to monitor water and to provide safe, piped, drinking water. That this is a very recent phenomenon, and not ubiquitous even in Europe, is well known. Many still remember holidays in the 1960s and 1970s when British or American citizens were advised to avoid dangerous tap water in Spain, Italy, Greece and even France. Only a few north European countries and America were relatively safe. Now, on the whole, the developed world has safe public drinking water.

Yet, according to a recent series on water and health, some 1.1

thousand million people, approximately one-sixth of the world's population, do not have access to safe drinking water. On average, it is 6 kilometres to the nearest water supply in large areas of Africa and Asia, from which people (mostly women) have to carry 10–16 kilograms of water each day or two. Much of this water is unsafe. Combined with the fact that four-tenths of the world population do not have access to adequate sanitation, this still leads to a vast amount of ill-health and death from waterborne diseases. The same programme alleged that half of the world's sickbeds were occupied by people with waterborne diseases, and that a child dies every fifteen seconds of waterborne disease, many of them in infancy.[159]

The problems persist. How is a human being living in an increasingly crowded world, and often in the vastly expanding cities of the Third World, to ingest a daily average of two pints of safe liquid when cold water is heavily polluted and raw milk both unsafe and unobtainable by most people? Coffee, chocolate, wine, whisky, sake, all these and many other drinks, as we have seen, are unsuitable or too costly. Until the water becomes safe there seems to be only one option, namely the one which the East Asians discovered over many centuries – to drink tea.

Tea has one major drawback. Although in itself it is usually relatively cheap and leaves can be re-used, tea needs boiling water. The water has to be boiled using fuel, usually wood. The fact that half the energy requirements for people in the Third World is for fuel for cooking and heating is an enormous drain on family resources. Having to boil water for tea adds to this expense.

Yet the alternative to tea drinking is unthinkable. If the two-thirds of the world's population who live in China, Japan, India and South East Asia were suddenly deprived of tea (for example, if the bush were to suffer some blight equivalent to what happened to potatoes in Ireland or grapevines in France) the death rates would soar. Many cities would collapse, infants would die in large numbers. It would be a catastrophe.

And so it does not seem unreasonable to suggest that any government or charity concerned with improving the conditions of large swathes of the world's poor could do worse than look into the possibilities of encouraging the distribution of powdered or leaf tea. Simultaneously, they should investigate ways in which this invigorating, social and healthful drink could be produced with the minimal use of fuel. If history repeated itself, this action could save more lives and create more happiness than any other 'medicine' that could be provided. At the same time, the unsatisfactory conditions on the tea gardens that produce tea need to be investigated, so that the tea garden labourers who provide this extraordinary medicine are more properly rewarded in every way.

Today, in the advanced industrial nations with clean, piped water supplies and the wealth to buy other drinks, the problem of waterborne disease has largely disappeared. From this we might conclude that the health-giving properties of tea have finished playing their part. They may have helped to make our world possible, but surely now tea is mainly an energy restorative and no longer a medicine?

In industrial, urban nations, the major killers are the diseases of middle and older age, particularly cancers of various types, heart diseases (coronary) and brain conditions (strokes). It is now beginning to be suggested that the tea bush's evolutionary strategy had, by pure accident, developed substances that were useful. Contained within the complex batch of polyphenols and flavonoids, which make up much of the solids of tea, are not only antibacterial and antifungal agents, but also a series of antioxidants, vitamins and other chemicals. Their nature and effects are as yet little understood, but as they are studied and tested they increasingly suggest that tea may have other properties beyond making liquids safe to drink. Many degenerative diseases seem to be mitigated by tea drinking, or so the research is starting to suggest.

Much of the health, inspiration and happiness of the human species has arisen out of this modest green bush. A vast industry that produces, transports, auctions, advertises and sells this leaf has emerged and held many nations on earth in its grip. Tea provides up to three-quarters of the world's population with much of their daily liquid requirements.

It is a plant which has made millions of people's lives tolerable, even pleasurable. The rich could enjoy the scented teas and social grooming; the poor could struggle through another day in the factories, mines, plantations and fields with the help of tea. Without it their children would often have died in far larger numbers and their exhausted bodies and minds would find it even more difficult to cope.

And yet so much suffering and indignity for millions of workers on tea plantations has been caused in order to produce the 'green gold' whose value made others rich. It is astonishing to think of what lies behind what seems such an innocent, mild, brown or green liquid. De Quincey was right to describe tea as 'bewitched water'.

Notes

Chapter 2: The Story of an Addiction
  1 Goodwin, *Gunpowder*, 61

Chapter 3: Froth of the Liquid Jade
  1 Hardy, *Tea Book*, 138
  2 Ukers, *Tea*, II, 398
  3 Ukers, *Tea*, II, 398
  4 Okakura, *Tea*, 3
  5 Lu Yu, *Classic*, 60
  6 Wilson, *Naturalist*, 97–8
  7 Wilson, *Naturalist*, 98
  8 Okakura, *Tea*, 47
  9 Okakura, *Tea*, 44
 10 Jill Anderson, quoted in Weinberg and Bealer, *Caffeine*, 36
 11 Ukers, *Tea*, II, 399
 12 Ukers, *Tea*, II, 432
 13 Ukers, *Tea*, II, 400
 14 Quoted in *Encyclopaedia Britannica*, 1910–11, 'Tea', p.482
 15 Williams, *Middle*, II, 53
 16 For an excellent account, see Okakura, *Tea*. For a longer

description of the tea ceremony, see
www.alanmacfarlane.com/tea

17	Frederic, *Daily Life*, 75; Kaisen, *Tea Ceremony*, 101

18	Weinberg and Bealer, *Caffeine*, 133

19	Paul Varley in *Cambridge History of Japan*, 3:460

20	Morse, *Japanese Homes*, 149–51

21	From Hammitzsch, *Zen* , 59–60

22	The quotations are from Okakura, *Tea*, 29-30, 54,
	80–1,129

23	Morse, *Japanese Homes*, 151–2

Chapter 4: Tea Comes to the West

24	The account given here is very brief. A much fuller one is
	contained in Macfarlane, *Savage Wars*, 144-9, and also on
	www.alanmacfarlane.com/tea

25	Bowers, *Medical Pioneers*, 36

26	Ferguson, *Drink*, 24

27	Ukers, Tea, I, 40

28	Dr Nicolas Tulpius, *Observationes Medicae*, Amsterdam,
	1641, quoted in Ukers, *Tea*, I, 31–2

29	Ukers, I, p.32; *Les Grandes Cultures*, p.216

30	Quoted in Porter and Porter, *In Sickness*, 220

31	Short, *Dissertation*, 40–61

32	Lettsom, *Natural History*, 39ff

33	Quoted in Braudel, *Structures*, 251; for further statistics of
	a more detailed kind, see Macfarlane, *Savage Wars*, 145
	and figures on the website

34	Drummond and Wilbraham, *Food*, 203

35	Earle, *Middle Class*, 281

36	Davis, *Shopping*, 210

37	Kames, *Sketches*, III, 83

38	Quoted in Drummond, *Food*, 203

39 Quoted in Marshall, *English People*, 172

40 Ukers, *Tea*, I, 47

41 de la Rochefoucauld, *Frenchman*, 23, 26

42 Quoted in Drummond, *Food*, 204

43 Quoted in Wilson, *Strange Island*, 154

44 On the interesting widespread use of tea in the Netherlands from the 1660s onwards, see Ukers, *Tea*, II, 32, 421

45 The importance of a previous history of hot drinks, and of the relative affluence of the British middle classes, is discussed by Burnett, *Liquid Pleasures*, 186

Chapter 5: Enchantment

46 There is a description of it in 'The tale of a teabag' by Fran Abrams, in the *Guardian* (*G2* magazine), 26 June 2002

47 Ukers, *Tea*, I, 46; the story of Lyons tea houses is in Ukers, II, 414

48 Burgess, *Book of Tea*, 10

49 Troubridge, *Etiquette*, II, 2

50 Messenger, *Guide to Etiquette*, 66

51 Maclean, *Etiquette and Good Manners*, 66

52 Stables, *Tea*, 77

53 Talmage, *Tea-Table*, 10

54 Quoted in Kowaleski-Wallace, *Consuming*, 19

55 Burnett, *Liquid Pleasures*, 49–50, 63

56 Williams, *Middle Kingdom*, II, 54

57 Ovington, *Tea*, dedication

58 Sumner, *Popular*, 42

59 Sigmond, *Tea*, 135

60 Stables, *Tea*, 111

61 Pascal Bruckner, quoted in Burgess, *Tea*, 126

62 Raynal, quoted in Ukers, *Tea*, I, 46

63 Scott, *Story of Tea*, 195

64 Hobhouse, *Seeds*, 1999, 136, 138-9
65 Burnett, *Liquid Pleasures*, 51
66 The advertisement is reprinted in Ukers, *Tea*, I, 42
67 Davis, *Chinese*, 375
68 Mintz, *Sweetness*, 214

Chapter 6: Replacing China

69 See photographs in Ukers, *Tea*, I, 300, 464
70 Gordon Cumming, *Wanderings*, 317–8
71 Wilson, *Naturalist*, 93
72 Quoted in Ukers, *Tea*, I, 465
73 Gordon Cumming, *Wanderings*, 317–8
74 Dyer Ball, *Things Chinese*, 644
75 Ball, Account, 352-3
76 Isabella Bird, *Yangtze*, 142–3
77 Wilson, *Naturalist*, 95
78 Ball, *Account*, 354
The monetary units are as follows, reading from the left: tael (a monetary unit formerly used in China, equivalent in value to this weight of standard silver); mace (one tenth of a tael); cent (one tenth of a mace) candareem (one tenth of a cent)
79 The section on the Opium Wars is largely based on Henry Hobhouse, *Seeds*, 1999, 144–52
80 Davis, *Chinese*, 370
81 Hobhouse, *Seeds*, 1999, 152
82 Bramah, *Tea*, 81 A fruit the size of a small apple with a thick, pulpy purple rind encasing segments of succulent white flesh encasing seeds of varying sizes
83 Ball, *Account*, 334–5
84 Fortune, *Tea Districts*, II, 295

Chapter 7: Industrial Tea

85 Charles Bruce's Report is in the *Report of the Agricultural and Historical Society, 1841*, India Office Tracts, no.320
86 Bruce's Report

Chapter 8: Tea Mania

87 St Andrews University Library, Scotland
88 Carnegie letters, India Office Library, BL

Chapter 9: Empire of Tea

89 *The March of Islam AD 600–800* (Amsterdam, 1988), 108
90 Griffis, *Mikado's Empire*, II, 409–10
91 Scidmore, *Jinrikisha*, 254
92 See Macfarlane, *Savage Wars*, chapters 7, 9
93 Morse, *Day*, II, 192
94 Arnold, *Seas*, 543
95 Black, *Arithmetical*, 164
96 Heberden, *Observations*, 34–5, 40–1
97 Place, *Illustrations*, 250
98 Kames, *Sketches*, I, 245
99 Blane and Rickman are both quoted in George, *London*, 329, n. 103
100 George, *Some Causes*, 333–5
101 Burnett, *Liquid Pleasures*, 56, 187
102 Ukers, *Tea*, I, 67
103 Scott, *Story of Tea*, 100, 99; Reade, *Tea*, 65
104 M. A. Starr, MD, Emeritus Professor of Neurology, Columbia University, New York, in the New York Medical Record, 1921. Quoted in Ukers, *Tea*, I, 556
105 Burgess, *Book of Tea*, 16
106 *The Lancet*, London, April, 1908, p. 301: quoted in Ukers, *Tea*, I, 554

107 No.746, dated 25th October 1879, to the Secretary to the
Surgeon-General, Calcutta: medical appendix from
Maitland's *Report*

108 *The Lancet*, London, April, 1908, pp. 299–300; quoted in
Ukers, *Tea*, I, 554

109 Professor Edward Parkes, quoted in Ukers, *Tea*, I, 553; the
link to malaria is discussed in Chapter 13, 'Tea, Body and
Mind'. At present it is just a conjecture

110 *Chambers Encyclopaedia*, 'Tea', 481

111 Quoted in Reade, *Tea*, 16

Chapter 10: Industrial Tea

112 The passages are taken from Ball, *Account*, 336, 342,
357–8, 361

113 *Daily Telegraph* special issue, 28 February 1938, vii

114 Harler, *Tea*, 64

115 Based on Ukers, I, 157–8

116 Dyer Ball, *Things Chinese*, 647; for a useful diagrammatic
representation of this, see Forest, *Tea*, 189

117 An anonymous informant, quoted in Gardella, *Harvesting*

118 Dyer Ball, *Things Chinese*, 648

Chapter 11: Tea Labour

119 Money, *The Cultivation and Manufacture of Tea*

120 Henry Cotton's Scrapbook, see bibliography

121 In India Office Library, MSS/EUR/F/174

122 In India Office Library, MSS/EUR/F/970

123 In India Office Library, MSS/EUR/F/1036

124 Pilcher, *Navvies of the 14th Army*

125 Tyson, G. *Forgotten Frontier*

Chapter 12: Tea Today

126 See Chatterjee, *Time for Tea*. For another interesting account of conditions in tea, see *Guardian* , *G2*, 25 June 2002, 'The Tale of a Teabag' by Fran Abrams

127 The following account is based on some brief investigations carried out in 2001. In the interviews I conducted (all of which I filmed and re-analysed) I tended to cover a central range of topics, with some extra, specific, questions for each informant

128 Names of the informants whose filmed interviews are transcribed here have been changed, except for Smo Das, which is his real name

129 The following compressed account is largely based on Hazarika, *Strangers*

130 Hazarika, *Strangers*, 264

131 Details are given in Hazarika, *Strangers*, especially 263–4

Chapter 13: Tea, Body and Mind

132 Williams, *Middle Kingdom*, II, 52

133 Morse, *Day*, II, 192

134 Morse, 'Latrines', *American Architect and Building News*, xxxix, no.899, 172

135 Morse, *Day*, II, 192

136 Goodwin, *Gunpowder*, 37

137 King, *Farmers*, 323,77

138 King, *Farmers*, 323–4

139 *Encyclopaedia Britannica*, 1910–11, 'Tannin'

140 Ukers, *Tea*, I, 557

141 Ukers, *Tea*, II, 301

142 Ukers, *Tea*, I, 547, 514

143 Ukers, *Tea*, I, 520, 540

144 H. C. Wood, Jr., MD, Professor of Pharmacology of the

Medico-Chirurgical College, Philadelphia: *Tea and Coffee Trade Journal*, New York, October, 1912, 356

145 M. A. Stare, M D, Emeritus Professor of Neurology, Columbia University, New York, in the *New York Medical Record*, 1921

146 R. Pauli, PhD, Professor of Psychology in the University of Munich, quoted in the *Tea and Coffee Trade Journal*, New York, July, 1924, 54–6.

147 Quoted by Ukers, *Tea*, I, 539

148 See the table in Ukers, I, 542

149 See Weinberg and Bealer, *Caffeine*, chapter 16

150 Stagg and Millin, 'Nutritional', 1975

151 A fuller account behind this brief summary is to be found on *www.alanmacfarlane.com/tea*

152 Of course, the manganese content will vary considerably, depending on the quantity of manganese in the soil in which the tea bushes are growing.

153 See www.galaxymall.com/books/healthbenefits/greentea.html

154 See *www.alanmacfarlane.com/tea* for a summary of some of the reported health benefits as described on the Internet

155 Quoted in Hylton, *Rodale Herb Book*, 360

156 The figure of 500, and a description of their nature, is to be found in *Green Tea* by Ling and Ling, 71. Chapter 5, on 'The Pharmacological Effects of Green Tea', contains a recent survey on research on the medical effects of tea

Chapter 14: Bewitched Water

157 Ukers, *Tea*, I, 390–1; Harler, *Tea*, 58, 78; *Chambers Encyclopaedia*, 'Tea', 482

158 BBC, Radio 4, 29 July 2001, *Water Story*

Bibliography and Further Reading

Supplementary materials on the World Wide Web

A number of topics mentioned in the text are dealt with in more depth in a set of appendices on my website: www.alanmacfarlane.com/tea
These include:

Tea; a view from South India, October 2002
Modern methods of tea growing and processing
Some possible effects of tea on health
Medical effects of tea reported on the Internet

There are also (for those with broadband connections) some films of tea production and the authors talking about tea and related matters.

Manuscript sources

Chapter 7 'Green Gold': India Office Tracts, vol.320 for Charles Bruce's account. Copies of papers received 22 February 1839, HMSO. For Tea Committee, sf/A30.B7E 39,63 in St Andrew's University Library, Scotland.

Chapter 8 'Tea Mania': The Carnegie letters are in the India Office Library at the British Library, MSS/EUR/C682. The report on coolie immigration is at the same F/174/968.

Chapter 11 'Tea Labour': Reports on all the Commissions of Enquiry are to be found at the India Office Library, British Library, in MSS/EUR/F174. Of special interest are those of Rege (1006), Desphende (1007), Lloyd Jones (1008), TUC (1036), Cotton (589,597,1165), Dowding (970), Royal Commission (1030), Shadow Force (1313), Report on Emigrants (968). Henry Cotton's Scrapbook is in MSS/HOME/Misc/D1202.

Some of the above correspondence has been reprinted in *The Colonization of Waste-Lands in Assam, being a reprint of the official correspondence between the Government of India and the Chief Commissioner of Assam*. (Calcutta, 1899)

Books and articles

Unless specified otherwise, place of publication of books is London.

Allen, Stewart L., *The Devil's Cup: Coffee, the Driving Force in History* (1999)

Antrobus, A. A. *History of the Assam Company* (1957)

Arnold, Sir Edwin, *Seas and Lands* (1895)

Baildon, Samuel, *Tea Industry in India* (1882)

Bailey, F. M., *China, Tibet, Assam* (1945)

Bald, Claud, *Indian Tea* (1940)

Ball, Samuel, *An Account of the Cultivation and Manufacture of Tea in China* (1848)

Bannerjee, Sara, *The Tea Planter's Daughter* (1988)

Barker, G. A., *A Tea Planter's Life in Assam* (1884)

Barpujari, H. K., *Assam in the Days of the Company* (1980)

Barua, B. K., *A Cultural History of Assam* (1951)

Bird, Isabella, *The Yangtze Valley and Beyond* (1899; Virago reprint 1995)

Black, William, *An Arithmetical and Medical Analysis of the Diseases and Mortality of the Human Species* (1789)

Bowers, John Z., *Western Medical Pioneers in Feudal Japan* (Baltimore, 1970)

Bramah, Edward, *Tea & Coffee: a Modern View of Three Hundred Years of Tradition* (1972)

Brand, Dr Van Someren le (ed.), *Les Grandes Cultures du Monde* (Flammarion, Paris, early twentieth century)

Braudel, Fernand, *The Structures of Everyday Life* (1981)

Breeman, J., *Taming the Coolie Beast* (Oxford, 1989)

Brewer, John and Porter, Roy (eds), *Consumption and the World of Goods* (1993)

Brown, Peter B., *In Praise of Hot Liquors: The Study of Chocolate, Coffee and Tea-Drinking 1600–1850* (1996)

Burgess, Anthony (preface), *The Book of Tea* (Flammarion, no date, by various authors)

Burnett, John, *Liquid Pleasures: A Social History of Drinks in Modern Britain* (1999)

Cambridge History of Japan, Vol. III, 'Medieval Japan'. ed. Kozo Yamamura, Cambridge University Press, 1990

Chamberlain, Basil Hall, *Japanese Things: Being Notes on Various Subjects Connected with Japan* (Tokyo, 1971)

Chambers Encyclopaedia, 1966, 'Tea'

Chatterjee, Piya, *A Time for Tea: Women, Labor, and Post/*

Colonial Politics on an Indian Plantation (2001)

Clarence-Smith, William Gervase, *Cocoa and Chocolate, 1765–1914* (2000)

Cotton, Henry, *Indian and Home Memories* (1911)

Cranmer-Byng, J. L. (ed.) *An Embassy to China: Being the journal kept by Lord Macartney during his embassy to the Emperor Ch'ien-lung 1793–4* (1962)

Crole, David, *Tea* (1897)

Daily Telegraph and Morning Post supplement, 28 February 1938. 'Empire Tea', various articles

Das, R. K., *Plantations Labour in India* (1931)

Davis, Dorothy, *A History of Shopping* (1966)

Davis, John Francis, *The Chinese: a General description of China and its Inhabitants* (1840)

Drummond, J. C. and Wilbraham, Anne, *The Englishman's Food, a History of Five Centuries of English Diet* (revised edn, 1969)

Dyer Ball, J., *Things Chinese* (1903; reprint Singapore, 1989)

Earle, Peter, *The Making of the English Middle Class* (1989)

Encyclopaedia Britannica, 11th edition, 1910–11

Ferguson, Sheila, *Drink* (1975)

Forrest, Denys, *Tea for the British: The Social and Economic History of a Famous Trade* (1973)

Fortune, Robert, *Three Years' Wanderings in the Northern Provinces of China* (1847)

___, *The Tea Districts of China and India* (1853)

Frederic, Louis, *Daily Life in Japan, at the time of the Samurai, 1185–1603* (1972)

Gardella, Robert, *Harvesting Mountains: Fujian and the China Tea Trade, 1757–1937* (1994)

George, M. Dorothy, 'Some Causes of the Increase of Population in the Eighteenth Century as Illustrated by London', *Economic Journal*, vol. xxxii, 1922

___, *London Life in the Eighteenth Century* (1965)

Goodman, Jordan, Lovejoy, Paul and Sherratt, Andrew (eds.), *Consuming Habits: Drugs in History and Anthropology* (1995)

Goodman, Jordan, 'Excitantia, or, How Enlightenment Europe took to soft drugs' in Goodman et. al. above

Goodwin, Jason, *The Gunpowder Gardens: Travels through India and China in search of Tea* (1990)

Gordon Cumming, C. F., *Wanderings in China* (Edinburgh, 1900)

Griffis, W. E., *The Mikado's Empire* (10th edn, New York, 1903)

Griffiths, Sir Percival, *The History of the Indian Tea Industry* (1967)

Grove, Richard, *Green Imperialism* (Cambridge, 1995)

Guha, A., *Planter-Raj to Swaraj: freedom struggle and electoral politics in Assam 1826–1947* (Delhi, 1977)

Hammitzsch, Horst, *Zen in the Art of the Tea Ceremony* (Tisbury, Wiltshire, 1979)

Hann, C. M. *Tea and the domestication of the Turkish State* (Huntingdon, 1990)

Hara, Y, 'Prophylactic functions of tea polyphenols', *Health and Tea Convention*, Colombo, 1992

Hardy, Serena, *The Tea Book* (Whittet Books, Surrey, 1979)

Harler, C. R., *The Culture and Marketing of Tea* (Oxford, 1958)

Hazarika, Sanjoy, *Strangers of the Mist: Tales of War and Peace from India's Northeast* (1994)

Heberden, William, *Observations on the Increase and Decrease of Different Diseases, and Particularly the Plague* (1801)

Hobhouse, Henry, *Seeds of Change: Six plants that transformed mankind* (1987, 1999)

Hylton, William H. (ed.), *The Rodale Herb Book* (Rodale Press, Emmaus, Pa., 1974)

Kaempfer, Engelbert, *The History of Japan* (1727; 1993 reprint, Curzon Press), tr. J.G.Scheuchzer, 1906

Kaisen, Iguchi, *Tea Ceremony* (Osaka, 1990)

King, F.H., *Farmers of Forty Centuries, or Permanent Agriculture in China, Korea and Japan* (1911)

Kiple, Kenneth E. and Ornelas, K.C. (eds), *Cambridge World History of Food* (Cambridge, 2000), vol. 1, 'Tea', pp.712–19 (by John Weisburger and James Comer)

Kowaleski-Wallace, Elizabeth, *Consuming Subjects: Women, Shopping and Business in the Eighteenth-Century* (New York, 1997)

Lettsom, John Coakley, *The Natural History of the Tea-Tree, with Observations on the Medical Qualities of Tea.* (1772)

Ling, Tiong Hung and Nancy T., *Green Tea and its Amazing Health Benefits* (Longevity Press, Houston, Texas, 2000)

Lu Yu, *The Classic of Tea: Origins and Rituals* (New Jersey, 1974), translated and introduced by Francis Ross Carpenter

Macfarlane, Alan, *The Savage Wars of Peace: England, Japan and the Malthusian Trap* (Blackwell 1997; Palgrave, 2002)

Macartney *Embassy to China*, see Cranmer-Byng

Maclean, Sarah, *Etiquette and Good Manners* (1962)

Maitland, P. J., *Detailed Report of the Naga Hills Expedition of 1879-80* (Simla, 1880)

Mann, Harold, *The Social Framework of Agriculture* (1968), chapters 6, 33,34

Marks, V., 'Physiological and clinical effects of tea' in *Tea: Cultivation to Consumption* (1992), eds. K. C. Willson and M. N. Clifford

Marshall, Dorothy, *English People in the Eighteenth Century*

(1956)

Messenger, Betty, *The Complete Guide to Etiquette* (1966)

Mintz, Sidney W., *Sweetness and Power: the Place of Sugar in Modern History* (1985)

___ 'The changing roles of food in the study of consumption', in Brewer and Porter above

Money, Lt-Col. Edward, *The Cultivation and Manufacture of Tea* (3rd edn, 1878)

Morse, Edward S., *Japan Day by Day: 1877, 1878–9, 1882–83* (Tokyo, 1936)

___, *Japanese Homes and Their Surroundings* (1886; New York, 1961)

___, 'Latrines of the East', *American Architect and Building News*, vol. xxxix, no.899, 170–4 (1893)

Okakura, Kakuzo, *The Book of Tea* (Tokyo, 1989)

Ovington, J., *An Essay upon the Nature and Qualities of Tea* (R. Roberts, 1699)

Place, Francis, *Illustrations and Proofs of the Principle of Population* (1822; George Allen and Unwin reprint, 1967)

Pilcher, A. H., *Navvies of the 14th Army* (unpublished account, copies in the South Asian Studies Library, Cambridge and the Indian Tea Association Records, India Office Library, F/174; it is quoted at some length in Percival Griffiths, op.cit.)

Porter, Roy and Dorothy, *In Sickness and in Health* (1988)

Reade, A. Arthur, *Tea and Tea-Drinking* (1884)

Rochefoucauld, François de la, *A Frenchman in England 1784*, ed. Jean Marchand (1933)

Scidmore, Eliza R., *Jinrikisha Days in Japan* (New York, 1891)

Schivelbusch, Wolfgang, *Tastes of Paradise* (New York, Vintage, 1992)

Short, Thomas, *A Dissertation Upon Tea* (1730)

—— *A Comparative History of the Increase and Decrease of Mankind* (1767)

Scott, J. M., *The Tea Story* (1964)

Sigmond, G. G., *Tea: Its Effects, Medicinal and Moral* (1839)

Smith, Woodruff D., 'Complications of the Commonplace: Tea, Sugar, and Imperialism', *Journal of Interdisciplinary History*, XXIII: 2 (Autumn 1992), 259–78

——, 'From Coffeehouse to Parlour; the consumption of coffee, tea and sugar in north-western Europe in the seventeenth and eighteenth centuries' in Goodman et. al. (see above)

Stables, W. Gordon, *Tea: the Drink of Pleasure and Health* (1883)

Stagg, Geoffrey V. and Millin, David J., 'The Nutritional and Therapeutic Value of Tea – A Review', *Journal of the Science of Food and Agriculture*, 1975, 26, 1439–59

Sumner, John, *A Popular Treatise on Tea: its Qualities and Effects* (1863)

Talmage, Thomas de Witt, *Around the Tea-Table* (1879)

Teatech 1993, *Proceedings of the International Symposium on Tea Science and Human Health, Tea Research Association, India,* 1993, various papers

Troubridge, Lady, *The Book of Etiquette*, 2 volumes (1926)

Tyson, G., *Forgotten Frontier* (1945)

Ukers, William H., *All About Tea*, 2 volumes (New York, 1935)

Weinberg, Bennet A., and Bealer, Bonnie, K., *The World of Caffeine: The Science and Culture of the World's Most Popular Drink* (2001)

Weisburger, John H. and Comer, James, 'Tea' in Kenneth F. Kiple and K. C. Ornelas (eds), *The Cambridge World History of Food* (Cambridge 2000)

Williams, S. Wells, *The Middle Kingdom*, 2 volumes (1883)

Wilson, Ernest Henry, *A Naturalist in Western China: with Vasculum, camera, and Gun* (1913)

Wilson, Francesca M. (ed.), *Strange Island: Britain through Foreign Eyes 1395–1940* (1955)

Journals

Economic and Social History Review, 4 & 5; *Assam Review and Tea News*; *Economic and Political Weekly*, 2 & 22 (Assam Company); *Journal of Calcutta Tea Trader's Association*; *Journal of the Asiatic Society* (Bruce); *Journal of the Agricultural and Horticultural Societies*, vols. 1, 10, 35; *Bengal Economic Journal* 1918 (Mann), *Englishman's Overland Mail*, 1860; *Planting Opinion* (from 1896)

Index